S0-CWV-837

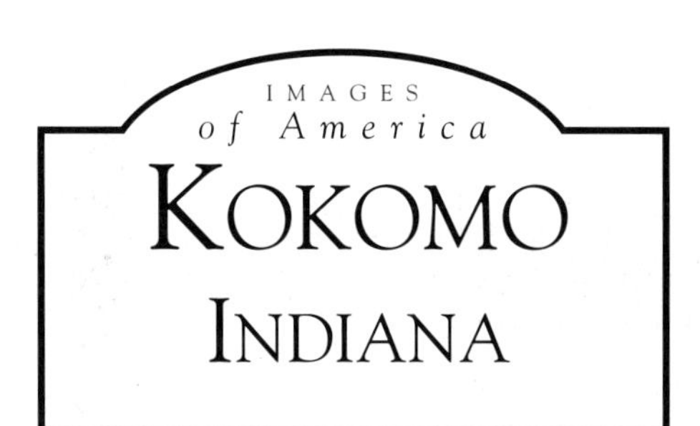
IMAGES
of America
KOKOMO
INDIANA

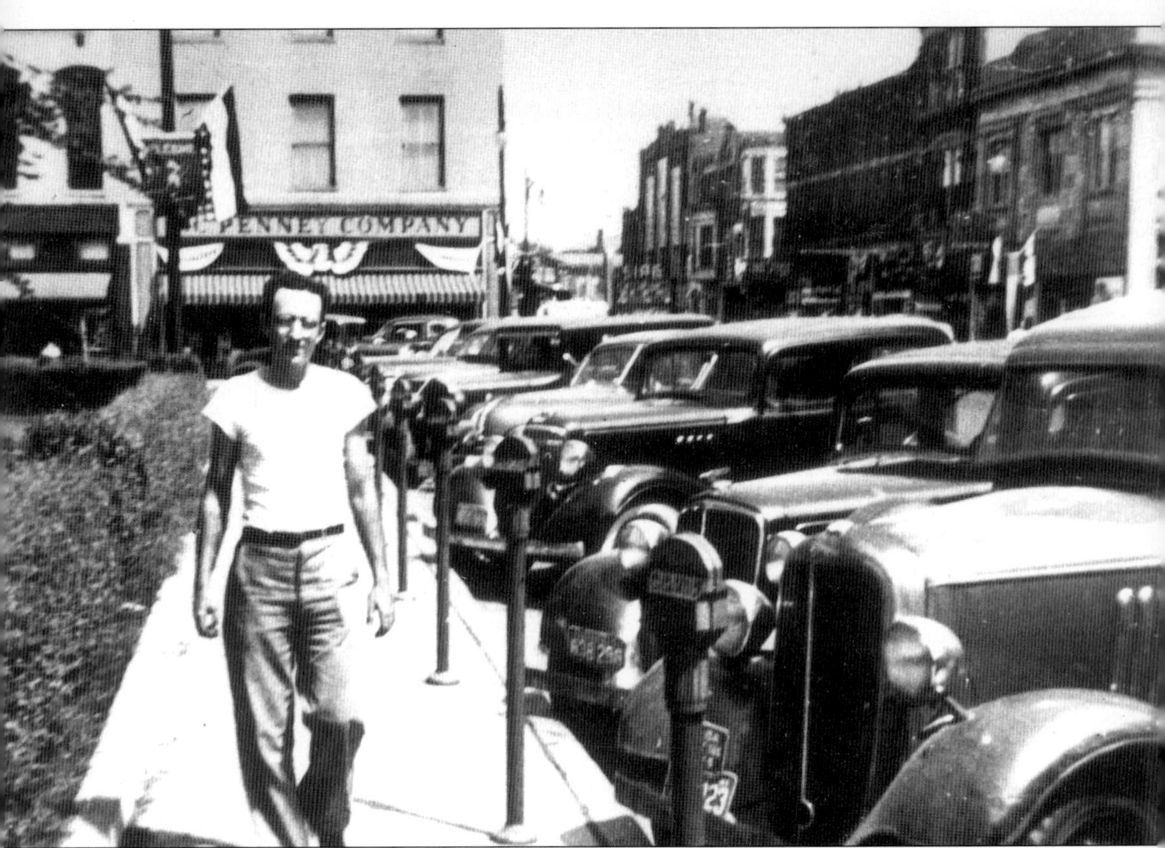

STROLLING THROUGH KOKOMO.

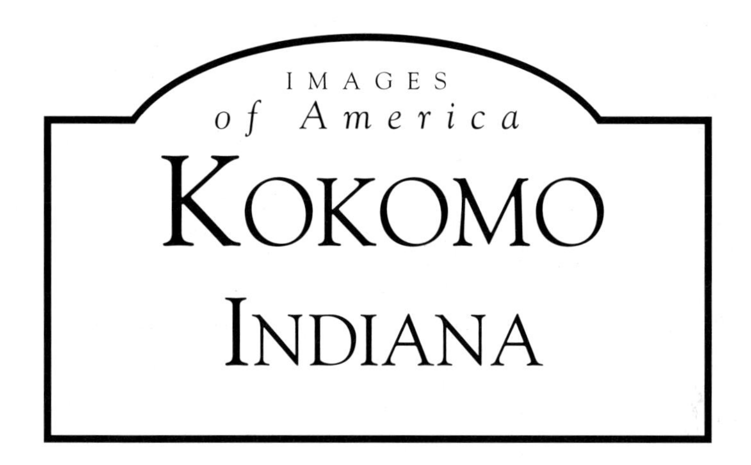

Thomas D. Hamilton

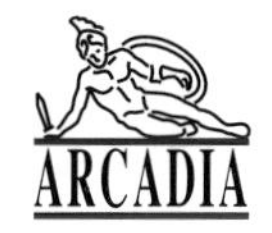

ISBN 0-7385-2026-8

First Printed 2002.
Reprinted 2003.

Published by Arcadia Publishing,
Charleston SC, Chicago IL, Portsmouth NH, San Francisco CA

Printed in Great Britain.

Library of Congress Catalog Card Number: 2002109584

For all general information contact Arcadia Publishing at:
Telephone 843-853-2070
Fax 843-853-0044
E-Mail sales@arcadiapublishing.com

For customer service and orders:
Toll-Free 1-888-313-2665

Visit us on the internet at http://www.arcadiapublishing.com

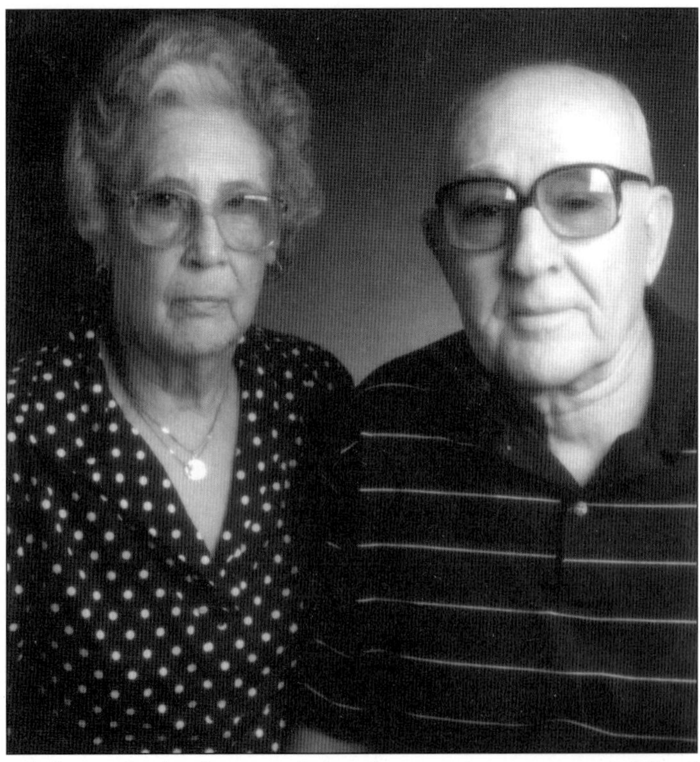

I would like to dedicate this book to my dad and mom who were married for 62 years. In his early years, Dad was one of Kokomo's favorite piano players. At the age of 89, he still entertains the people at Jefferson Manor, where he resides.

Contents

Acknowledgments		6
Introduction		7
1.	City of Kokomo	9
2.	Stores	23
3.	Theaters and Entertainment	31
4.	Restaurants	51
5.	Factories	59
6.	Bakeries	65
7.	Hotels	67
8.	Churches and Schools	69
9.	Business	75
10.	People	83
11.	Special	103

ACKNOWLEDGMENTS

Special thanks must be given to the following people:

Nancy Kennedy of Ryan Archives
John Eades
Charles Sullivan
Mrs. Robert Davies
Patty Host
Willie Lowry
The Kokomo Perspective, which has printed my weekly articles on Kokomo history for the last five years.
Tom Carey of *The Kokomo Tribune* who gave me my first break.

Most of all I want to thank my family:

Bob & Pam Hendershot
Richard & Cindy Russell
Robert & Sally Duke
Jeff & Donna Hamilton
Brian & Stacy Hamilton
Mike & Ella Cunningham

And most of all, my wife of 45 years, Barbara Richards Hamilton.

INTRODUCTION

Growing up in Kokomo, Indiana, is an experience a person can never forget. How can a dream be explained?

We were young and foolish and uptown Kokomo was ours forever. To try and explain the magic of the 1940s and '50s would take a genius. Norman Rockwell tried his best to paint it, but it would take a magic pen to write the story and capture the true depth, width, length, and height. How can dancing at the canteen and Moose Lodge each weekend be written? How can the perils of puppy love be penned?

Kokomo had six theaters—the Sipe, the Isis, the Indiana, the Fox, the Colonial, and the Wood. The Sipe must have been one of the best in the whole state of Indiana. Who could forget the balcony? We would put our arm around our sweetheart and leave it there, even long after it had gone numb. We would not even consider moving it! The sweet smell of her hair held us spellbound and made the discomfort worth it all. When she lifted her head up for a kiss, time stopped and we entered another dimension—a place where time did not exist.

We were young and foolish and never dreamt that it would ever end. If you were there, you can never forget it. Just to take a walk in uptown Kokomo was pure magic. At night, it only got better! The theaters all lit up and it was a sight to behold!

There were many drugstores, with their soda fountains, and they had puppy love written all over them! Where else could a fella take his gal and sip from the same glass, using two straws and gazing into each other's eyes?

The city bus was all a young boy needed to pick up his sweetheart and take her on a date. For 5¢, a boy could ride uptown and then get a transfer to pick up his date. Once they were back uptown, he could walk her around holding hands to let the whole world know that she was his. Everything looked good and smelled good! Was it her hair? Or perhaps the perfume she was wearing? Those were the days, my friend.

Time did not exist and we were sure that things would never change. The pretty hotels all lit up at night and the department stores with colorful displays in their windows. We thought the mighty W.H. Turner Co. and Montgomery Ward and the S.S. Kresge five and dime were all here to stay. Their automated money chutes and the many items they had for sale are all just memories now.

We loved uptown Kokomo and it was ours alone. In our young hearts we knew we had the best of everything. But, as we grew older, we watched in sadness as time started to exist. It moved on and left behind a path of closed department stores, drug stores, theaters, and hotels.

All of the things we had loved so much began to vanish into thin air. Yesterday became a dream, but what a dream it was!

Those of us who grew up in the 1940s and '50s had something that no other generation will ever have. We can never forget it, can we? We can only hope to share it with our children and grandchildren through pictures and stories from the past. That is the purpose of this book. I hope that it will take the reader back in time.

Maybe, after looking at this collection of pictures, you will hear the echoes of the 1940s and '50s bouncing off the buildings as you walk around in uptown Kokomo.

"Come on you guys! Let's go to the Hob-Nob."

"How about some hamburgers at Hills Snappy Service?"

"Want to go to the dance? What about a movie? What about Duke's Restaurant?"

"Do you love me like I love you? Can we go steady? Do you think your dad will mind?"

The voices of Nat King Cole, Patti Page, Perry Como, Eddie Fisher, Doris Day, and Tony Bennett are coming from the uptown alleys. The sounds will forever be in our hearts. We floated down Main Street, with wings on our feet, to the tunes that they sang. No love could ever be like our love. The stars and the moon gave us their blessing and we did not realize the thin line between love and fascination.

Memories will last forever and pictures will bring those memories to mind. May you behold, once again, the days of youth. Remember walking down the streets holding hands, the bus ride home, wading in the creeks, the theaters, the smell of leaves burning outside the classroom window. Remember the childhood friends who have gone away.

Remember… and be blessed.

This book is for you, from a friend who enjoyed living it.

Tom Hamilton.

One

City of Kokomo

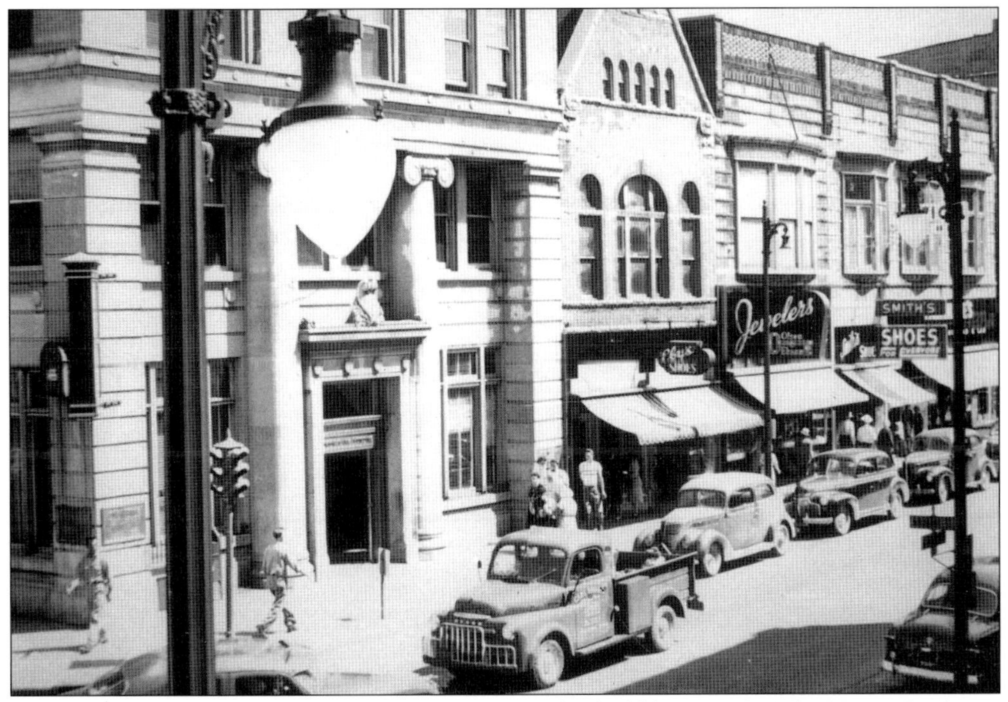

Main Street 1950. This is what uptown Kokomo looked like in 1950. The Union Bank was on the southeast corner of Main and Mulberry. The building has been torn down. Ameritrust Bank has a big glass building there now. None of the other stores in this block are there today.

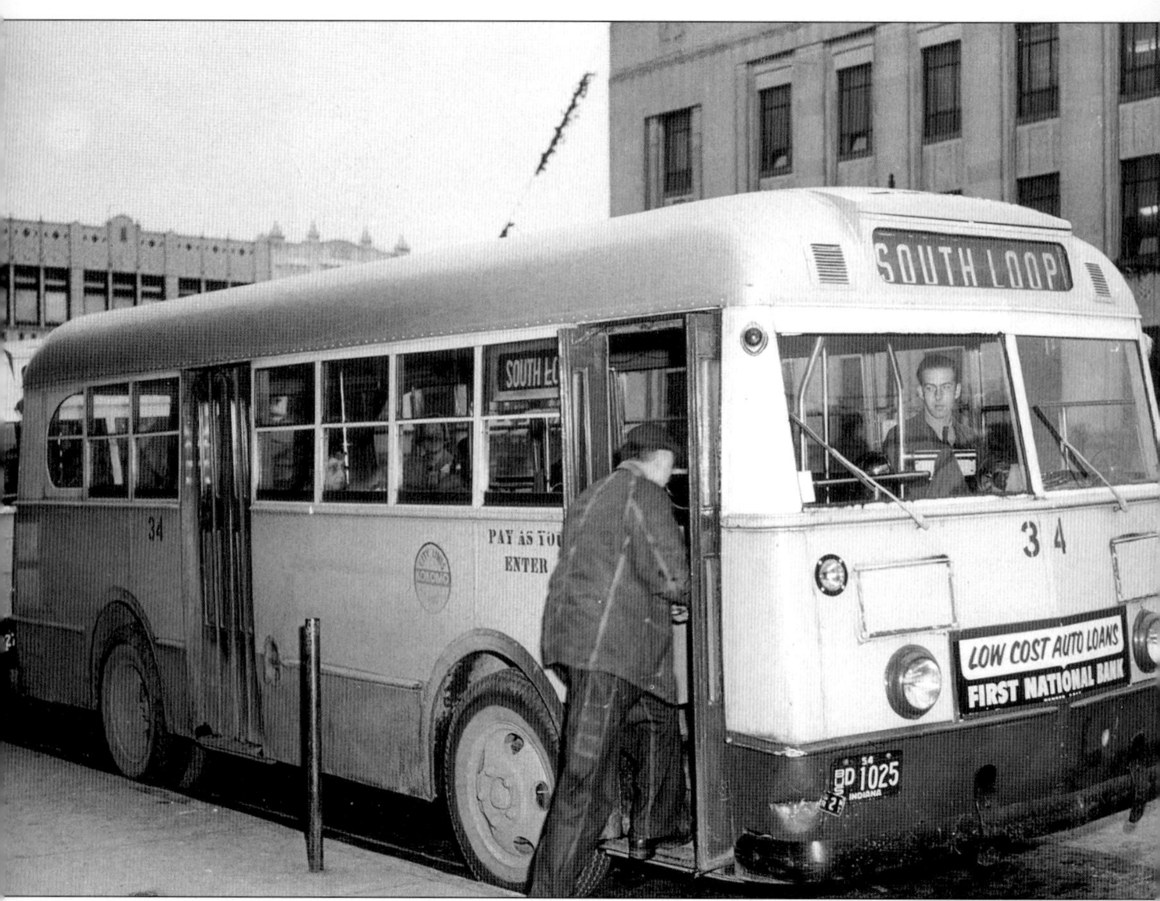

CITY BUS. Remember the city bus? For 10¢ we could take our sweetheart home from a date. Wasn't it fun holding hands on the bus? Sneaking a kiss wasn't a bad idea, was it? She said, "I think the bus driver saw us!" When he winked at us through his mirror and smiled, we knew he didn't care. The year was 1954 and the city bus picked us up on the northeast corner of Buckeye and Walnut. The driver is Harvey Phillips.

OLD COURTHOUSE. The Kokomo Courthouse is pictured here in the 1890s.

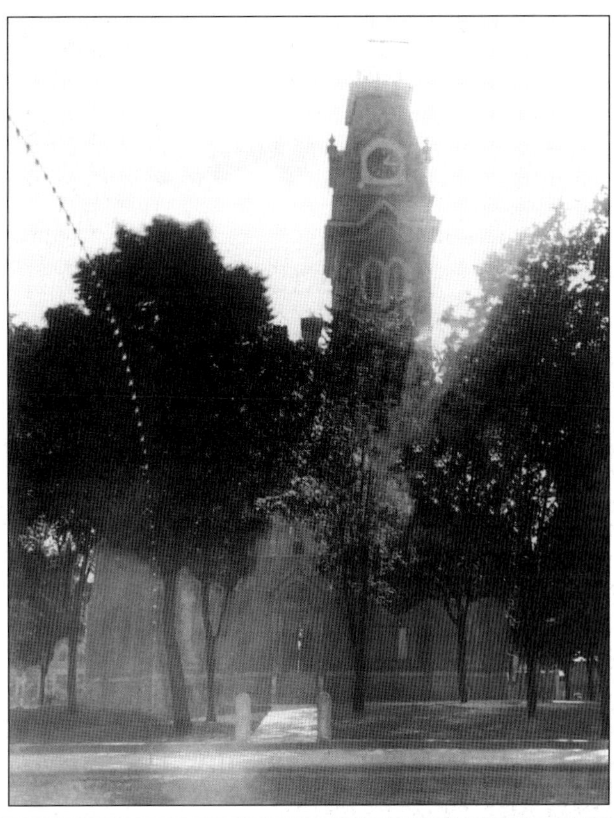

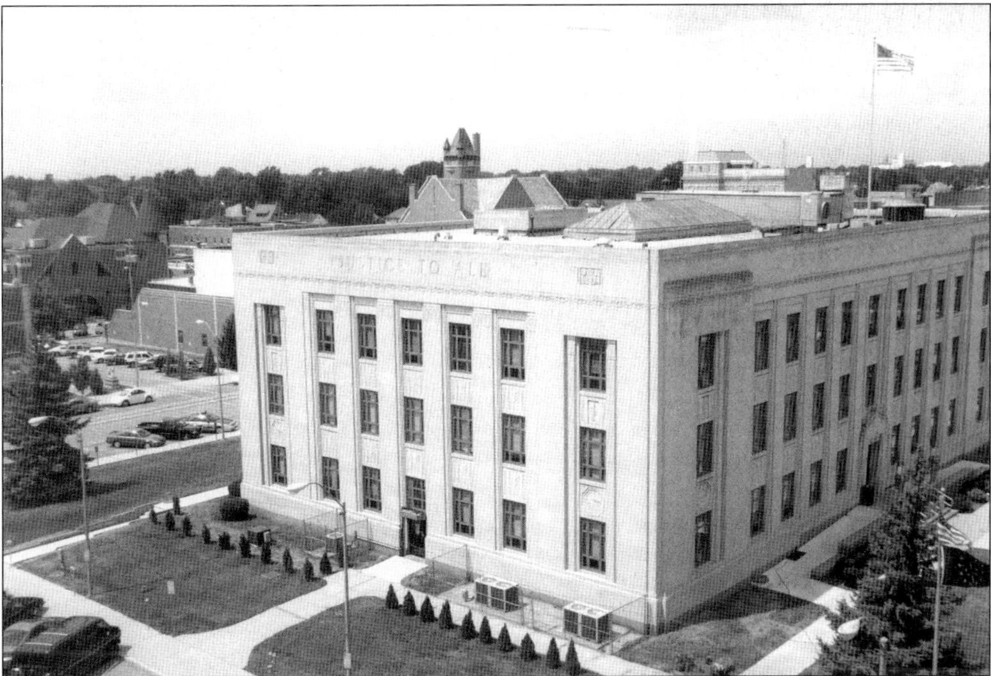

NEW COURTHOUSE. The Howard County Courthouse was torn down in 1927. A new one was built in 1937 in downtown Kokomo.

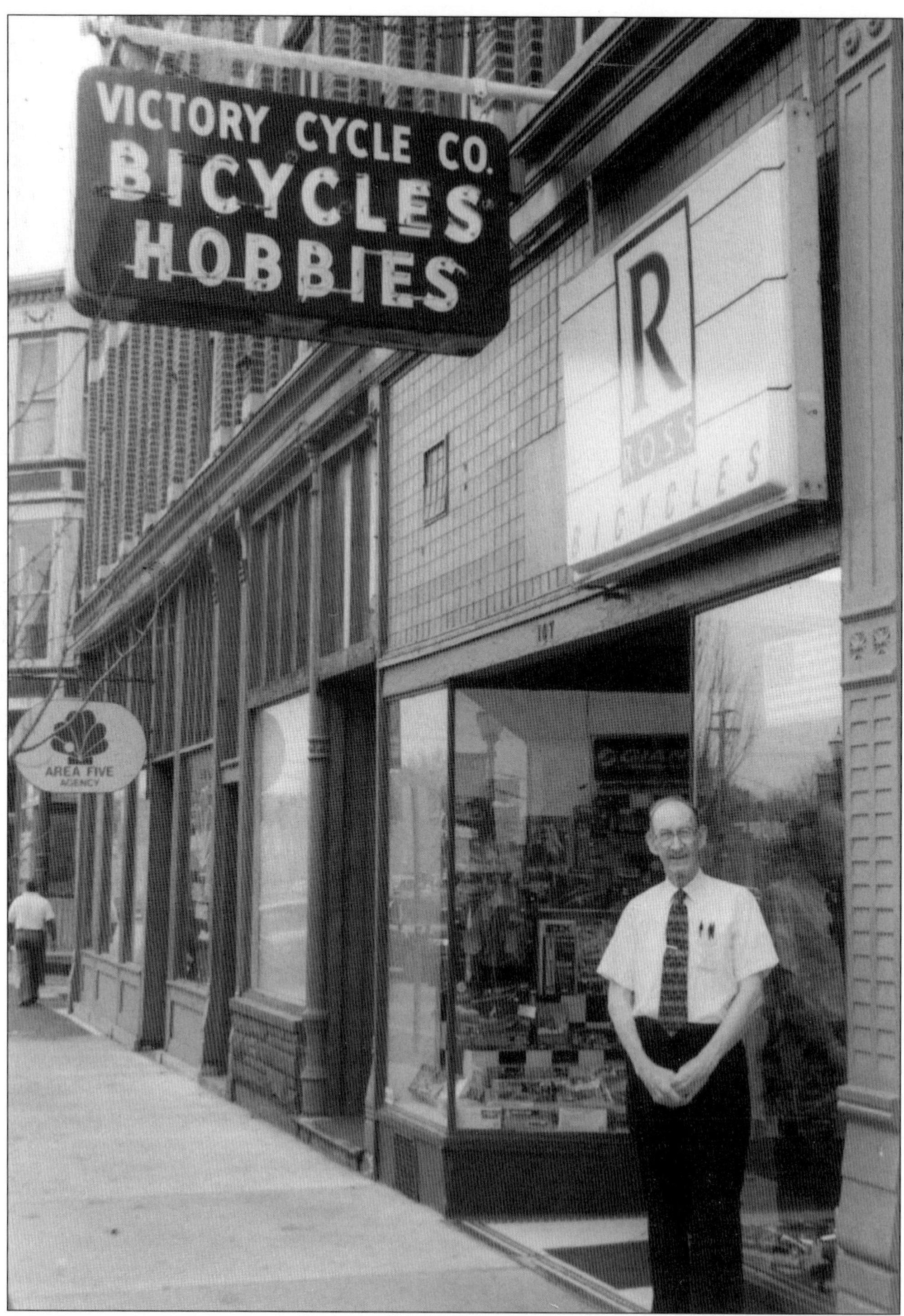

VICTORY CYCLE. Charlie Sullivan was the owner of Victory Cycle Co. through the 1950s. He was a well-known businessman. He retired in early 2000. Need a bike? See Charlie.

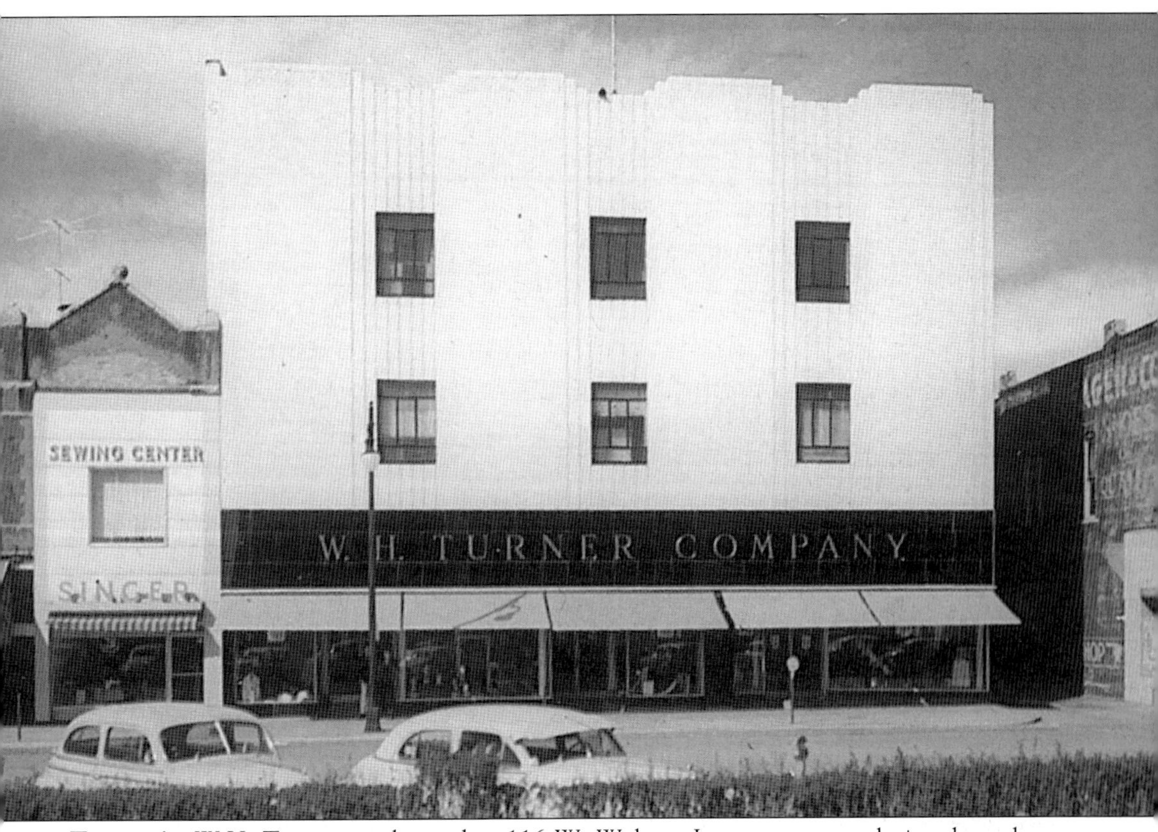

TURNER'S. W.H. Turner was located at 116 W. Walnut. It was a very exclusive dress shop. Singer Sewing was next door with fine fabrics.

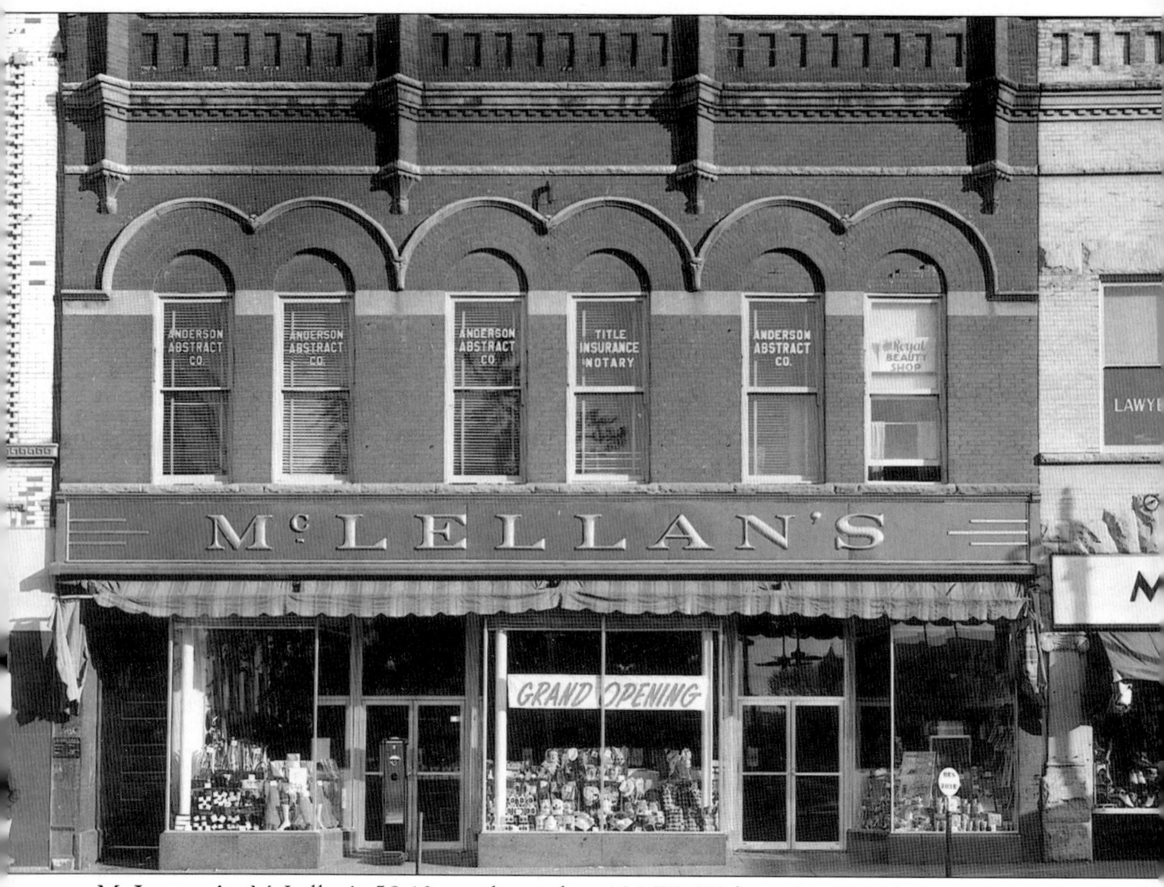

McLellan's. McLellan's 5&10 was located at 104 W. Walnut. It was a fun store to go for weekly supplies.

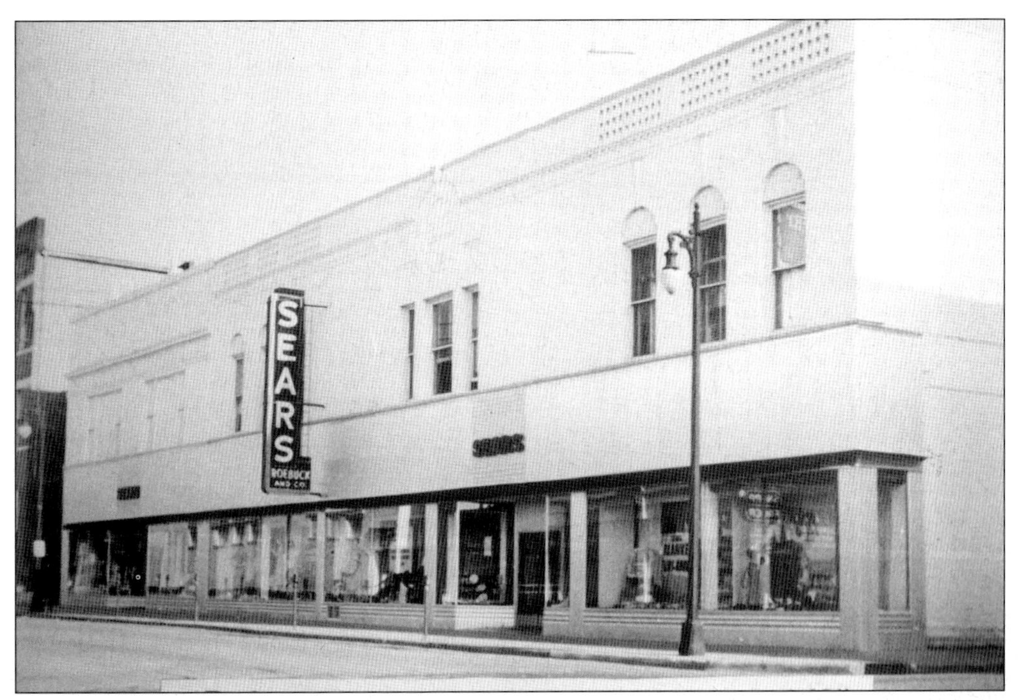

SEARS. Sears Roebuck was located at 118 E. Walnut. Now it is in the Markland Mall at the Bypass. The First of America Bank is located there now.

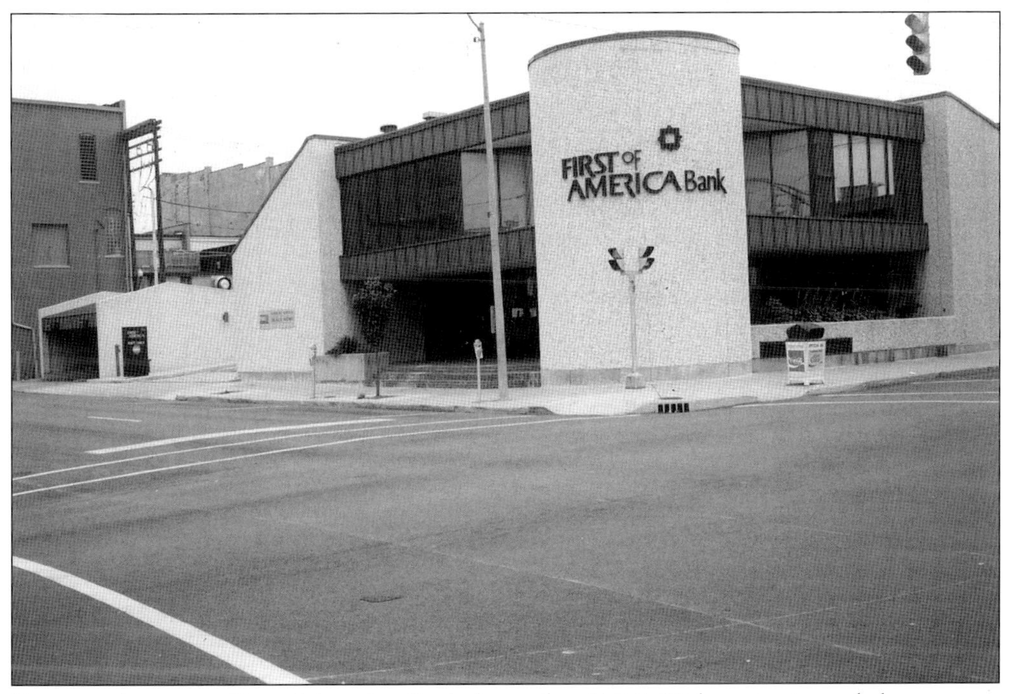

FIRST OF AMERICA. First of America Bank, located at 118 E. Walnut, is pictured above.

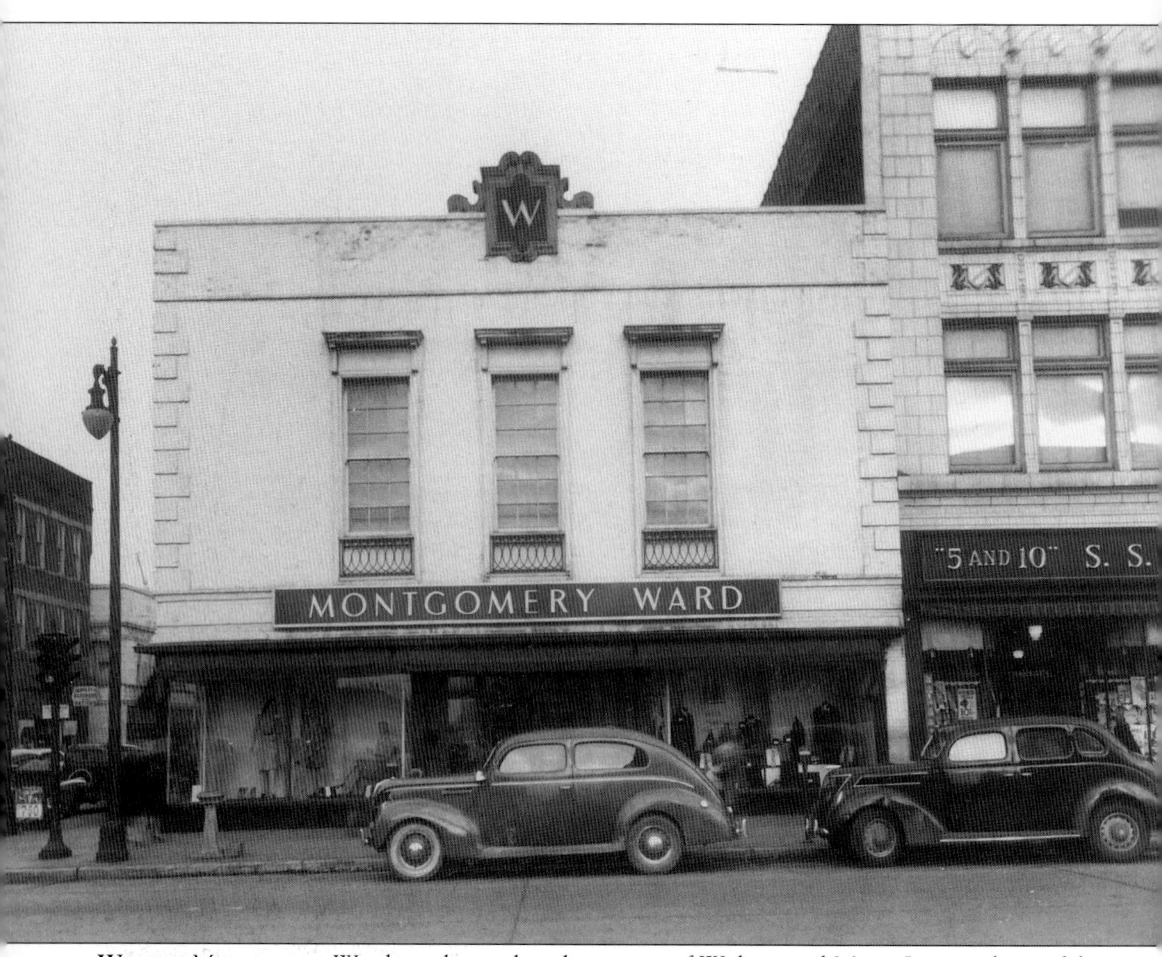

WARDS. Montgomery Ward was located at the corner of Walnut and Main. It was a beautiful place to shop.

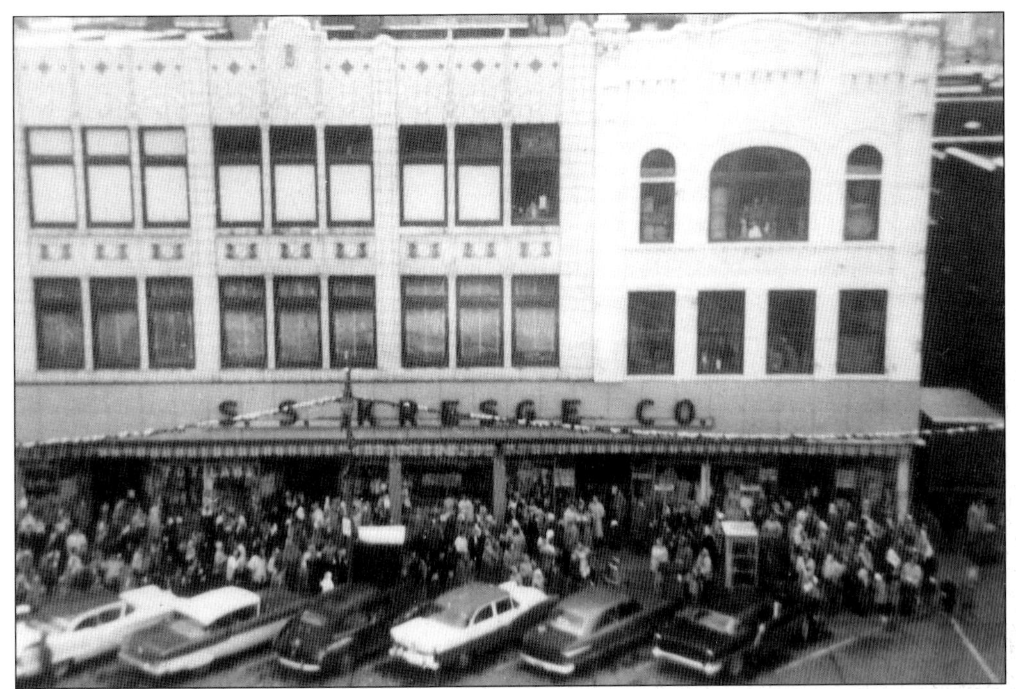

S.S. KRESGE'S. S.S. Kresge's was located at 116 N. Main. As you can tell by the crowd, uptown Kokomo was a fun place to be in the 1940s and '50s.

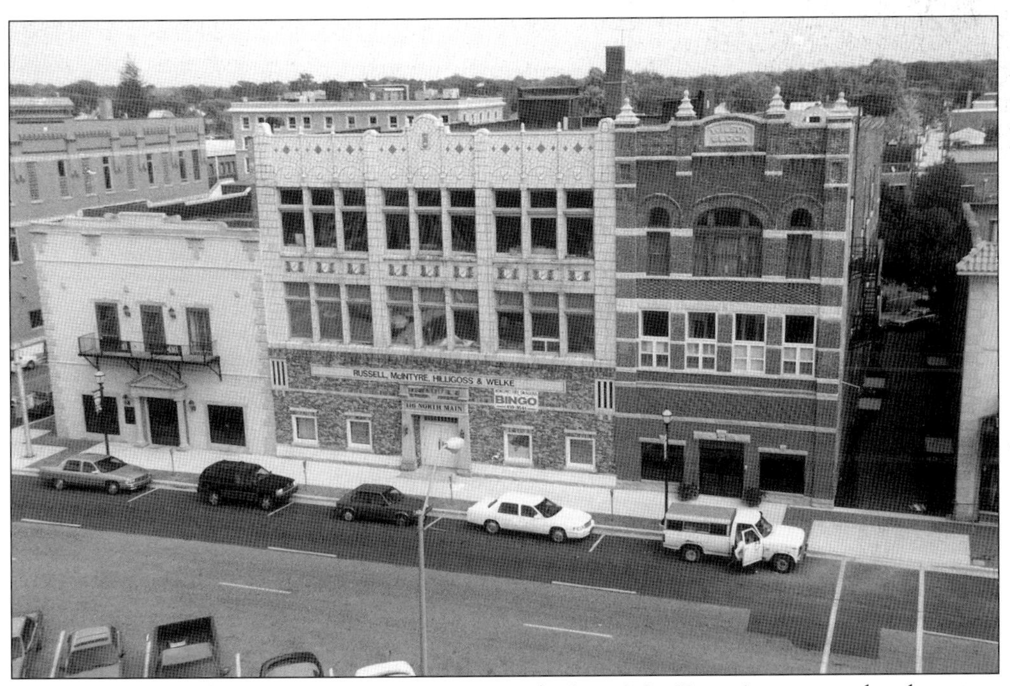

S.S. KRESGE'S. At one time in the 1940s and '50s, S.S. Kresge's was in this location. Montgomery Ward was on the southeast corner of Main and Walnut. This location is now occupied by Russell, McIntrye, Helligoss, and Welke Law Firms. Richard and Cindy Russell live in the condo above the firm.

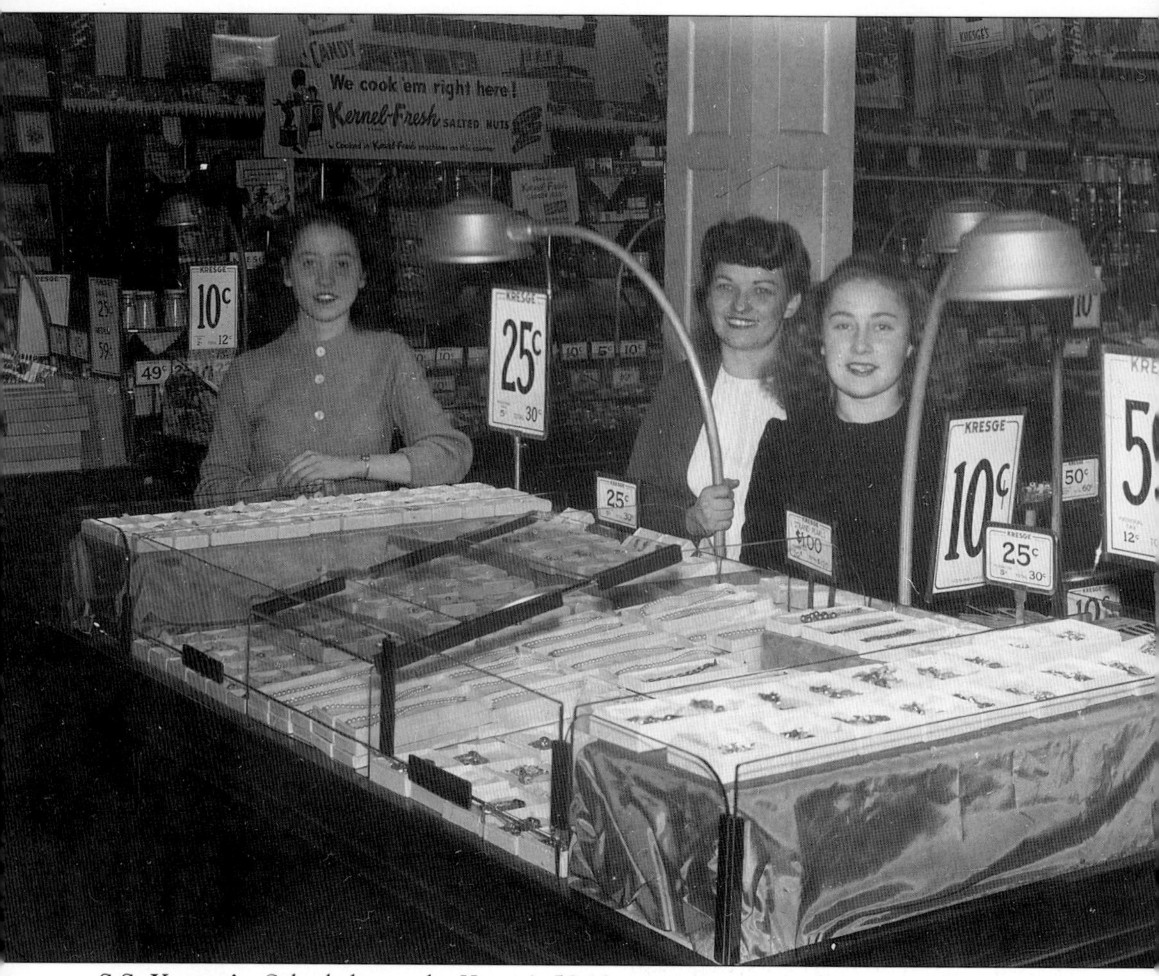

S.S. KRESGE'S. Sales ladies at the Kresge's 5&10 store. Are you in this picture? Do you know who they are?

Rip-roaring '40s and '50s

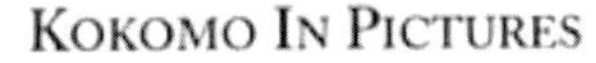

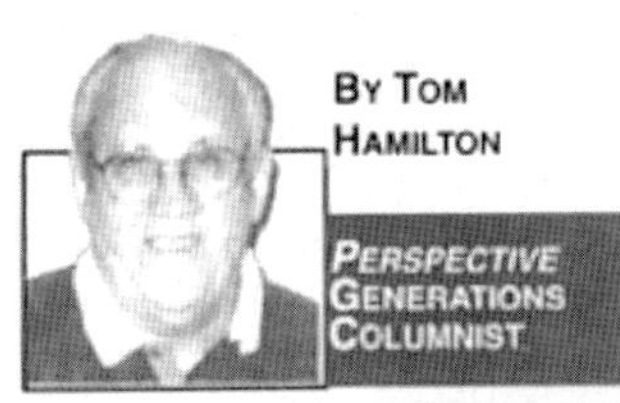

The S.S. Kresge Store was located at 116 North Main St., and what a store it was!

How well I remember the lunch counter and the joy of eating there. They had the best of everything. Fresh baked pies, sandwiches, sundaes, beverages and their grilled cheeseburgers were out of this world. And, wasn't it fun going up and down the aisle? You name it. They had it.

I can remember the Saturday afternoon crowds. People standing outside on the sidewalk talking and friends meeting to go to the movies. It was called the five and dime store. I'm not sure, but I think it opened in 1931 and closed its doors on December 24th, 1980. In our hearts, we thought that it would stay opened forever!

Can you remember the friendly people who worked there? They all seemed so happy. Here are a couple of pictures of the employees. Are you one of them?

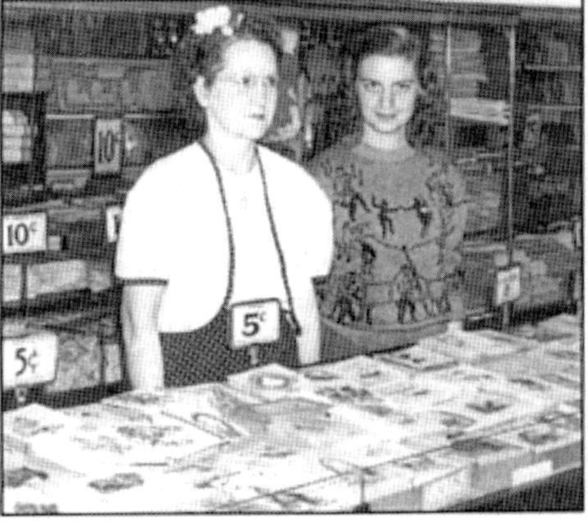

And, don't forget the Woolworth Store that was located at 108 North Main St. And, McLellan was located at 104 West Walnut. These all were listed in my 1947 phone book as the five cent to one dollar stores. Those were the days, my friends. The days of our youth. Uptown Kokomo was ours forever. For five cents, the city bus took us anywhere we wanted to go. We had the best of everything. There never will be another world like ours. To try to explain the magic of the '40s and '50s would take a genius. Norman Rockwell is the only one who could paint it! It would take a magic pen to write the story and to get the true breadth, length, depth and height of puppy love and dancing at the Moose Lodge. It would be almost impossible.

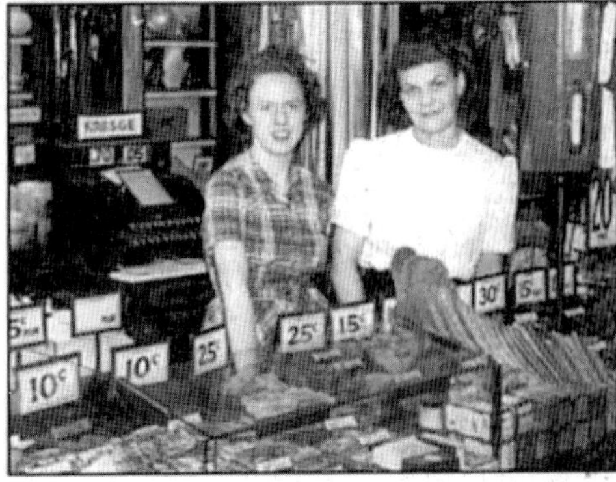

How can you explain your heart going pitter-patter? How could the smell of a young girl's clean hair send a young boy into orbit? And, wasn't it fun playing footsie under the table and floating down Main Street with wings on our feet? We were young and foolish and made a promise never to part.

Even today, as we walk uptown, the echo of the '40s and '50s bounce off the walls of the buildings. Come on you guys, let's go to the Hob Nob. How about a hamburger from Hills Snappy Service? Are you going to the dance at the Moose? The Sipe Theater is showing "Summer Stock" with Gene Kelly and Judy Garland. Do you love me, like I love you? Can we go steady? Do you think your dad will be okay with it?

The voices of Nat King Cole, Patti Page, Doris Day, Perry Como, Kay Starr, Eddy Fisher and Tony Bennett are coming from the uptown alleys.

The echo of the past, of the '40s and '50s will forever be in our hearts. Thank you very kindly for reading my articles. Feel free to call on me at anytime. My phone is burning off the hook, and I love it! I'm one lucky person to have friends like my readers.

I mentioned four months back how it would be nice to have a theater uptown. I'm happy to see others joining the bandwagon. I suggest the merchants help out with this idea. I have received calls with good ideas. Call the *Perspective* with yours!

As a columnist, Tom Hamilton writes about his memories of growing up and raising a family Kokomo, Indiana.

(From *The Kokomo Perspective*.)

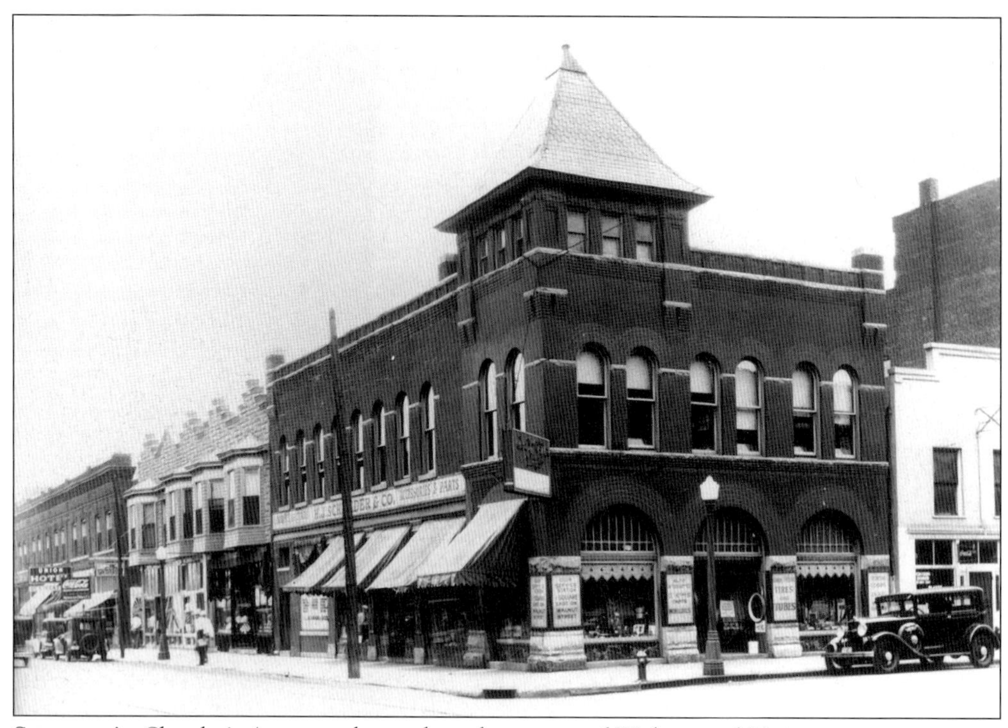

SHRADER'S. Shrader's Auto was located on the corner of Walnut and Union.

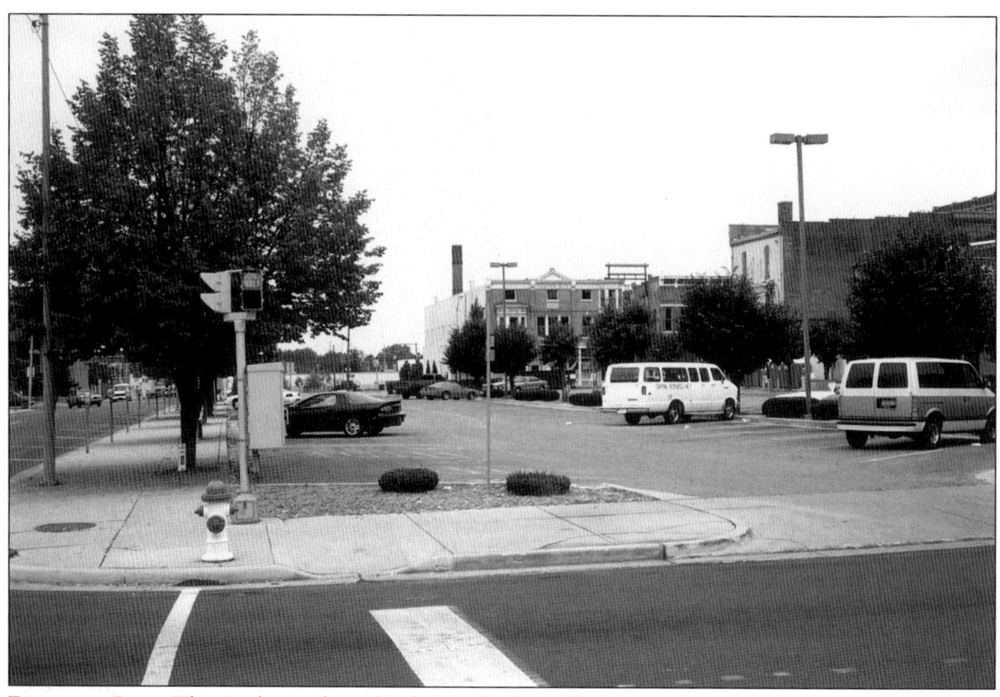

PARKING LOT. This is the parking lot located where Shrader's Auto Store once stood.

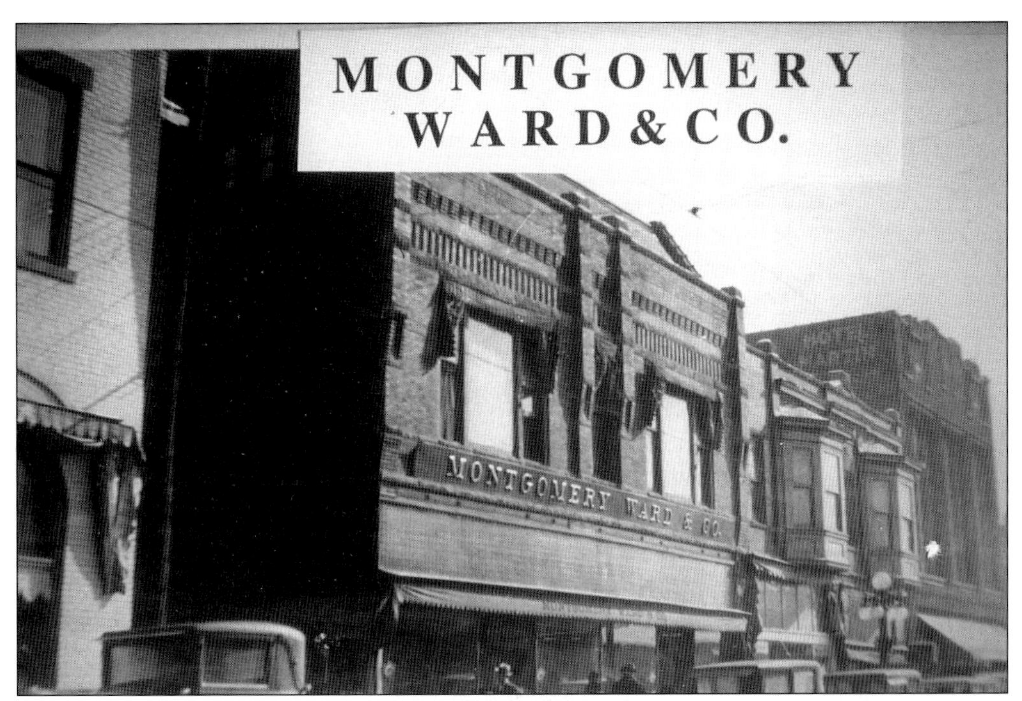

WARDS. In the 1900s, the Montgomery Ward Store was located at 112 S. Main where K&S was later located.

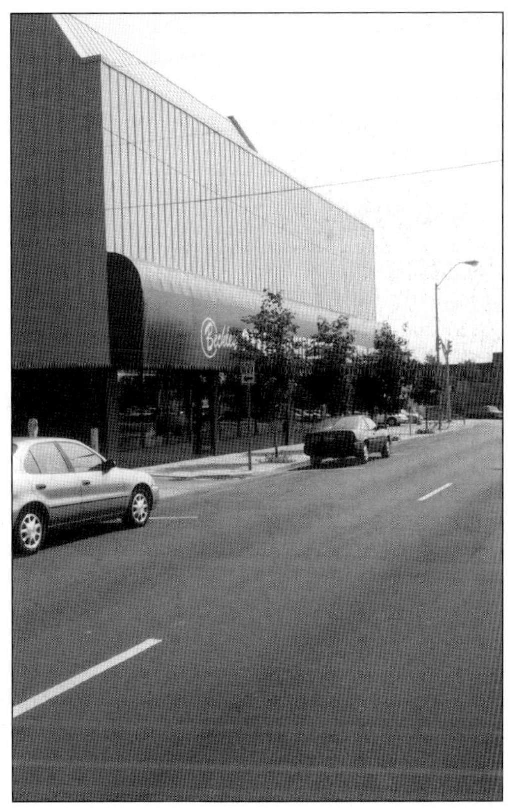

BECKLEY'S OFFICE EQUIPMENT. This location, 112 S. Main, is now Beckley's Office Equipment and Supplies.

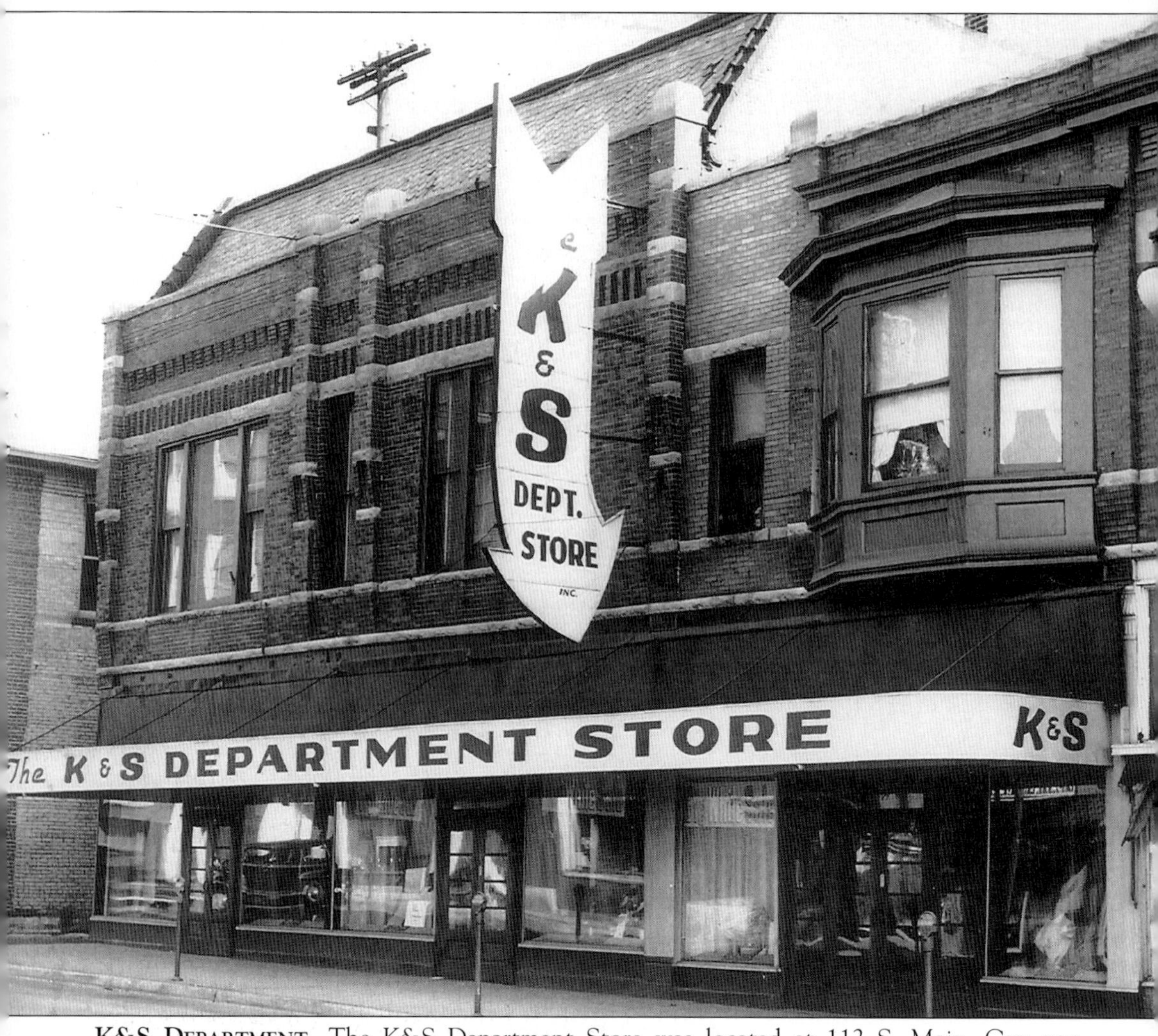

K&S DEPARTMENT. The K&S Department Store was located at 112 S. Main. Can you remember the money chutes? As a child, watching the money being put in a chute and traveling to the office and back to the customer with the receipt and change was a fascinating experience.

Two
STORES

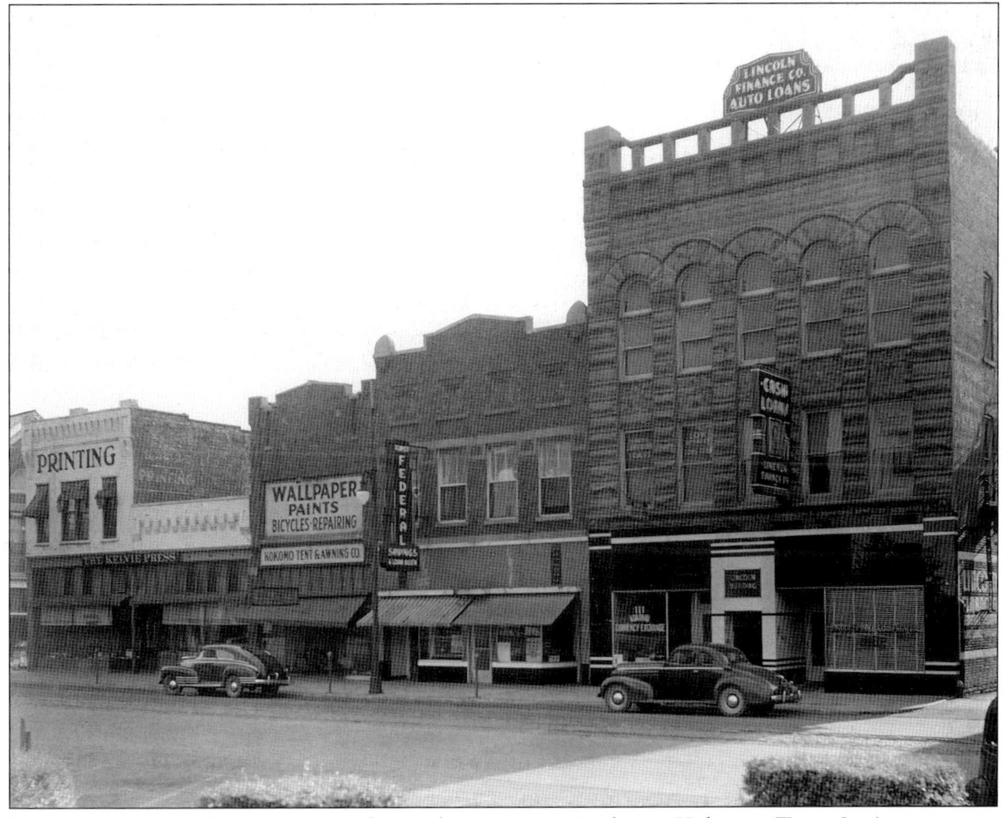

KELVIE PRESS. Kelvie Press was located at 101 N. Buckeye. Kokomo Tent & Awning was located at 105, First Federal at 107, and Lincoln Finance at 113 N. Buckeye. This picture was taken by Ryan Archives in 1945.

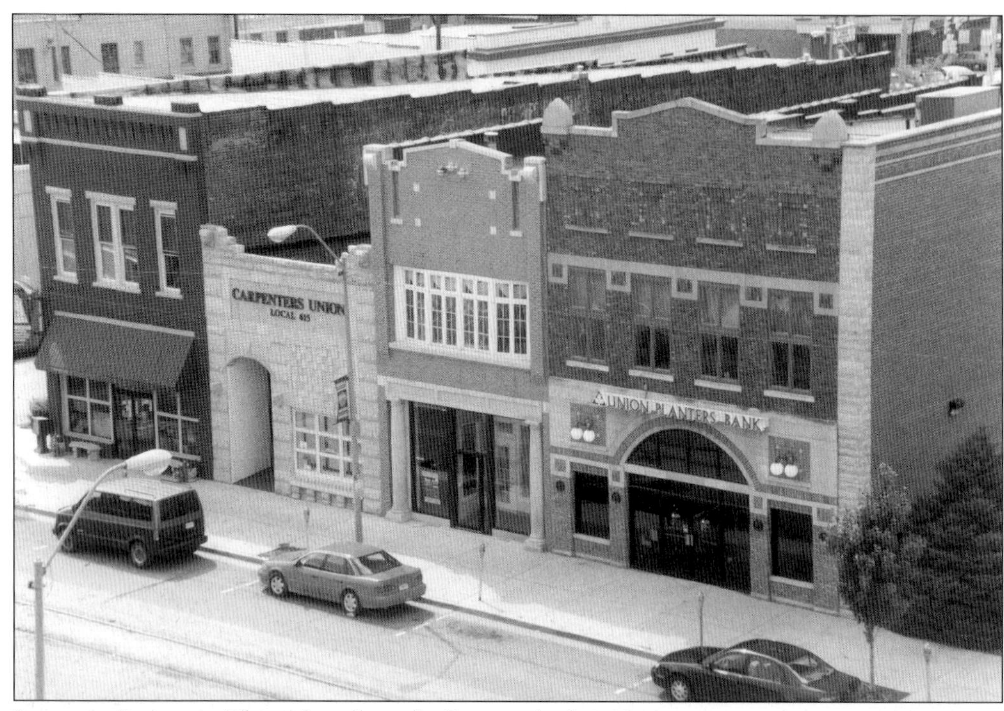

LINCOLN FINANCE. This is how Lincoln Finance looks today.

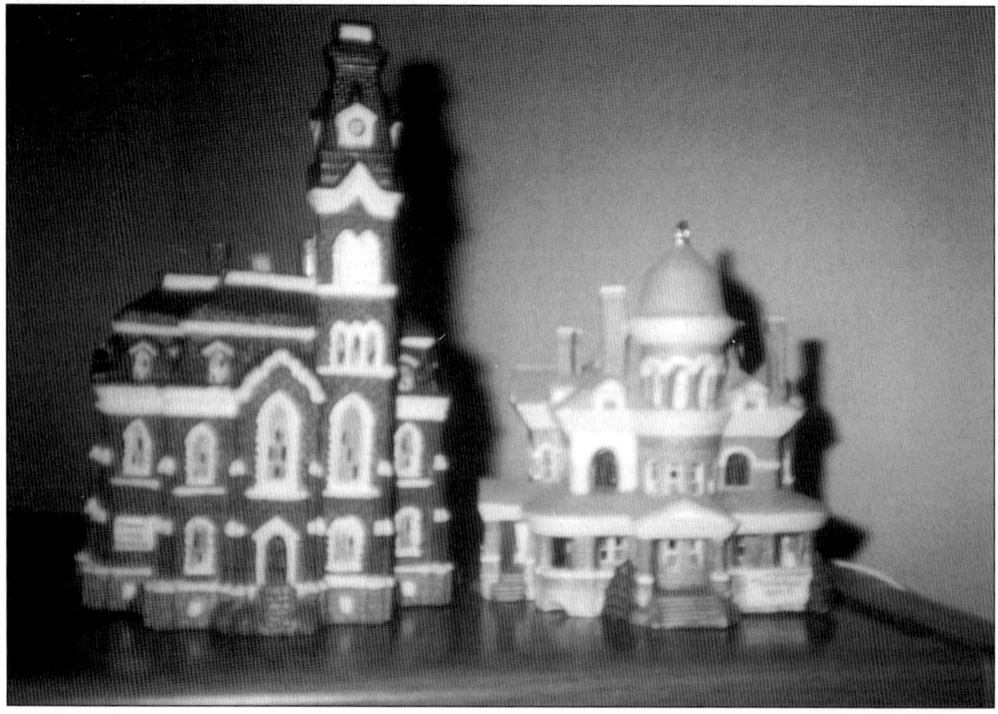

HOST ART & FRAMING. Patty Host Art & Framing has put together small models of Kokomo's buildings. Here are the old courthouse and Sieberling Mansion. The city hall building is the next one to be on display. Patty's address of business is 2322 Valentine Dr., Kokomo, Indiana.

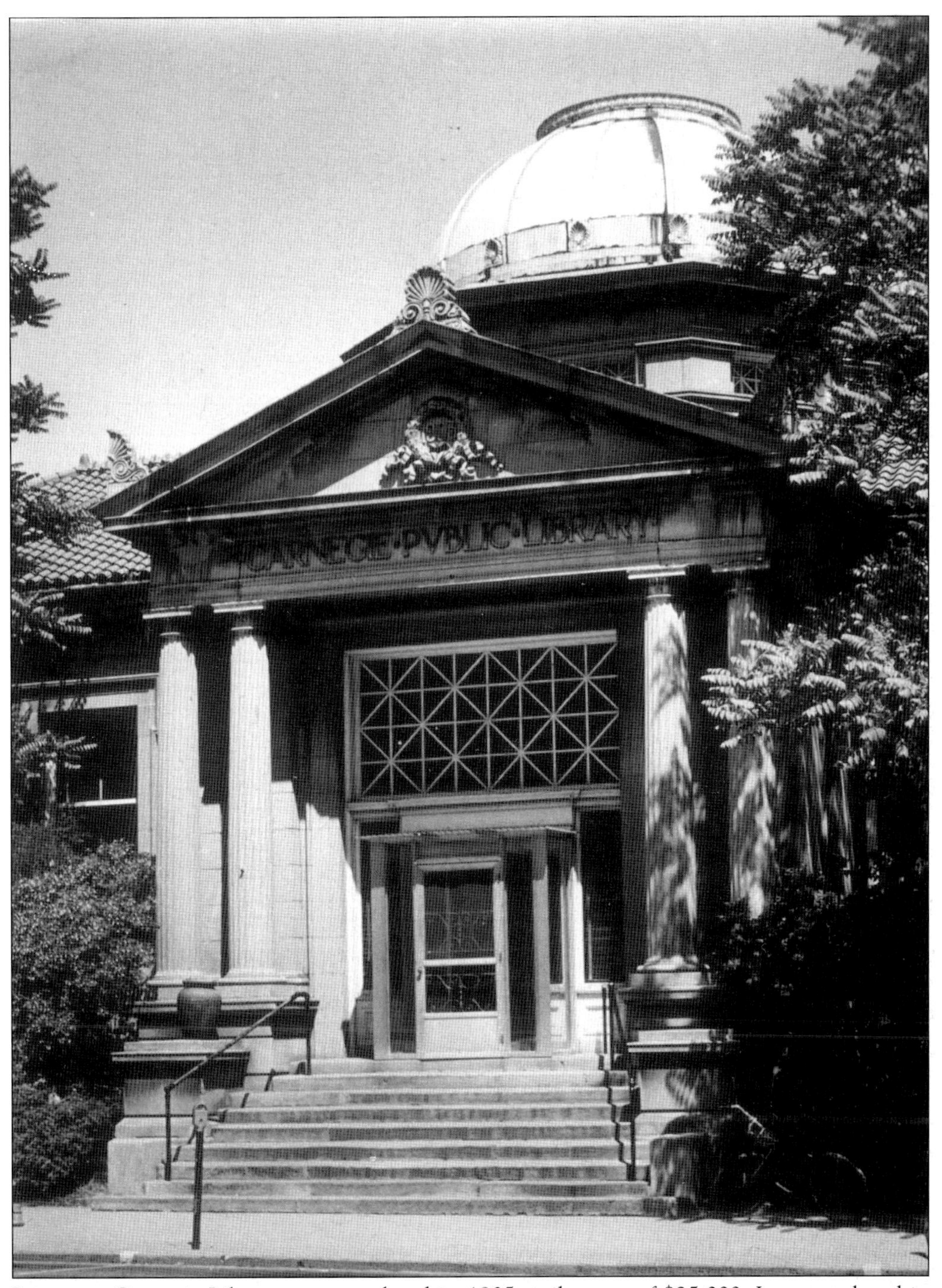

LIBRARY. Carnegie Library was completed in 1905 at the cost of $25,000. It was replaced in 1967 at the cost of $1,019,551. This is a big monetary difference. It was located on the southeast corner of Mulberry and Union.

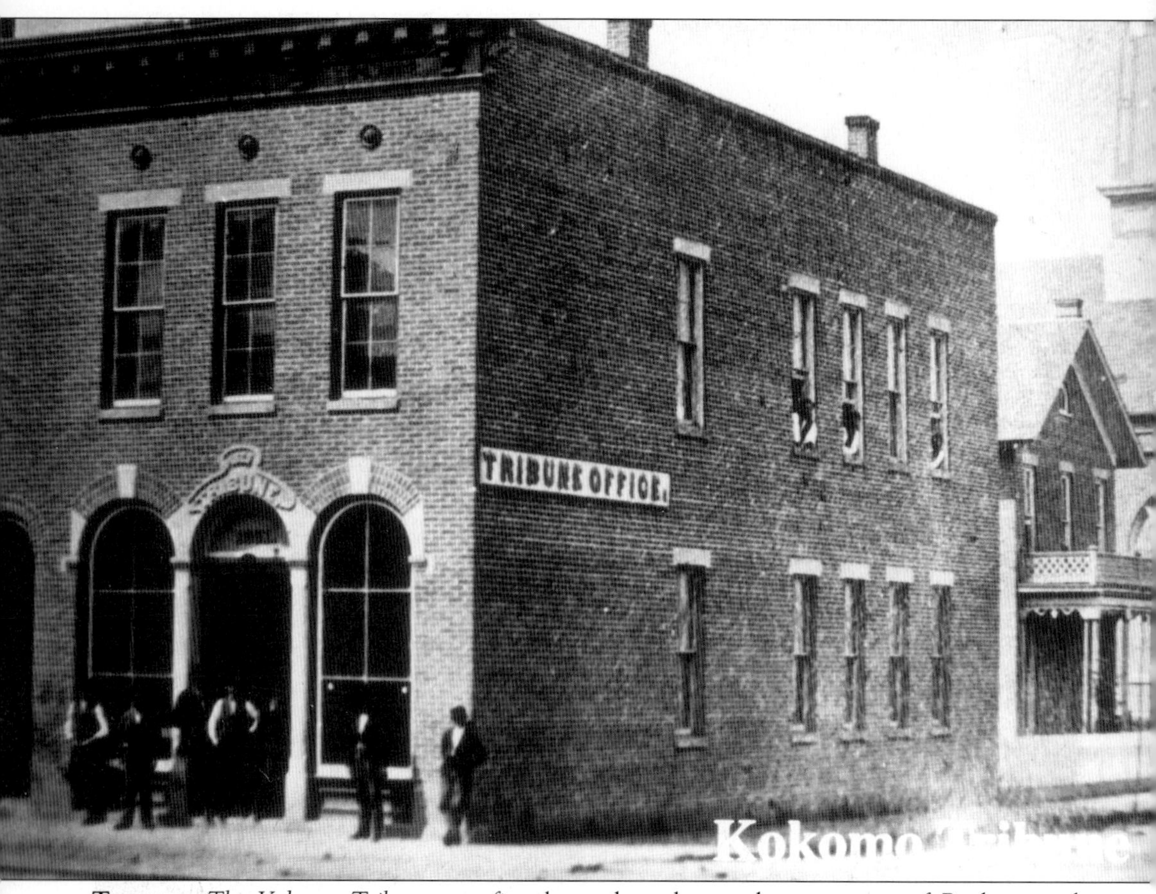

TRIBUNE. *The Kokomo Tribune* was first located at the southwest corner of Buckeye and Mulberry until 1892, when they moved to their present location at 300 N. Union.

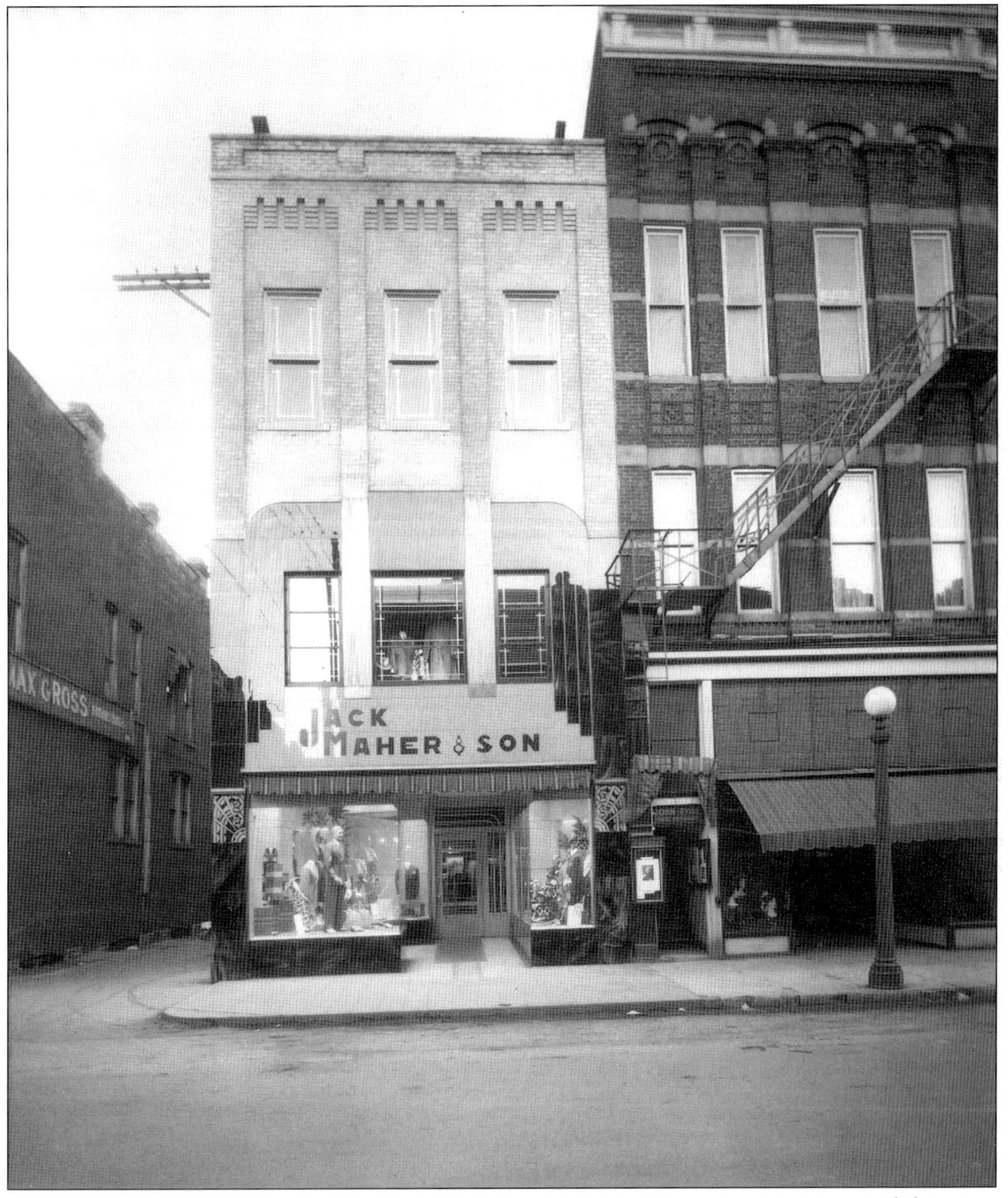

JACK MAHER. Jack Maher & Son was located at 210 N. Main Street. It was one of the most famous clothing stores to ever hit Kokomo. John Ryan's studio was upstairs at 208 N. Main. Ryan took this picture in 1949. The ladder from the building is still there today. Jack Maher & Son and Ryan's Studio are no longer there. It's just an empty building now.

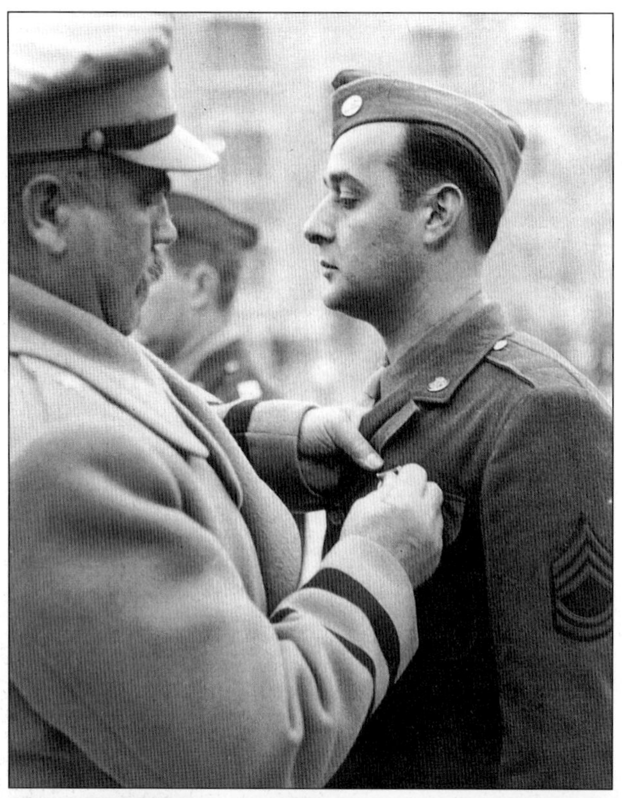

ROBERT FREED. Citation for Legion of Merit was awarded to Robert Freed for outstanding service in Sicily. This medal is the highest decoration bestowed by the Army for non-combatant service. Robert Freed trained 2,000 Sicilians with a squad of 212 GIs. He met and married Frances Congress in Fairmount, West Virginia. They have been married for 60 years and have 5 children. They own Palmers Jewelry.

ROBERT FREED'S FAMILY. This is the Robert Freed family. They own Palmers Jewelry Store. They have been in Kokomo for 60 years. They have been good for Kokomo, and love the city and its people.

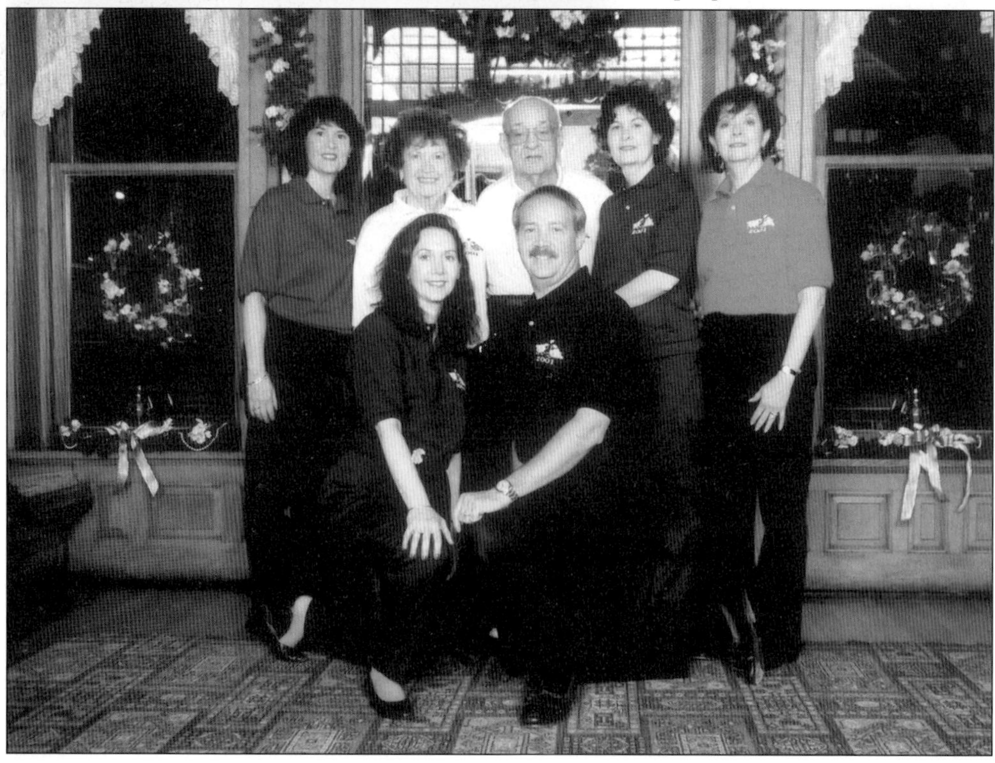

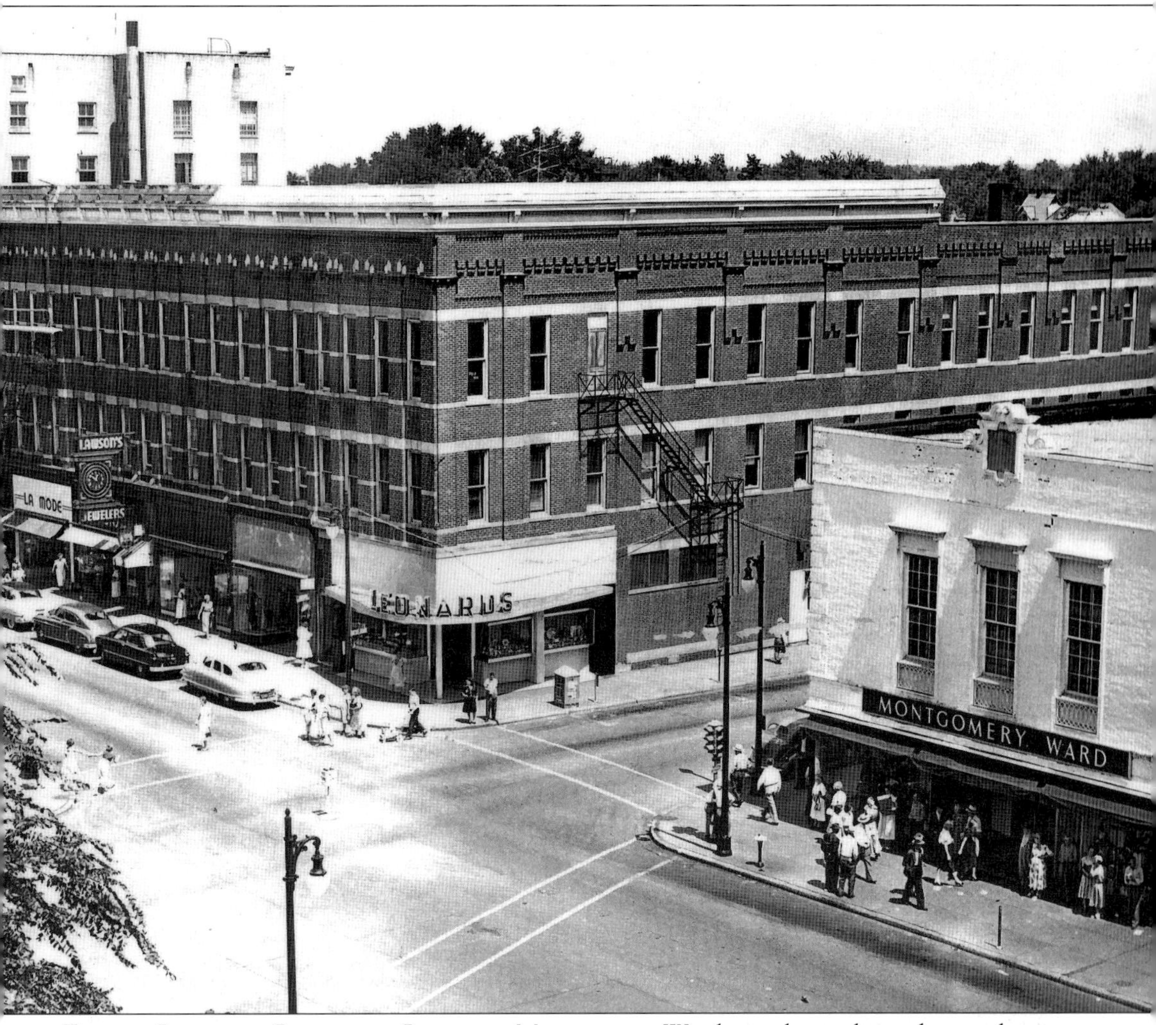

ENGELS JEWELRY—LEONARDS JEWELRY. Montgomery Ward was located on the southeast corner of Walnut and Main. Leonards Jewelry was on the northeast corner. None of these stores are there today. Engel's Jewelry is located where Leonards was. John Palumbo and David Granson are the owners. This picture was taken in 1948.

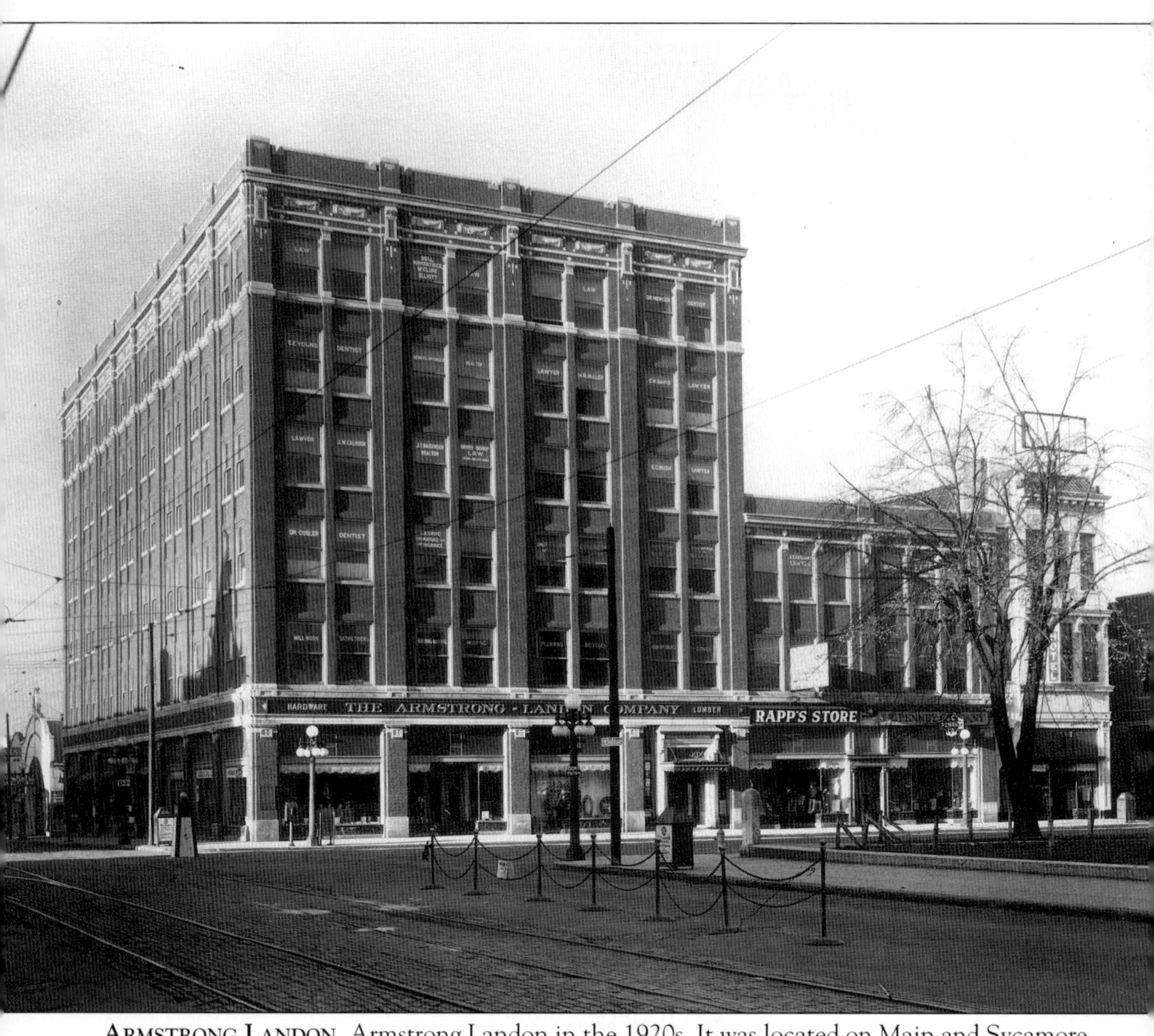

ARMSTRONG LANDON. Armstrong Landon in the 1920s. It was located on Main and Sycamore Streets. It is now the home of the First National Bank. Rapp's, JC Penney, and Hotel Central were also here. This photo was taken by John Ryan.

Three
THEATERS AND ENTERTAINMENT

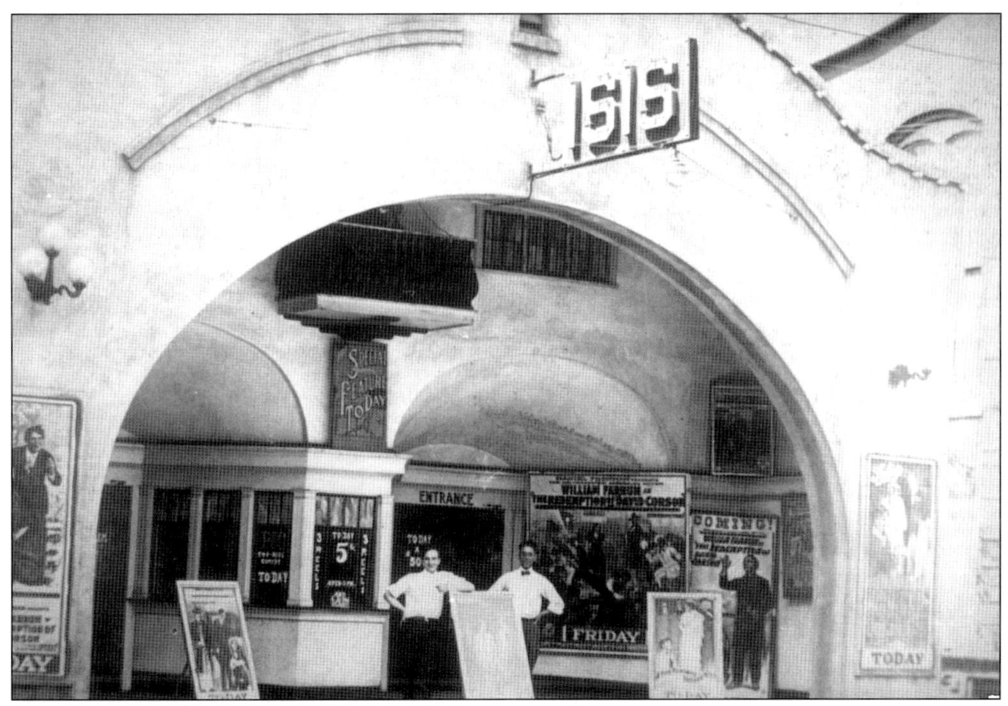

ISIS. Isis Theater was located at 111 S. Main. It is pictured here in its heyday in the 1900s and just before it was closed in 1960. The Isis had a balcony.

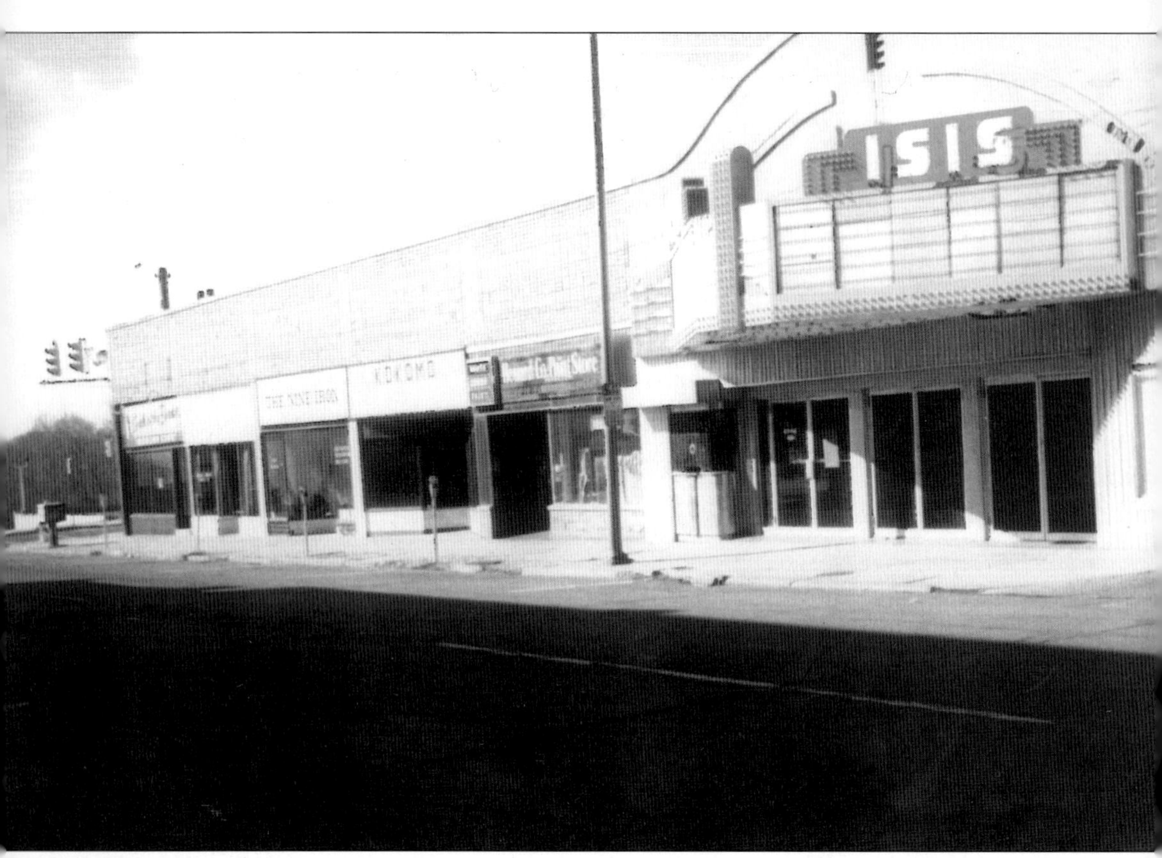

ISIS. Isis Theater before closing in the 1960s.

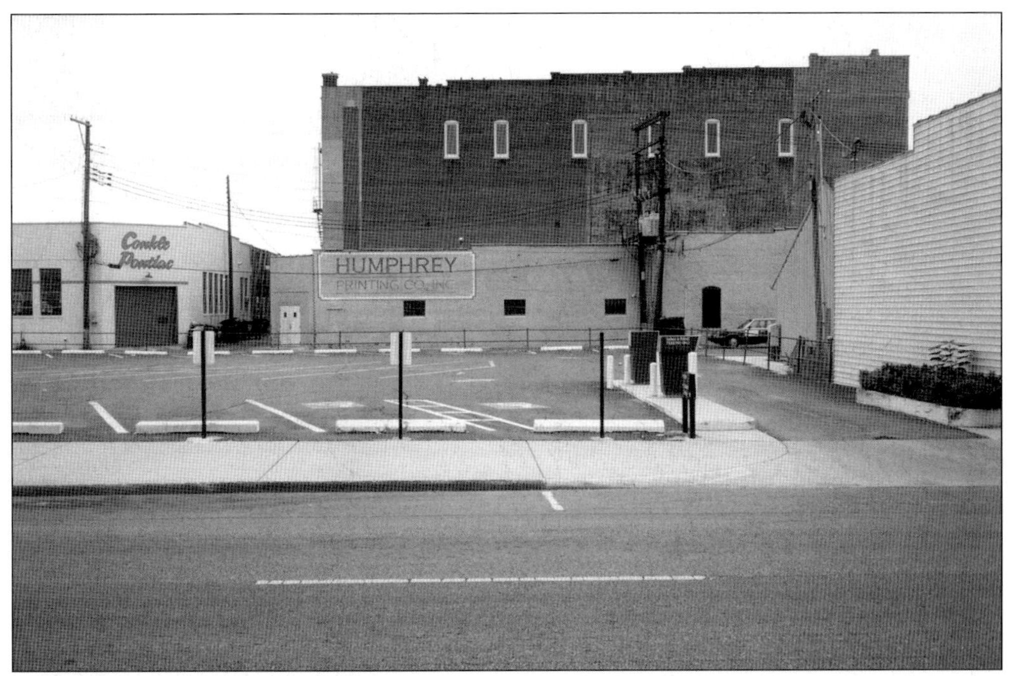

PARKING LOT. In 1947, the Fox Theater was here. In 2000, it was a parking lot.

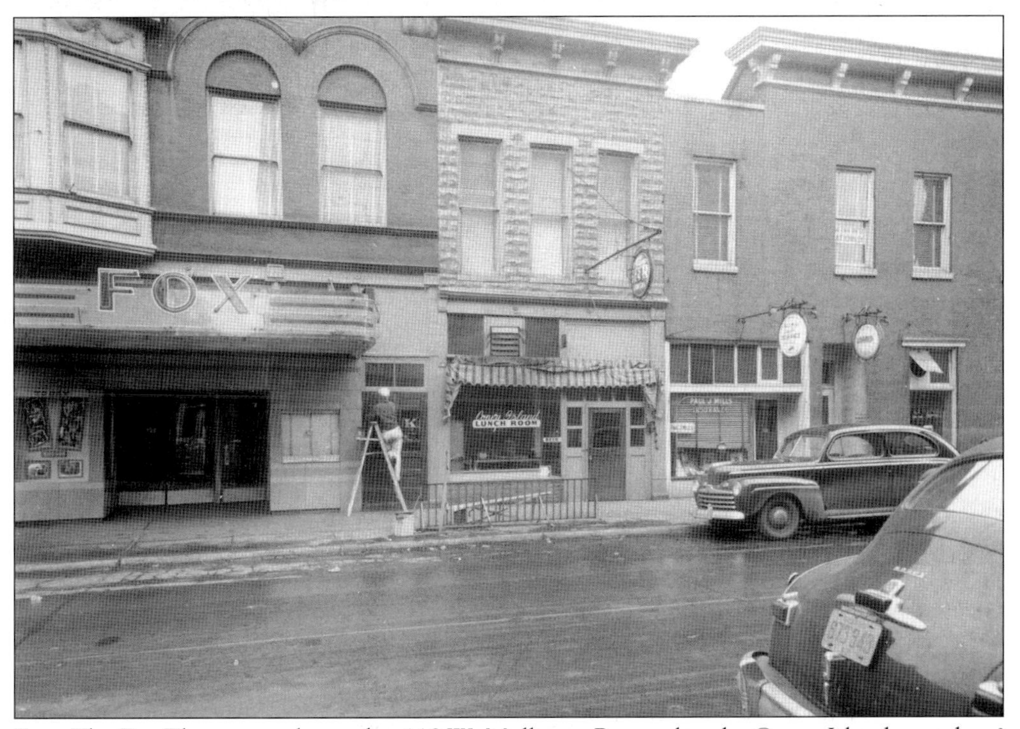

FOX. The Fox Theater was located at 110 W. Mulberry. Remember the Coney Island next door? Hot dogs were 5¢ in 1947, the year this picture was taken. Hoppy, Gene, and Roy showed up every weekend at the Fox. We would take our cap guns to the movies to help our favorite cowboys. Those were the days, my friend.

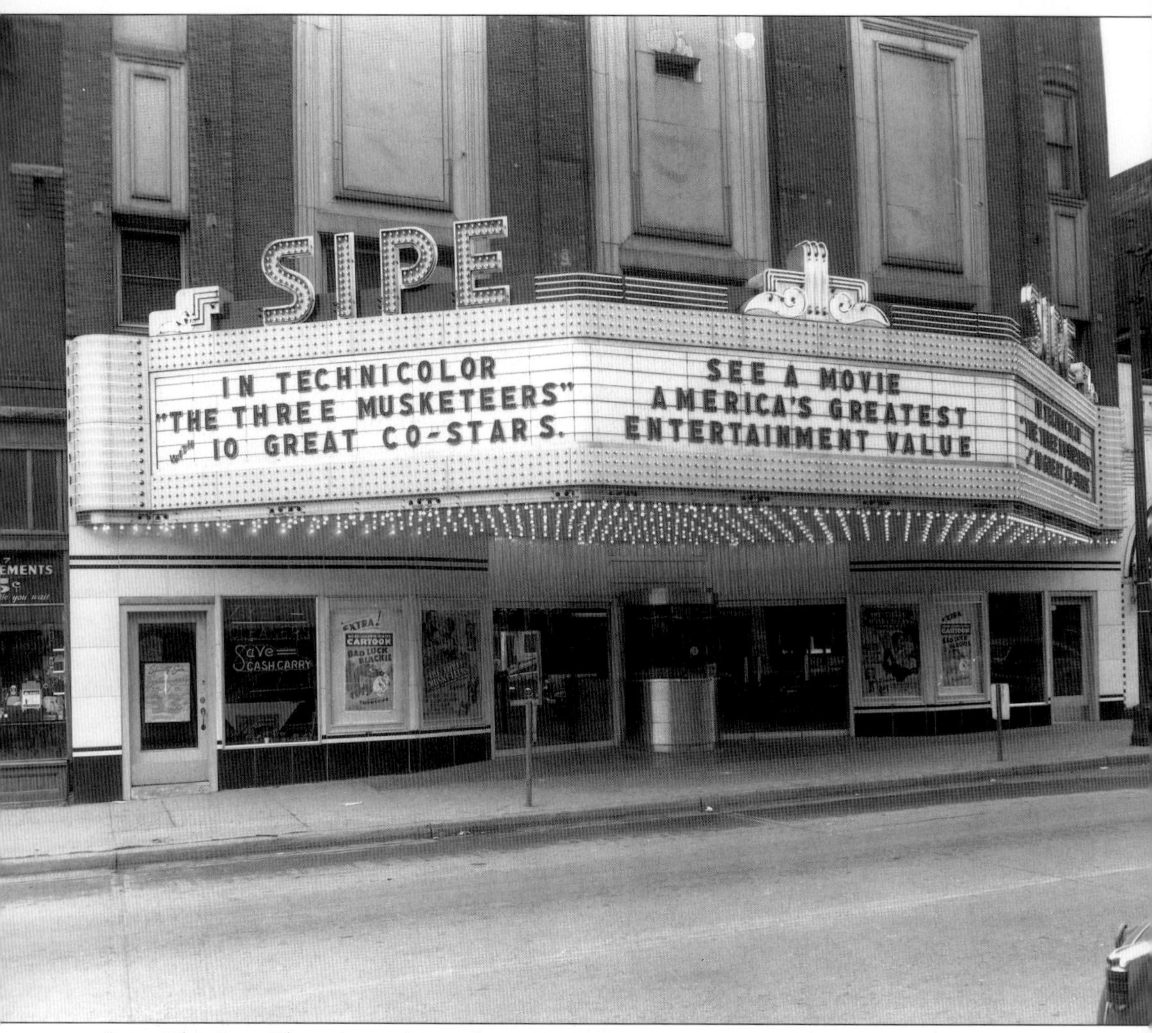

SIPE. The Sipe Theater was located at 127 E. Sycamore. It was the most beautiful theater in central Indiana. The balcony stairway was called "the Stairway to Heaven." We could have stayed in the balcony forever. The Sipe was like a magic wonderland.

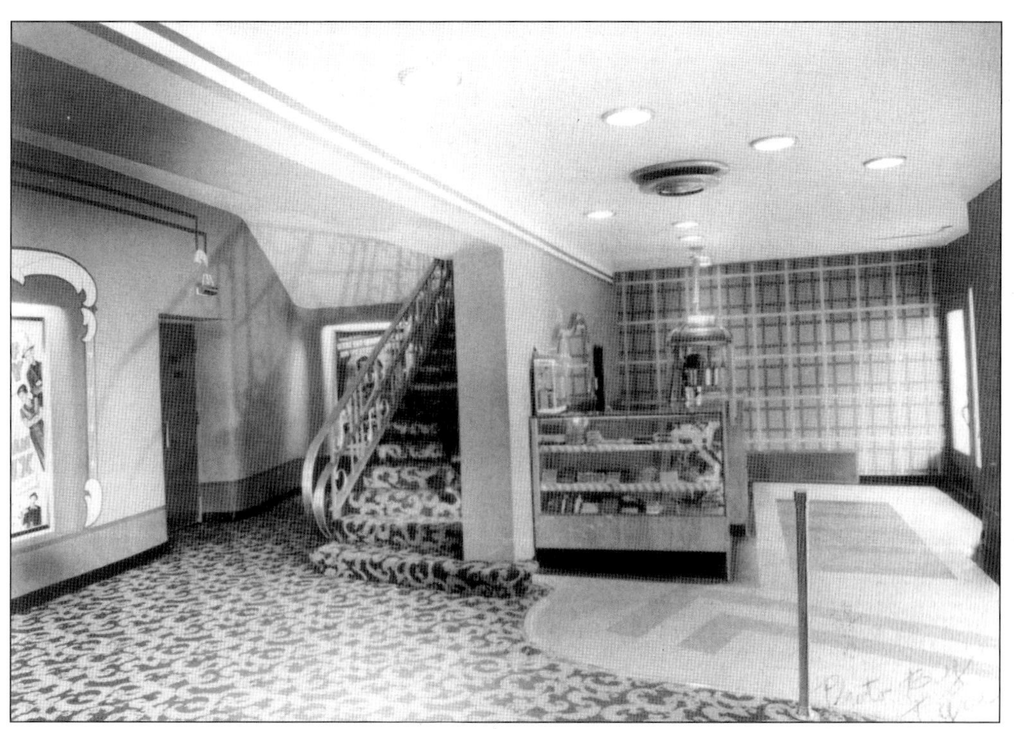

SIPE STAIRWAY. The stairway to the balcony at the Sipe Theater is pictured here.

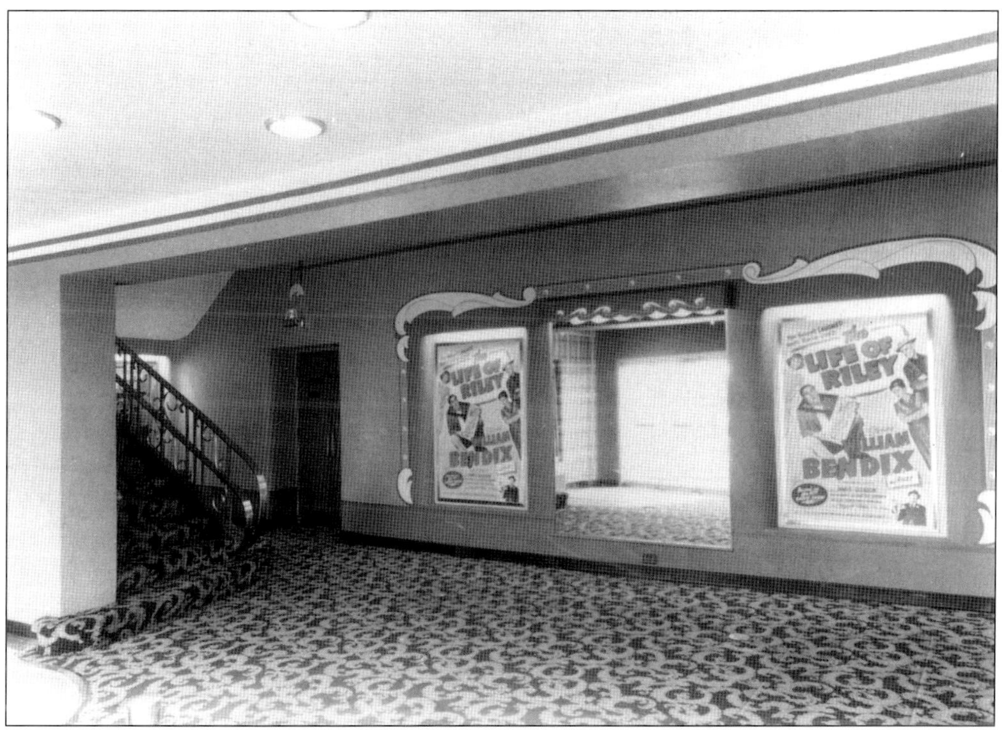

LOBBY. This was the lobby of the Sipe Theater.

Kokomo had a 'stairway to heaven'

■ Sipe Theater provided an oasis.

THOMAS HAMILTON

LOCAL COLUMNIST

How many can remember the balcony at the Sipe Theater? The year was 1948 and Kokomo was a teenager's dream. There was a dance every weekend, and Main Street was alive with excitement. But, we found the "stairway to heaven" at the Sipe.

Once inside the theater we would buy our popcorn and Coke and head to the stairway. The balcony was for those in love, and the Sipe had the best balcony in town. Once on the Balcony, we didn't care about the movie; we were too busy trying to get the courage to put our arm around our sweetheart. Once we got it there, it would get sore, or maybe even fall asleep, but we didn't dare move it. We held on for dear life.

Sometimes the younger kids would throw popcorn down at the "lovers" below, but it was worth the ridicule to have a girl's head on your shoulder. It was close enough for the sweet smell of her hair to muddle your senses. Sometimes it would take all the courage a fellow could muster just to hold the girl's hand, but to kiss her was wishful thinking. Ah, but the sweet smell of her hair and her bashful blush was something only a 15 year old could understand and appreciate. We could have stayed on the balcony forever. Time did not exist.

Do you remember the girls I'm speaking of? Were you one of them? Did you date one of them? They wore long skirts, bobby socks and saddle Oxfords. When a fella walked down the stairs of the balcony with his girl, he wanted everyone to see them. He wanted the world to know that they had been on the balcony together and that she laid her head on his shoulder.

When we left the balcony at the Sipe, we floated down Main Street with wings on our feet. We loved Kokomo and Kokomo loved us. We had Fenn's Soda Shop, Hooks Drug Store and a dance over at the Moose. We had the world on a string. We could go to Kresge's and get a Coke or a hot dog for a nickel and a hamburger for a dime. Surely this would last forever and the stairway to the balcony would always be there.

The balcony is now just a dream and we found that time waits for no one. Even now, when my sweetheart of 40 years snuggles up close on the couch, lays her head on my shoulder and I smell the sweet smell of her hair, I remember the balcony. I sneak my arm around her and leave it there, no matter what. Who cares what's on TV? I've got my girl in my arms and wings on my feet. How lucky can a guy get?

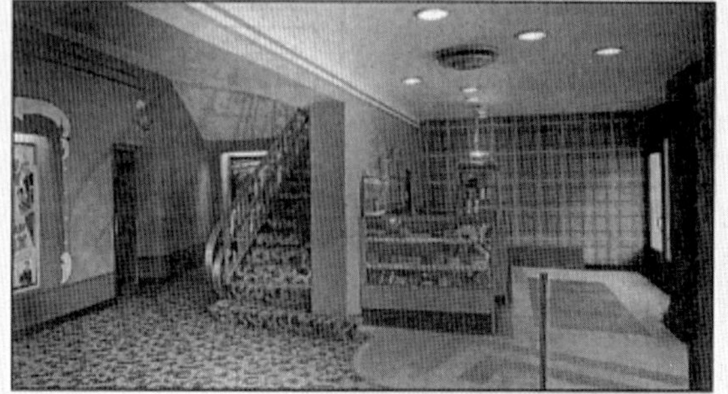

Inside the Sipe Theater, staircases led to "heaven." (Photo provided by Ryan Archives)

(From *The Kokomo Perspective*.)

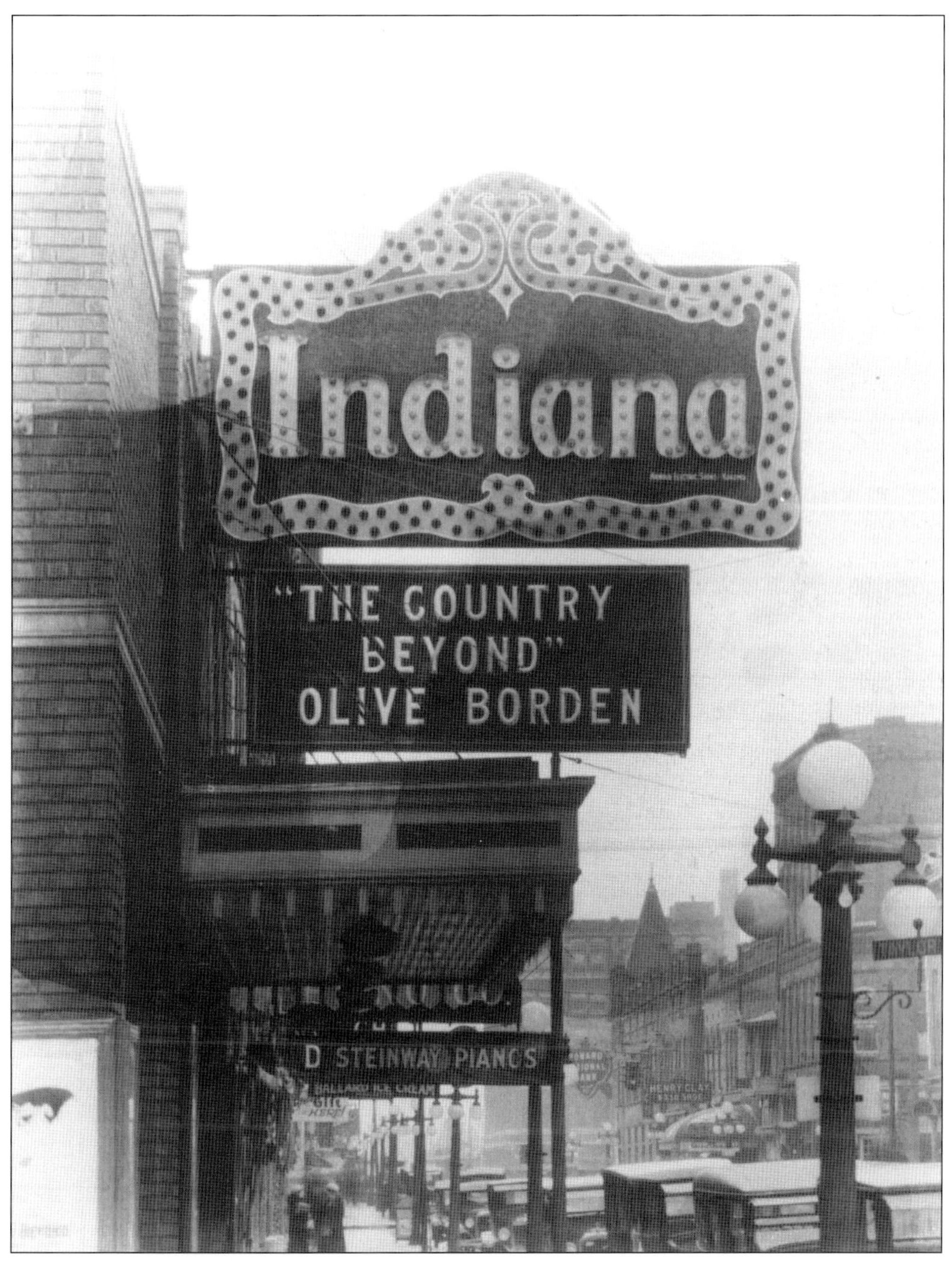

INDIANA. Indiana Theater was located on the southeast corner of Taylor and Main Streets. This picture was taken in the 1900s. Photo taken by Ryan.

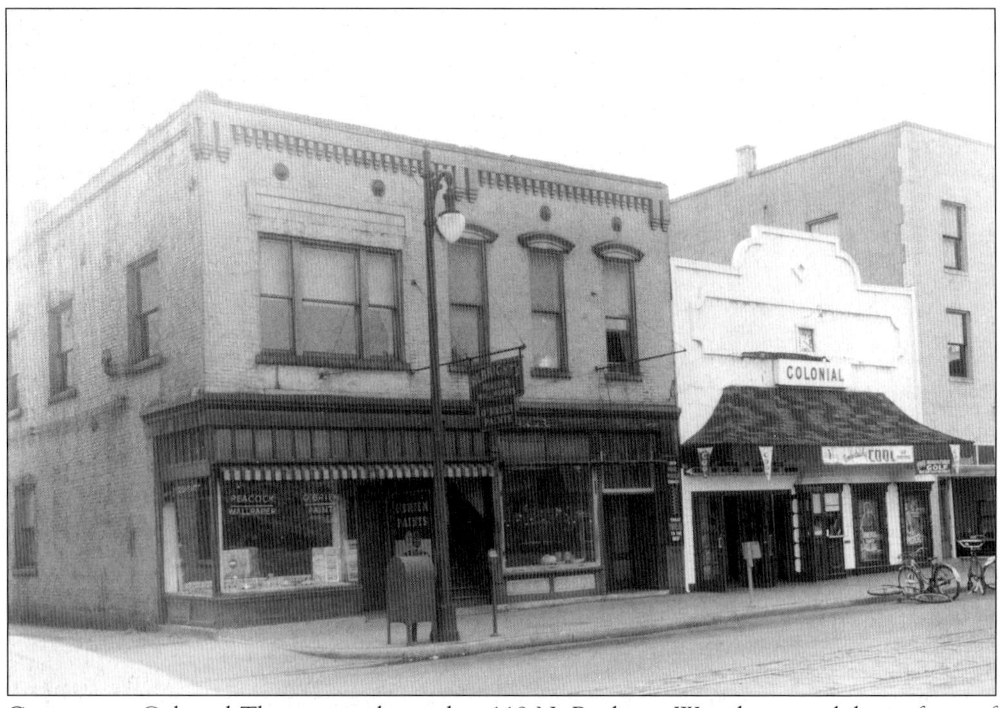

COLONIAL. Colonial Theater was located at 119 N. Buckeye. Was that your bike in front of the theater? O'Brien's wallpaper was next door. The year was 1951.

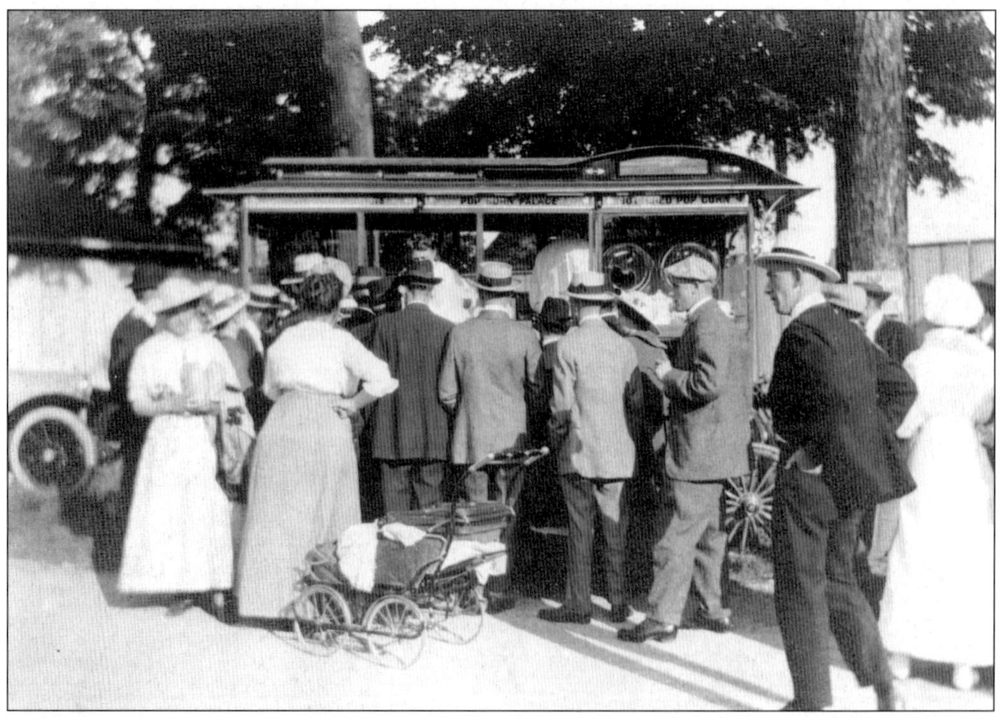

POPCORN. The Popcorn Machine was parked in front of the Indiana Theater in the 1950s, but it was used since the early 1900s. Photo taken by Ryan.

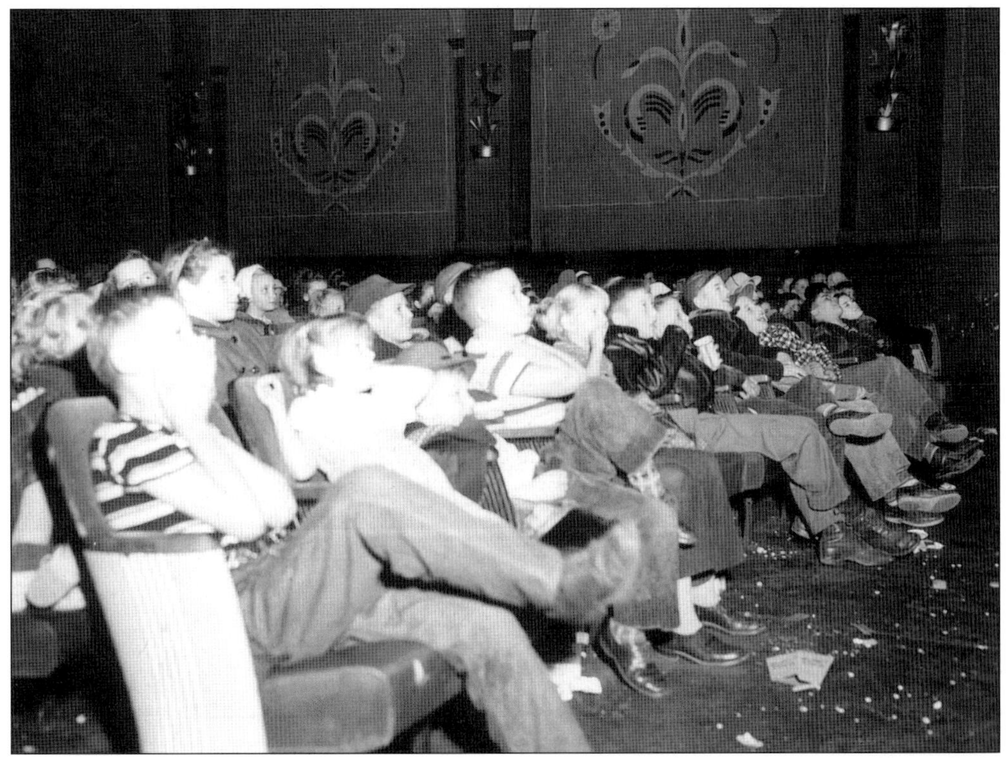

INSIDE INDIANA. These pictures were taken inside the Indiana Theater. It sure looks like a happy group of kids. Are you in this picture? It was taken in the early 1940s.

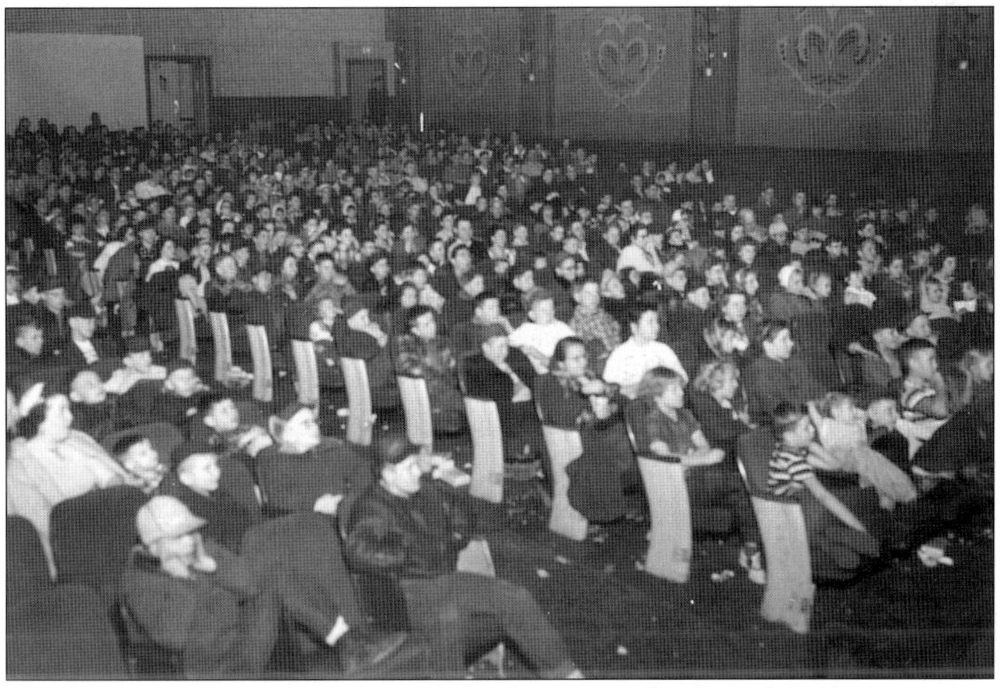

INSIDE INDIANA. This photograph of Indiana Theater was taken by Herb Sanders.

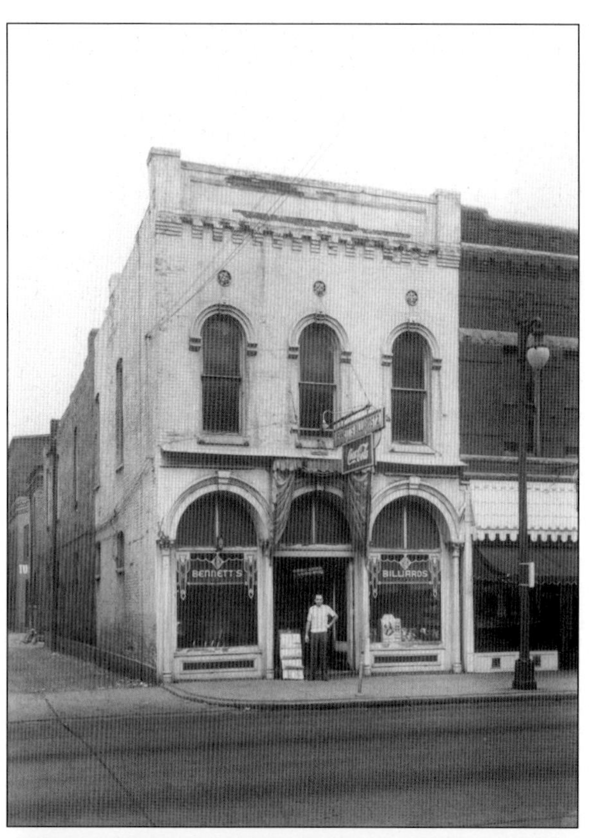

BENNETT'S POOL HALL. Bennett's Pool room was located at 100 N. Union St. (Photo courtesy of the Ryan Archives.)

WALKER'S POOL HALL. Walker's Pool Hall was located at 112 W. Mulberry.

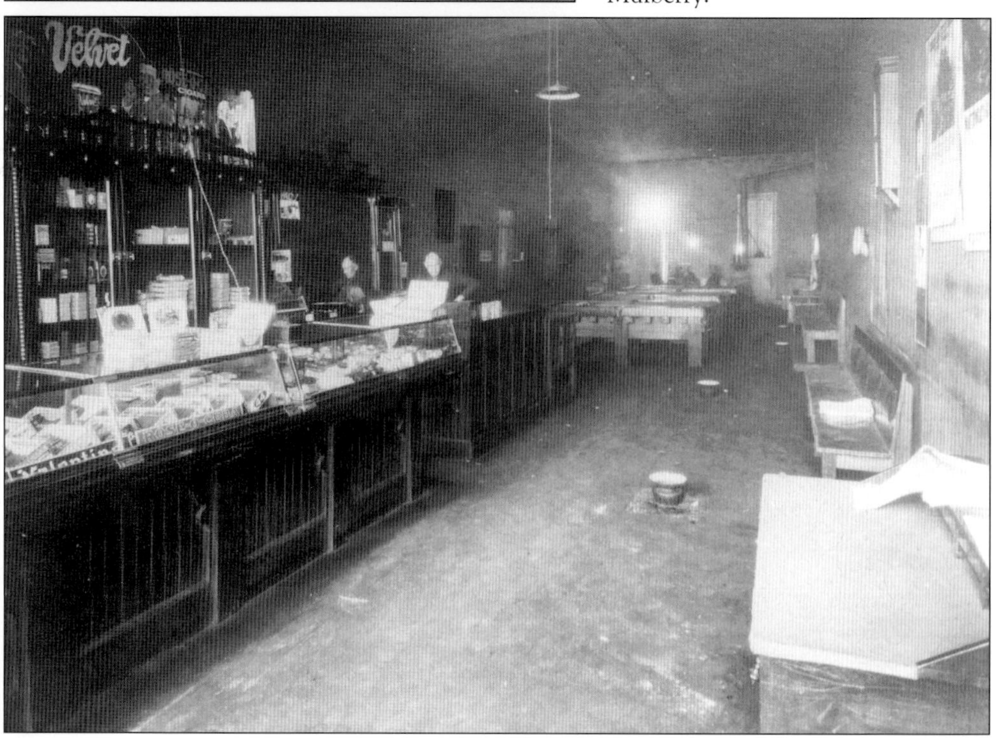

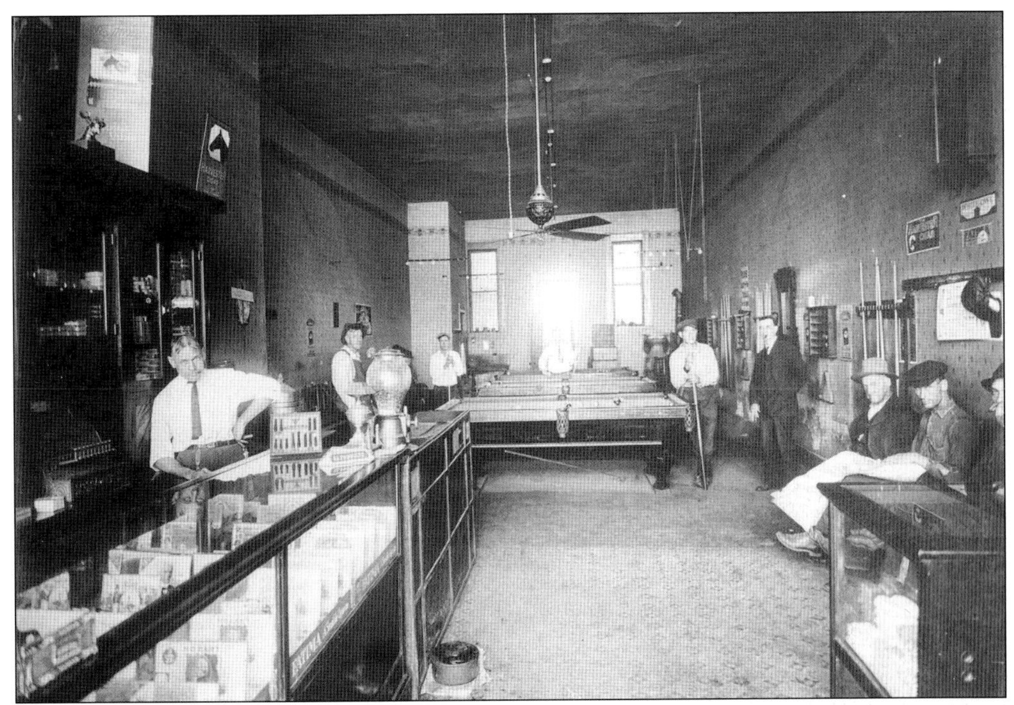

Rudy's Pool Hall. Rudy's Pool Hall in the 1900s, located at 116 W. Mulberry, was a place where a man could bring his four daughters in to watch him play pool.

Playing pool was cool at Rudy's

Thomas Hamilton
Local Columnist

Every man in town who is 60 years, or older, can remember Rudy's Pool Hall. It was among several pool halls in Kokomo in the later part of the '40s. Back then, playing pool or snooker was a popular past-time.

Everyone got along well at Rudy's. They had to; Rudy would not allow fighting of any kind, or horseplay. He was a swell guy and would even loan you a few bucks if you were in a pinch. I remember that Rudy had wavy hair and that he liked everyone. I also remember that he only had one arm, but he could rack the balls with the best of them! He also loved the great American past-time of baseball. He kept a ticker tape running with all the game scores and displayed them on a chalk board for all to see. Rudy's last name was Henger. He was born in 1888 and died in 1966.

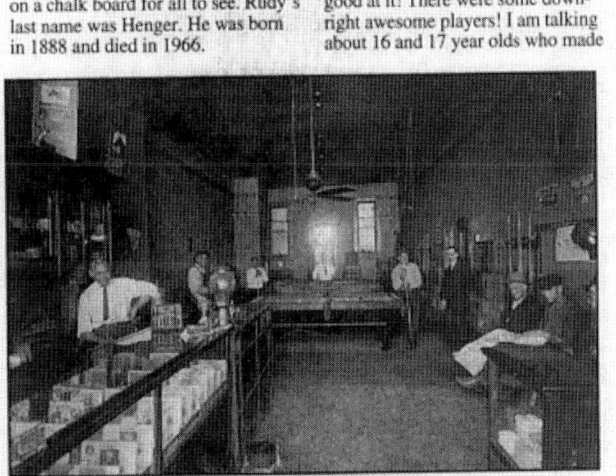

The guys who played at Rudy's were sharp dressers. Pegged pants, white shirts, and sweaters. We could play snooker and talk about our date from the night before. When you played snooker, you had better be good at it! There were some down-right awesome players! I am talking about 16 and 17 year olds who made three rail bank shots with ease! Sometimes is seemed like a shoot out at the O.K. Corral!

Only one time do I remember ever seeing any girls in the pool hall. I was in the back playing pool and in walked Andy Richards with four of his daughters. They were all dressed neat and clean. He had them all sit down in the chairs lined against the wall, as he shot billiards.

I was laughing and so were the rest of the guys. Those girls just sat there perfectly still while their dad played. We would try to get their attention, but they were well disciplined. When their dad finished playing, he simply hung the cue in the rack and walked out. The girls all rose and followed him in single file. We just fell over on the pool tables laughing our heads off, although later we did confess that they were all nice looking girls. I didn't want to admit it, but one sort of caught my eye.

Who can ever forget Rudy's? I cannot, because that is were I first saw my future wife without even knowing it at the time! I guess I learned a lesson that day. Whenever a young fellow laughs at a lady... she may just get the last laugh!

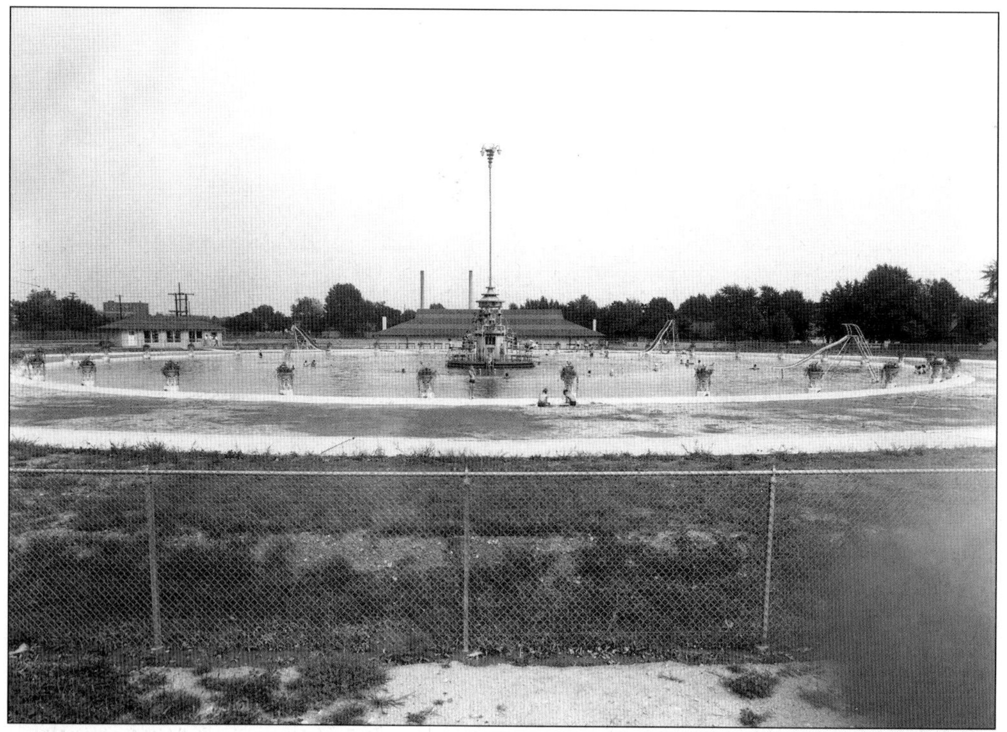

SEASHORE. This photograph of Kokomo Seashore Pool was taken in the 1930s by John Ryan. It was torn down in the year 2000 and another one is being built. The kids of the 1940s and '50s will never forget the Seashore. It was our home away from home!

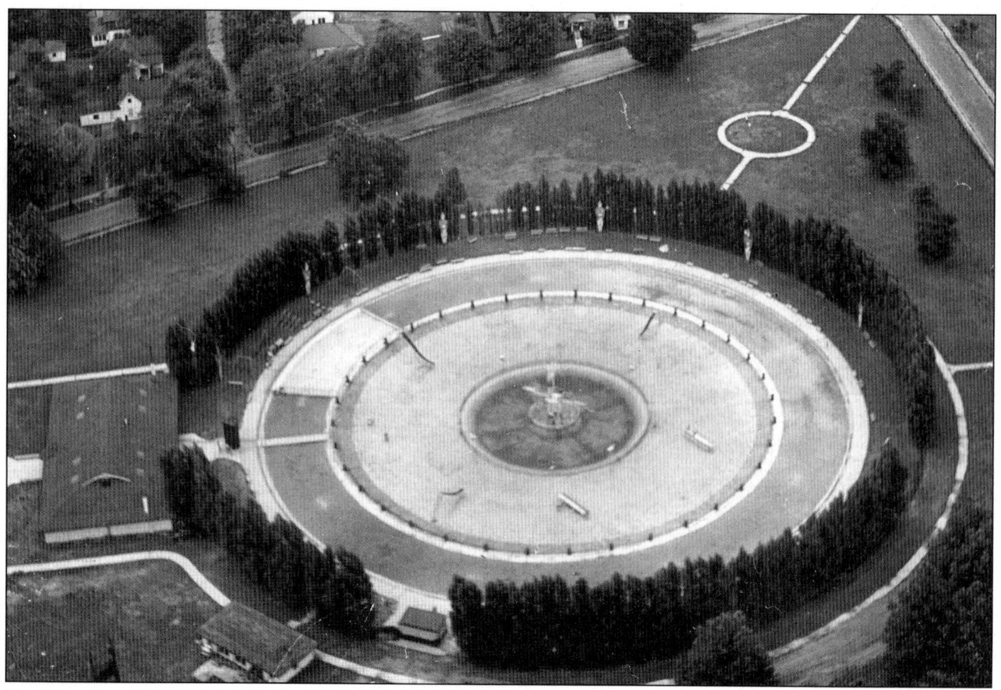

SEASHORE. This is an air shot of the Kokomo Seashore when it was first being put together in the early 1930s. (Photo courtesy of Ryan Archives.)

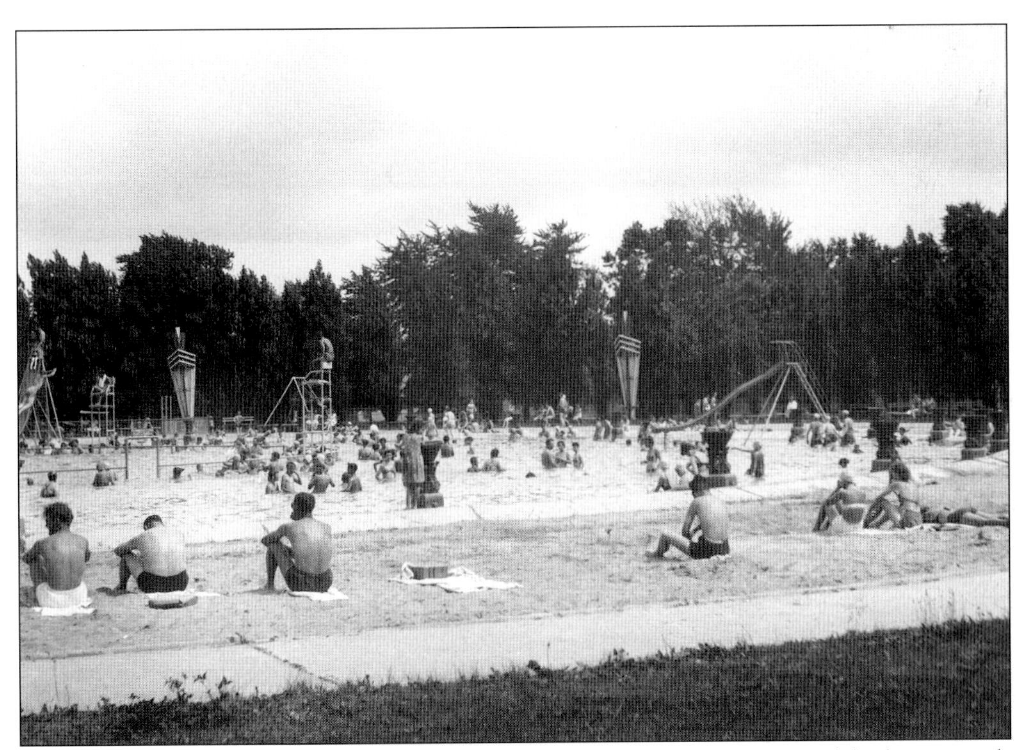

SEASHORE. The Kokomo Seashore opened in 1938. At the time, it was one of the largest pools in Indiana. It was a wonderful place to swim. When built, it cost $175,000. It was located on Park Avenue. It was torn down and replaced.

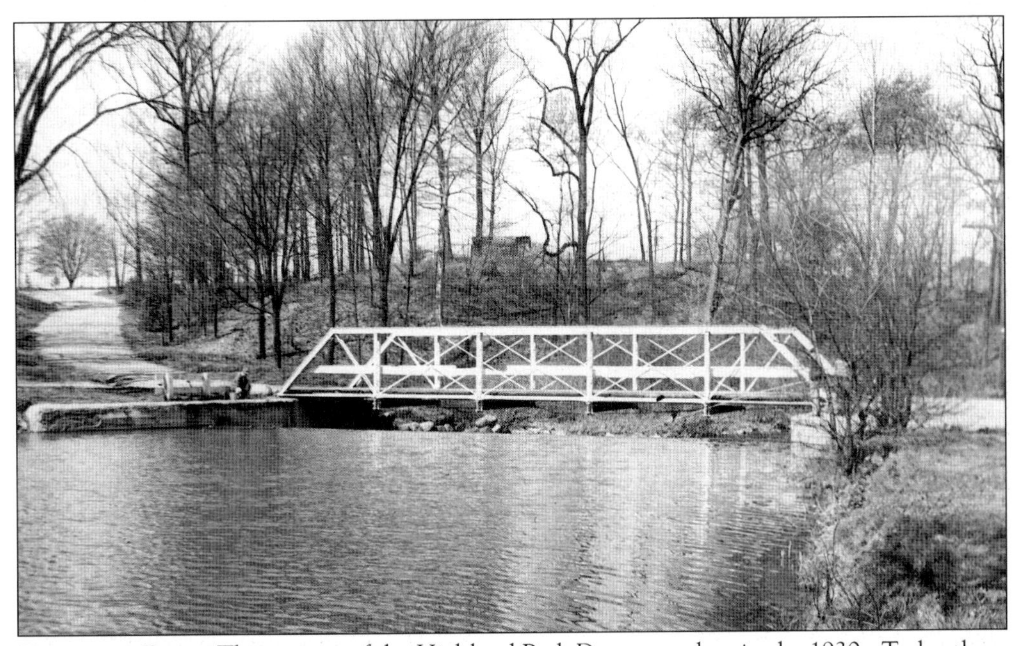

HIGHLAND PARK. This picture of the Highland Park Dam was taken in the 1930s. Today there are homes all around the park. If you look real close, you will see a man fishing. Wasn't it fun sneaking a swim at night?

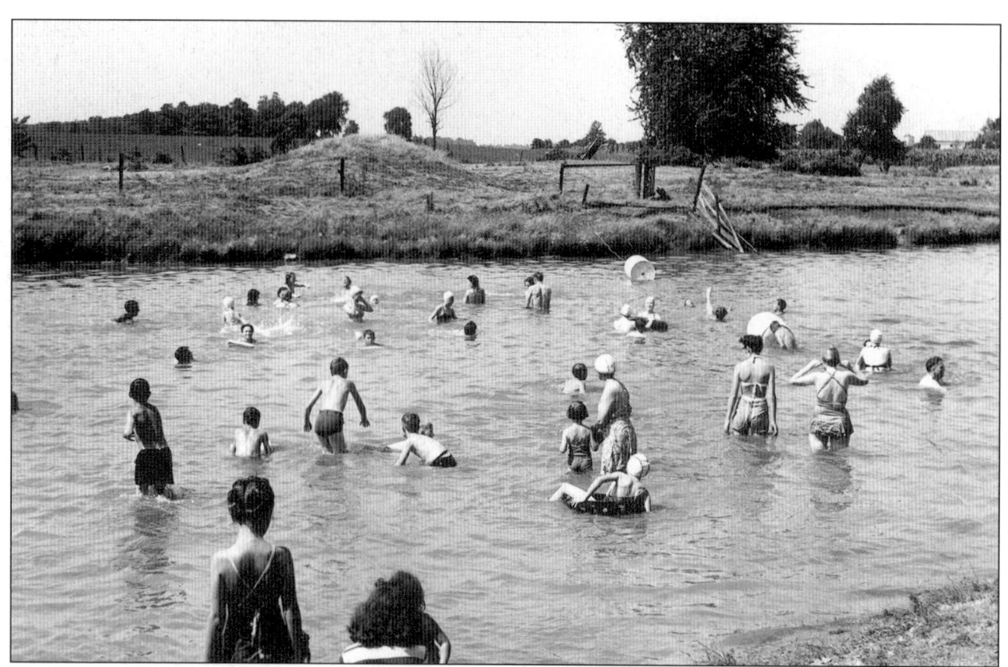

Wildcat Creek. Swimming in the Wildcat Creek was a pastime for young people in the 1950s.

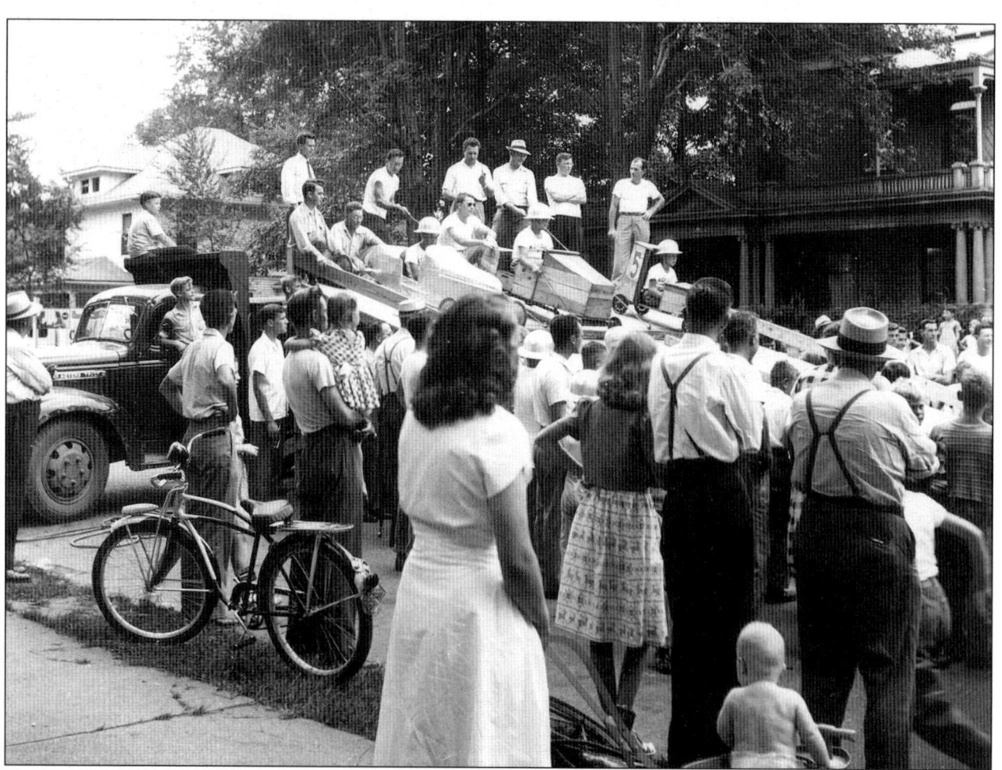

Soap Box Derby. These folks are getting ready for the Soap Box Derby. Families loved to be a part of this.

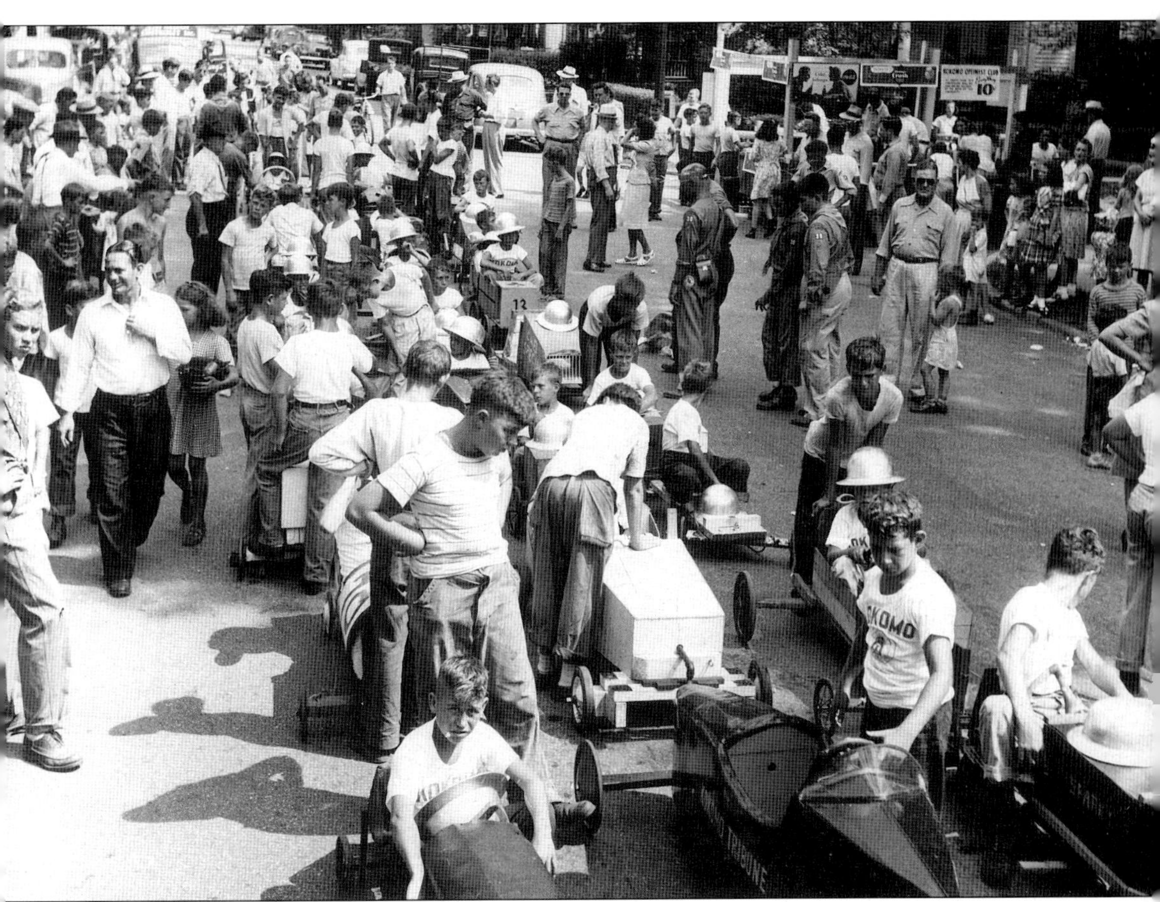

SOAP BOX. This is a picture of the Soap Box Derby, taken in Kokomo. The year was 1948. Do you know someone in this picture?

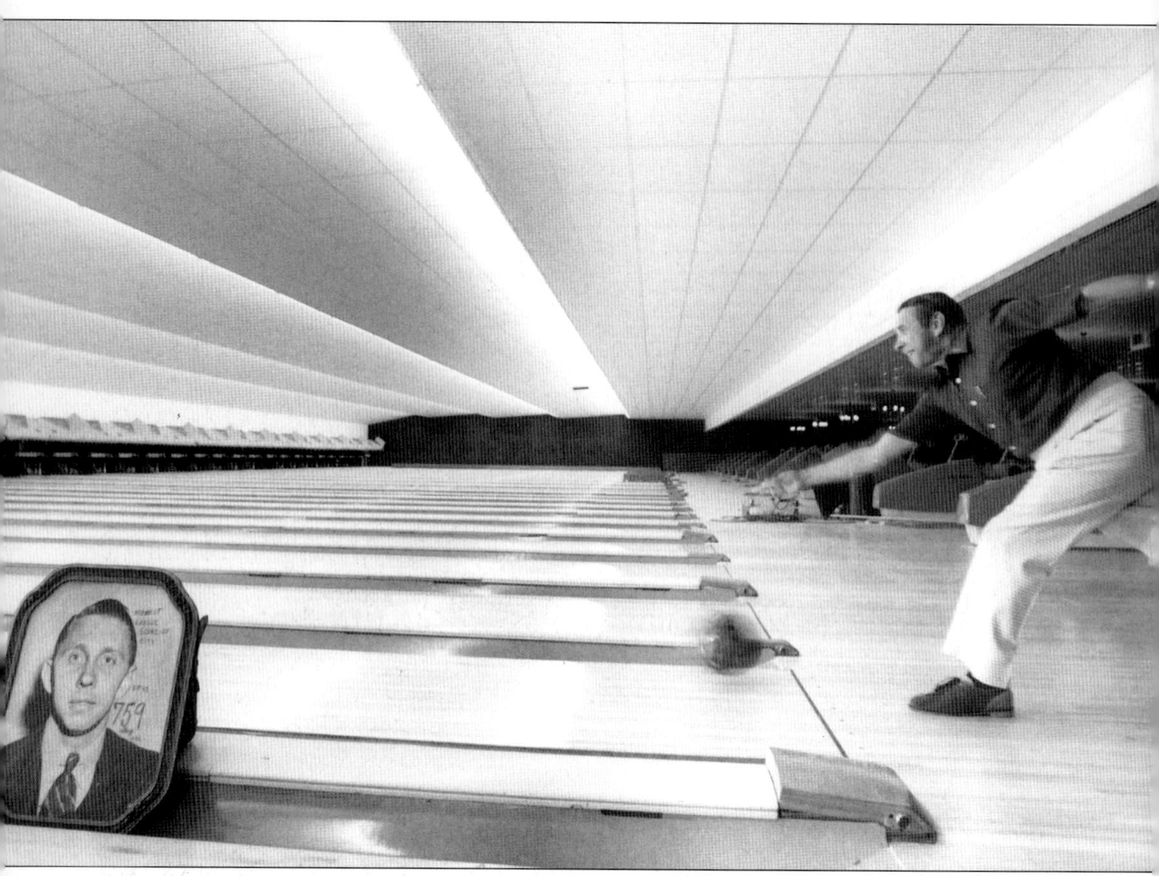

PLAY BOWL. Don Lowry bowled the first ball down the alley of this new bowling alley and it was a strike! It was also his birthday.

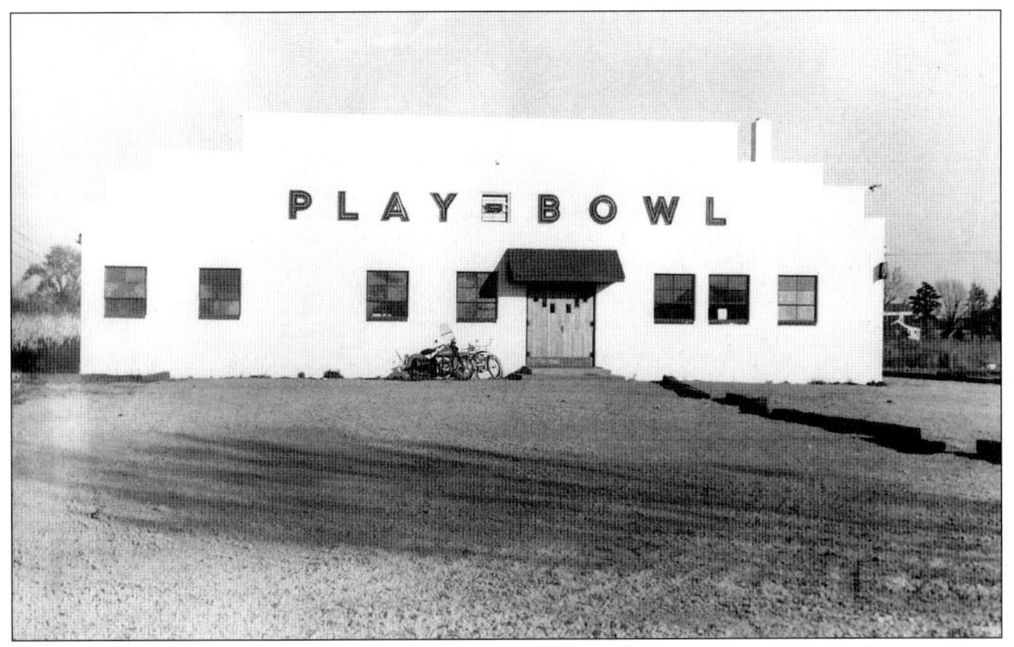

PLAY BOWL. This is the first Play Bowl Alley, located on the east side of US-31. Pictured here in 1952. It had 12 alleys. Don Lowry was the owner. He later opened a new Play Bowl at 301 W. Lincoln Road with 32 lanes. Lowry and his wife, Willie, gave pro-bowler Don Johnson his start in bowling.

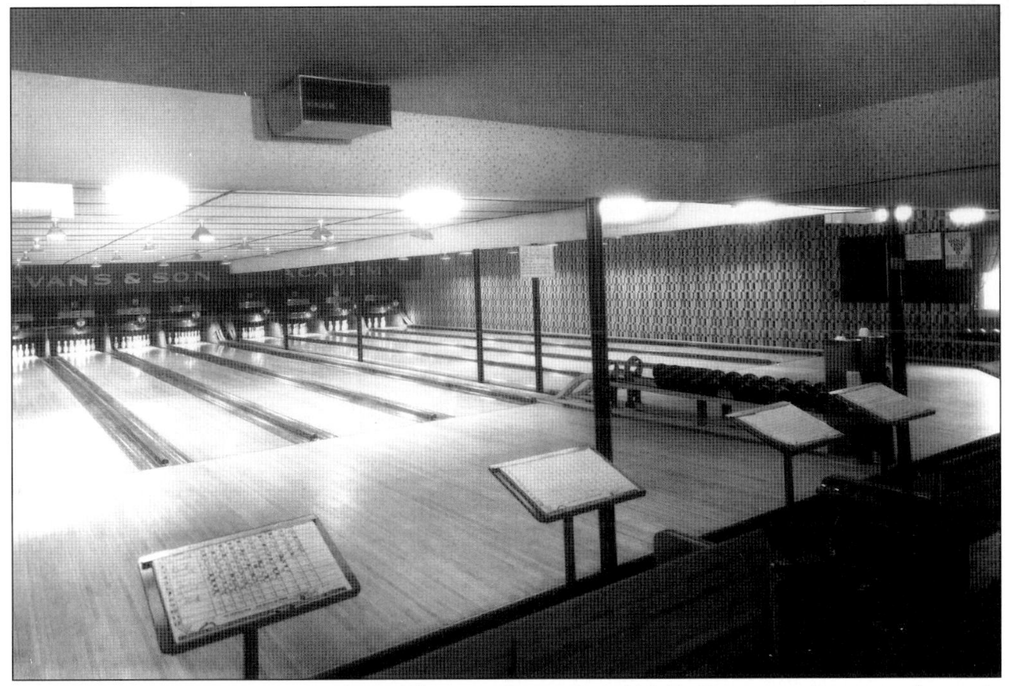

EVAN'S BOWLING. Evan's Bowling Alley was located at 212 E. Sycamore Street in the early 1940s. There were no automatic pin setters. Boys would set up the pins each time a person threw the bowling ball. (Photo courtesy of the Ryan Archives.)

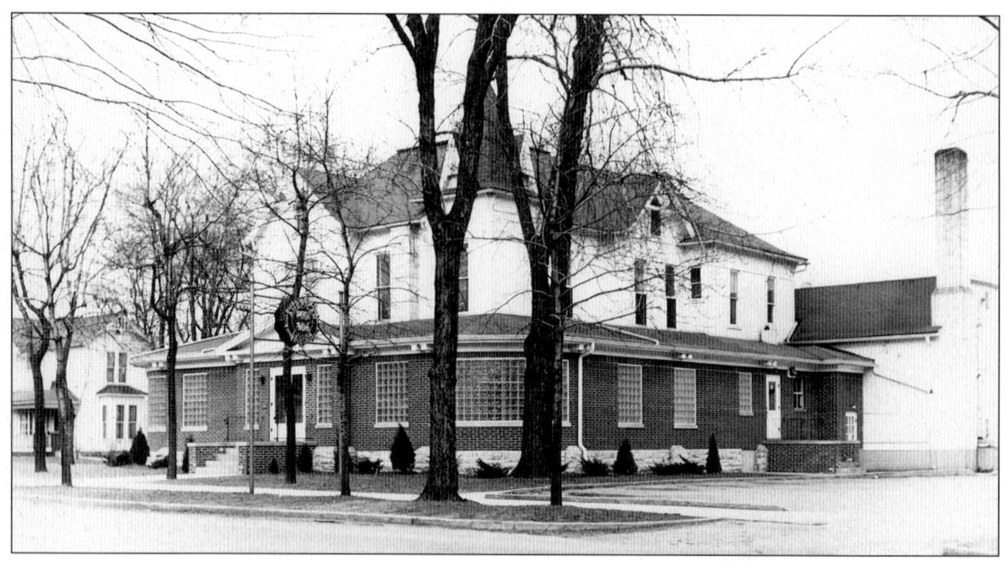

AMERICAN LEGION. The American Legion was located at 218 Apperson Way in 1948. They had a very good dance floor and it was also a great place to buy drinks and eat. In order to get in, you had to speak through a speaker and then a buzzer would open the door. (Photo courtesy of Robert Davies.)

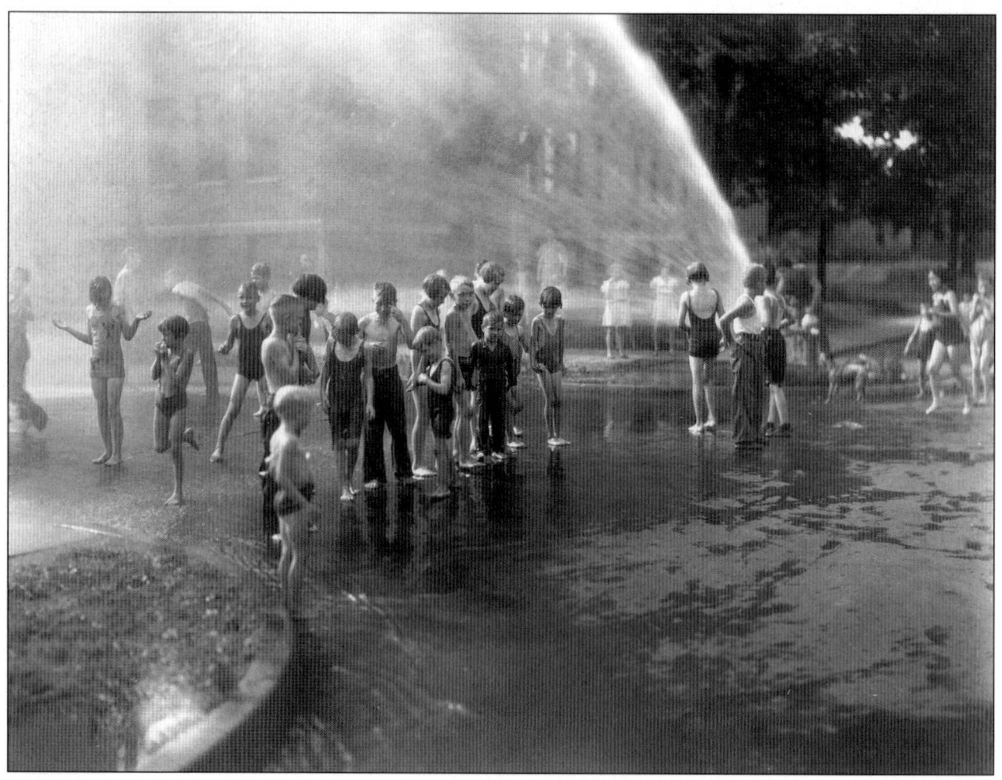

CHILDREN PLAYING. This was taken in 1936. This photo shows children playing in the water. It was taken at the corner of Harrison and South Bell. If you look real close you can see Meridian School in the background. (Photo courtesy of the Ryan Archives.)

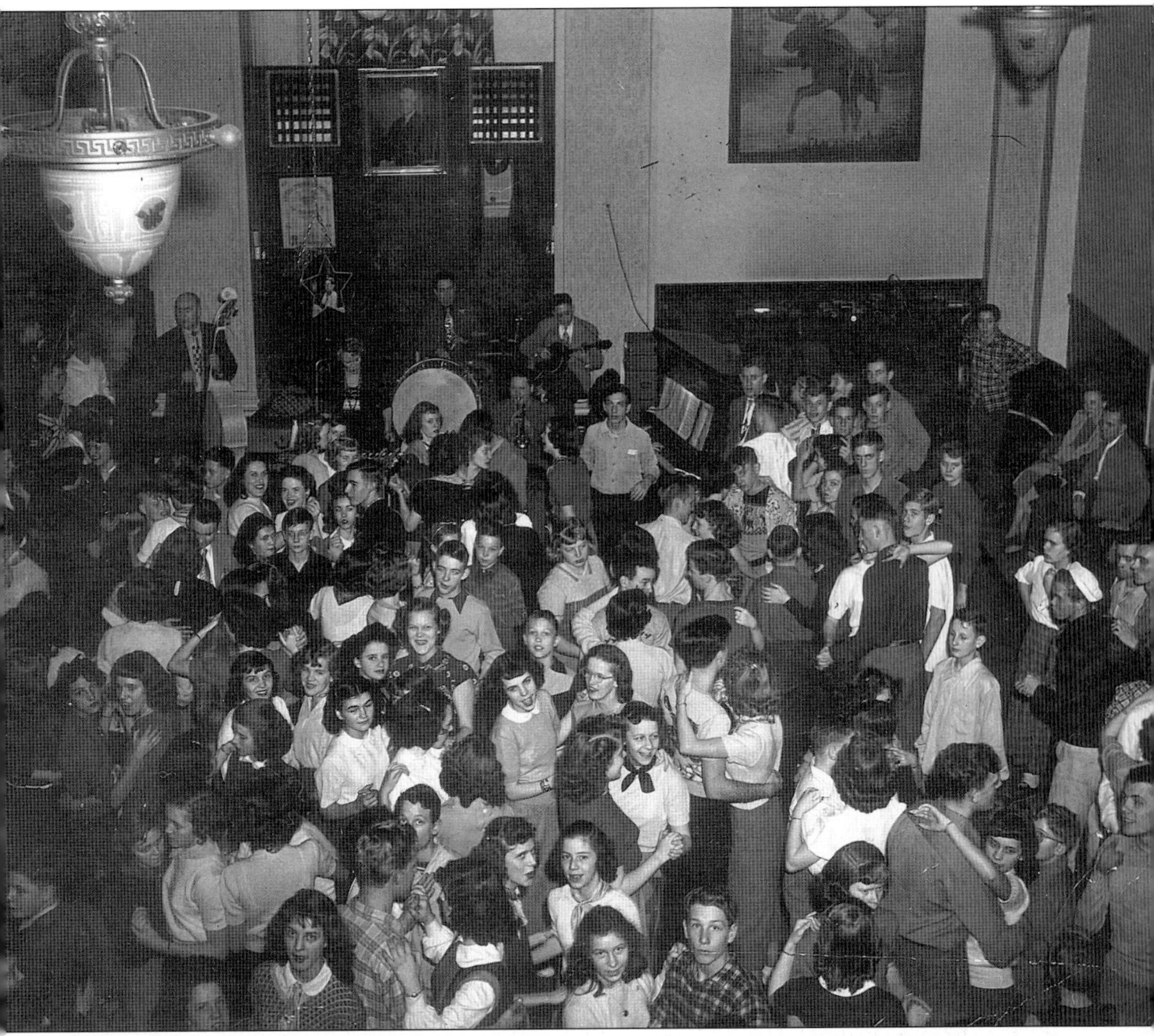

MOOSE. Who can forget the dances at the Moose Lodge? Can you remember Mr. LaVon Fipps? He was responsible for these teen dances. His wife, Helen, was the disc jockey. She paid for the records herself. All this at no cost to the teens! Are you in this picture? Thanks to Deloris Fipps Williams for the picture.

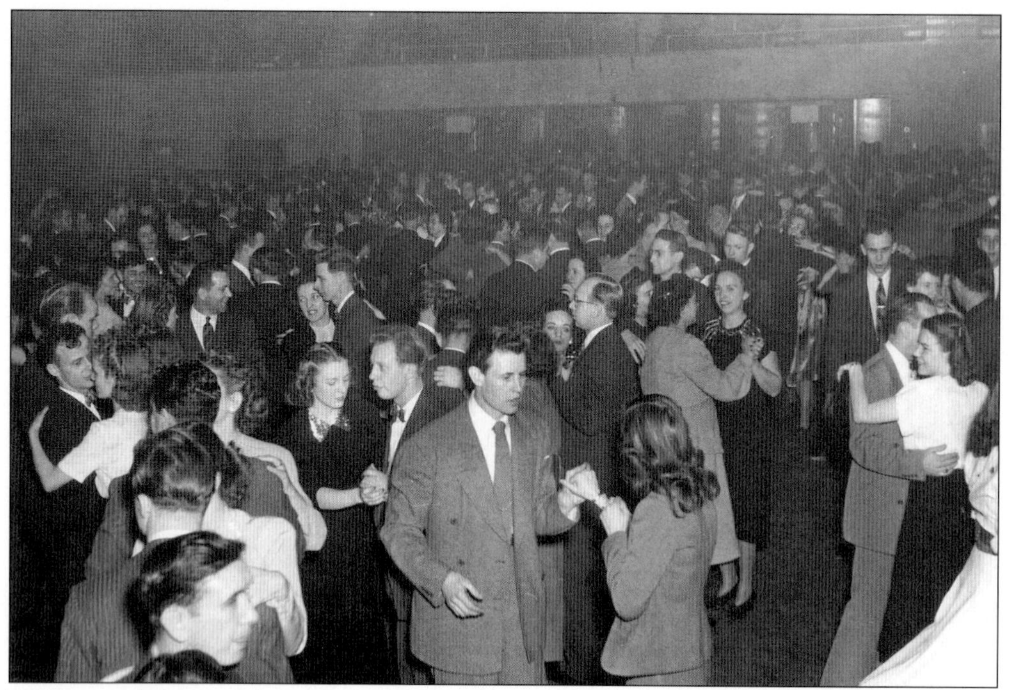

Dance at Armory. The year was 1948. The location was the National Guard Armory at 315 E. Markland Street. It was the Policeman's Ball. Were you there? The Kokomo High School played the basketball games there. Kokomo can be proud of the National Guard. It has been good to the city of Kokomo.

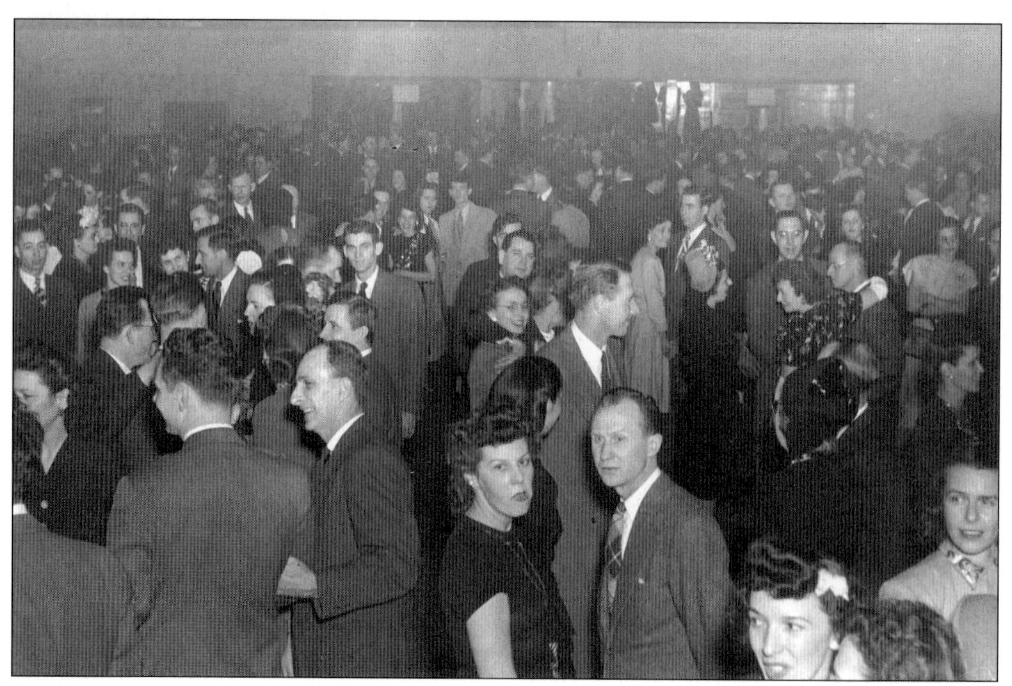

Dance at Armory. The Policeman's Ball at the National Guard in Kokomo, Indiana, 1948 is pictured here.

Four

RESTAURANTS

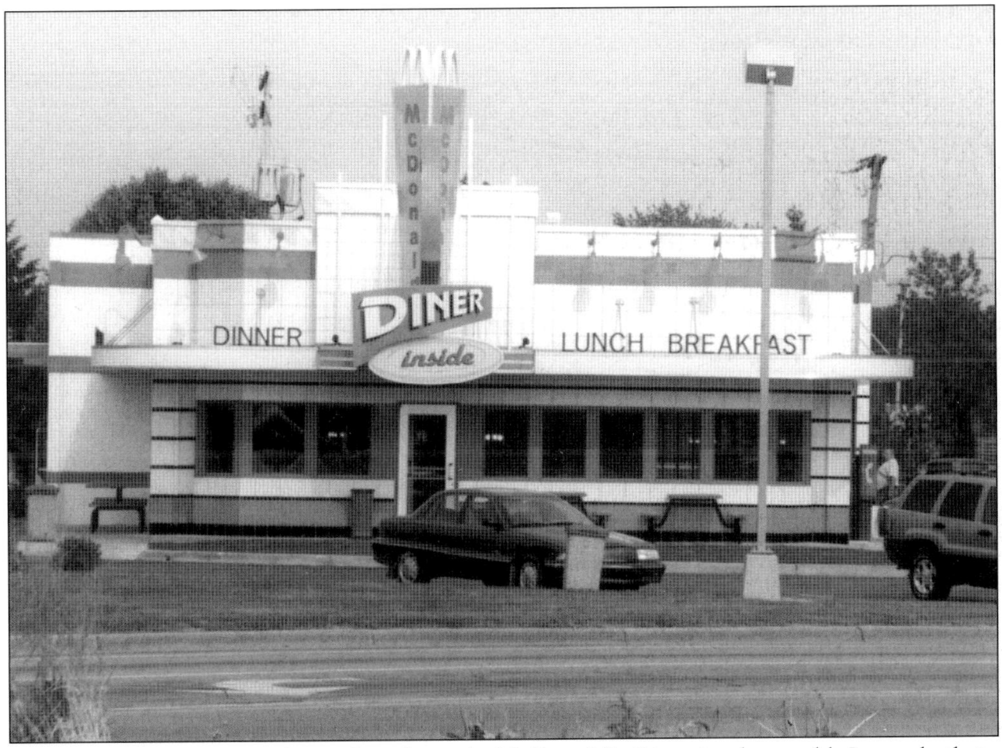

McDONALD'S DINER. Kokomo has the only McDonald's Diner in the world. It was built in 2000 and is doing a great business.

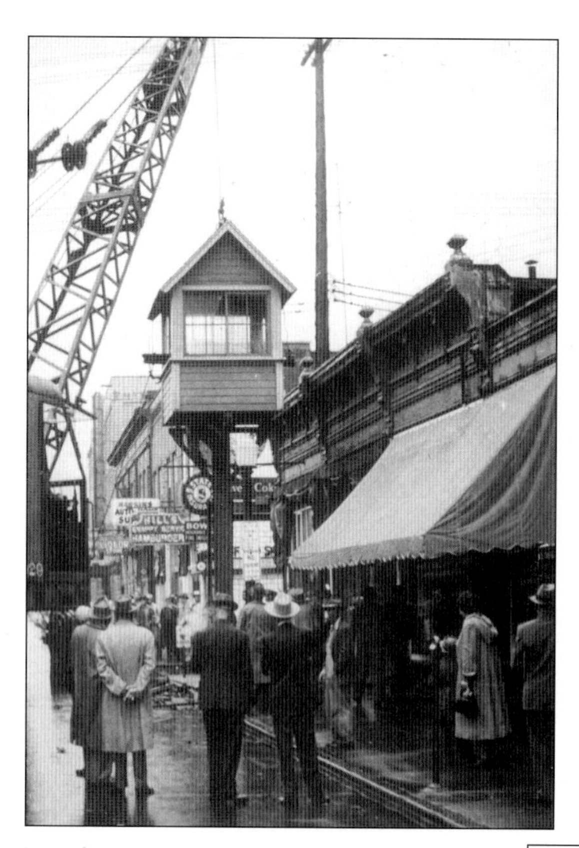

HILL'S. Can you remember Hill's Snappy Hamburgers? Hill's was located at 212 N. Buckeye Street. Their hamburgers were famous. Here is a picture taken in the early 1940s. People are watching the watch tower for the railroad to be set up. The tower is still here today. Hill's is now a parking lot.

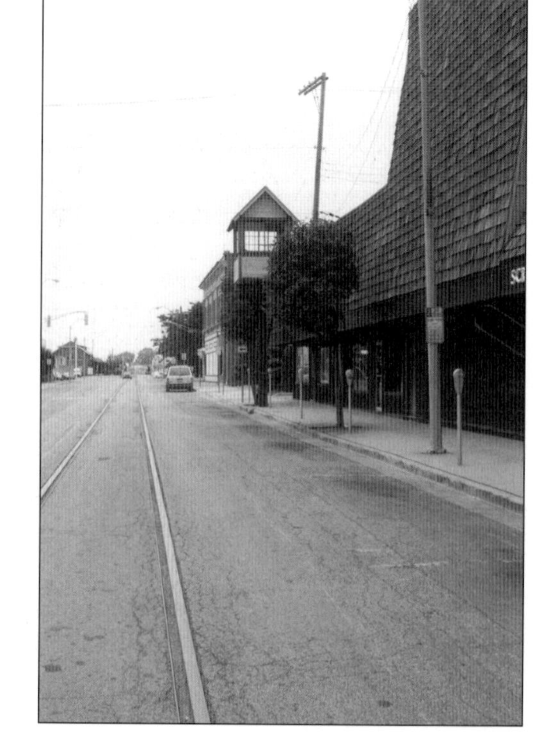

TOWER TODAY. Here is a picture of the tower today. I drove by there and thought: "Some nut might climb up there to see if it is locked." (It was).

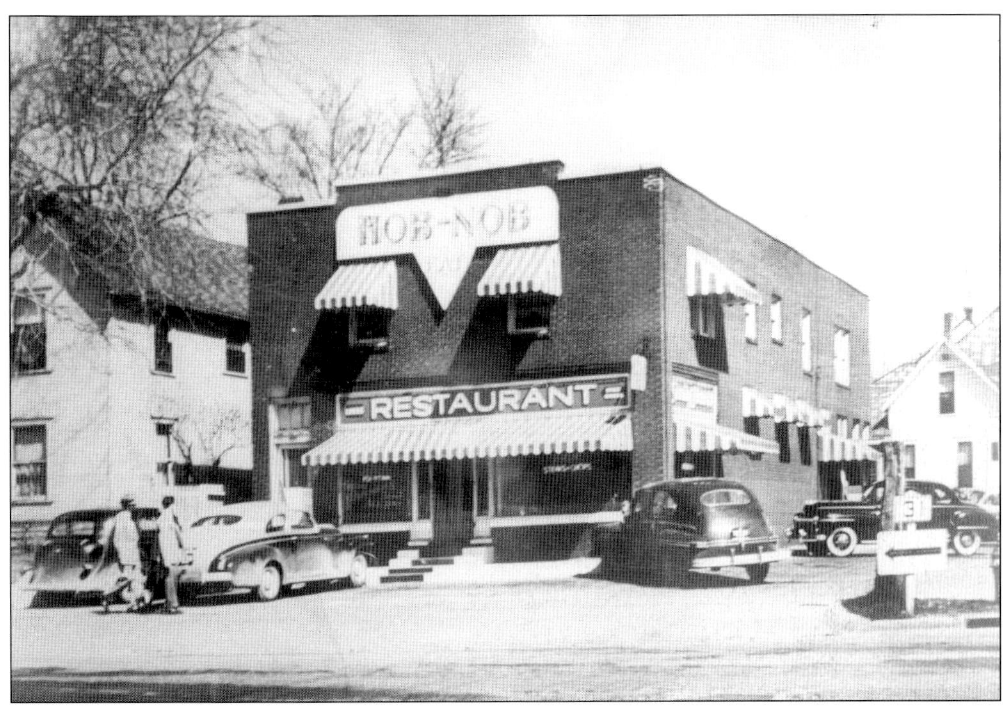

HOB-NOB. The Hob-Nob was located at 932 S. Washington. This was a wonderful place for teenage lovers to meet. This picture was taken in the mid-1940s. There is a Speedway station there today.

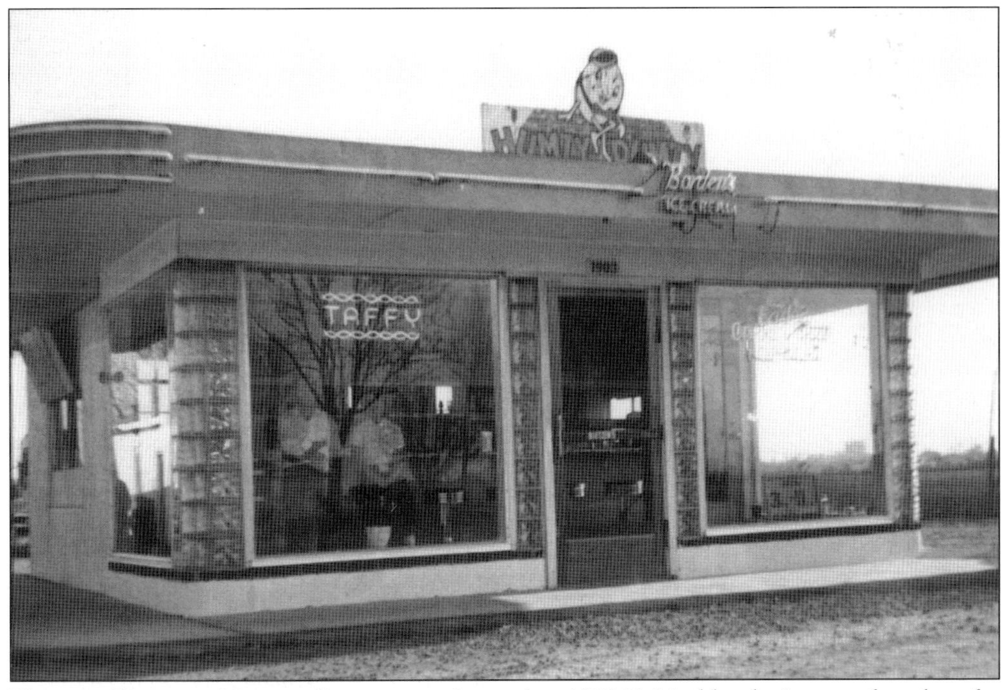

HUMPTY-DUMPTY. Humpty-Dumpty was located at 1903 E. Markland. It was a fun place for everyone.

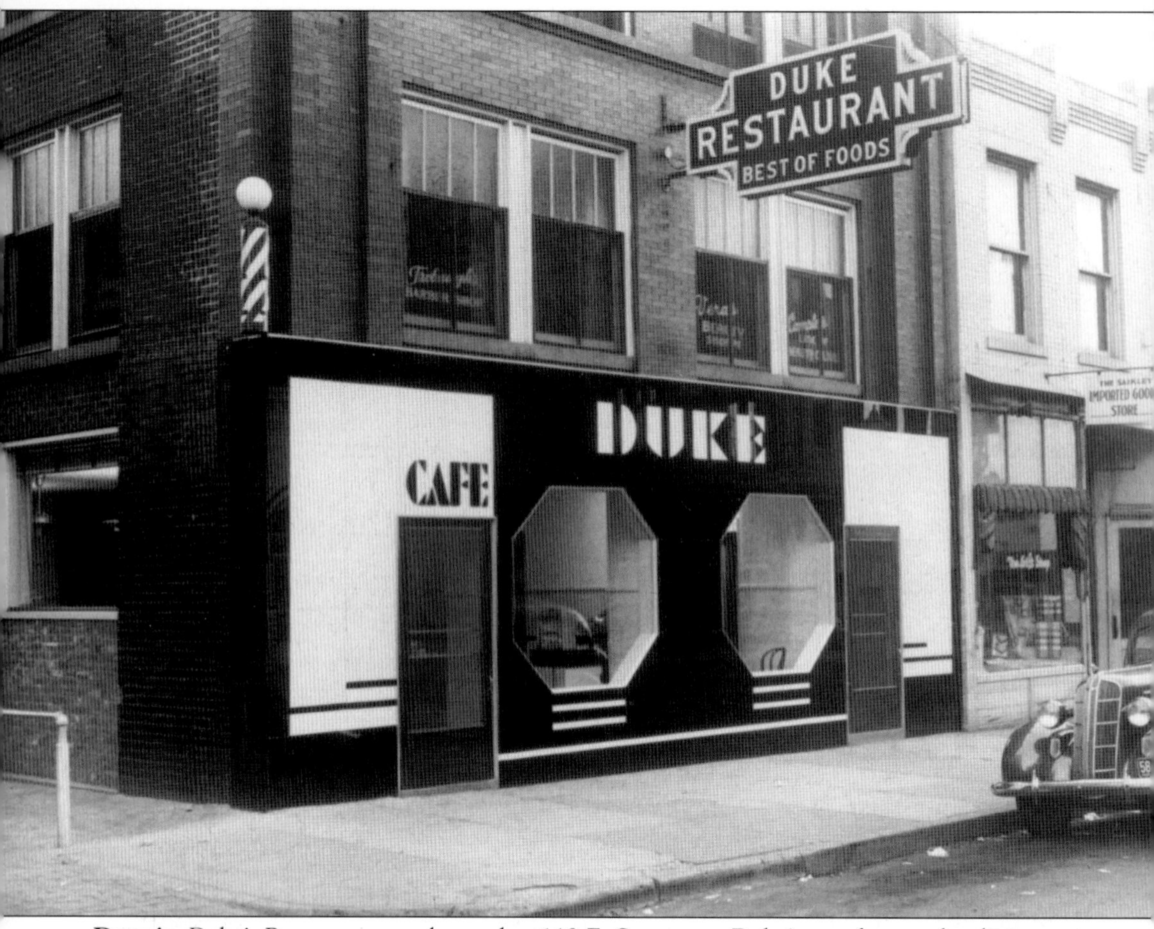

DUKE'S. Duke's Restaurant was located at 112 E. Sycamore. Duke's was famous for their sugar crème pie. Everyone knows about the pie, even people today talk about Duke's Restaurant. This picture by Ryan Archives was taken in the 1950s. It is now a parking lot.

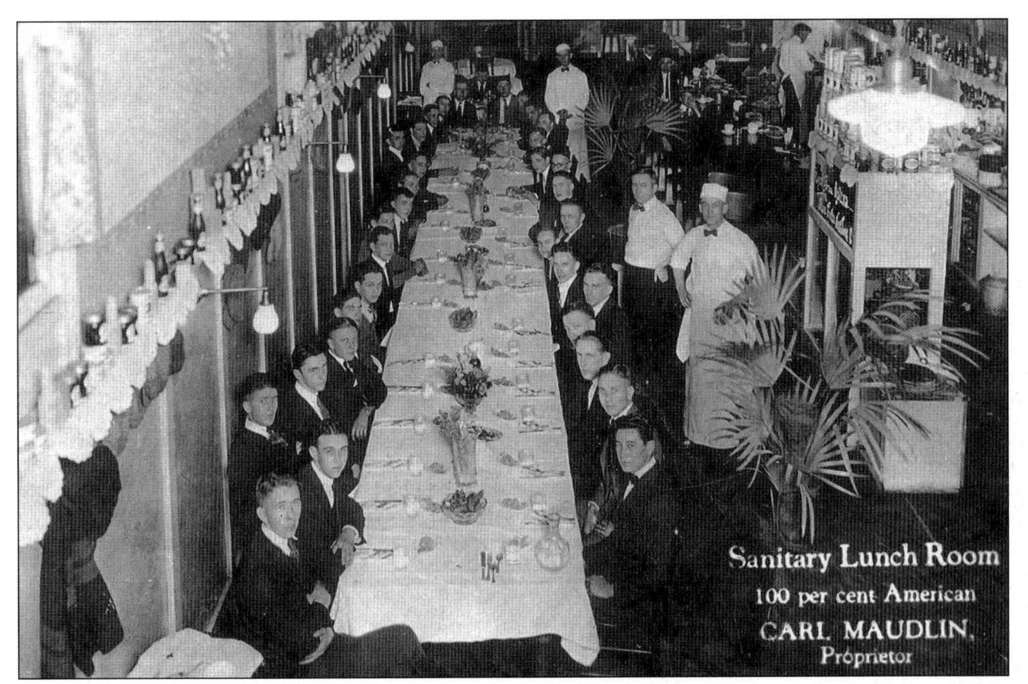

MAUDLIN'S. Maudlin's Lunch Room was located at 311 N. Main Street. This picture was taken in the early 1940s. Jamie's Soda Shop is there today.

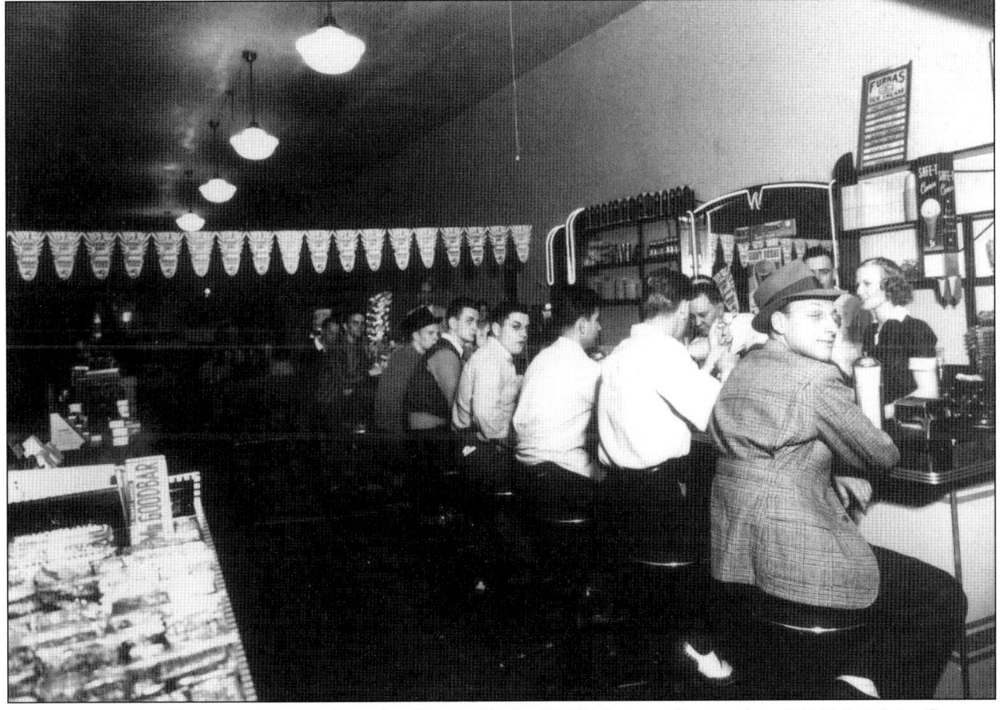

DORIS GRILL. Can you remember the Doris Soda Grill? It was located at 316 N. Main Street. This picture was taken in 1938 by John Ryan. It stayed open until 1954. Do you know anyone in this picture?

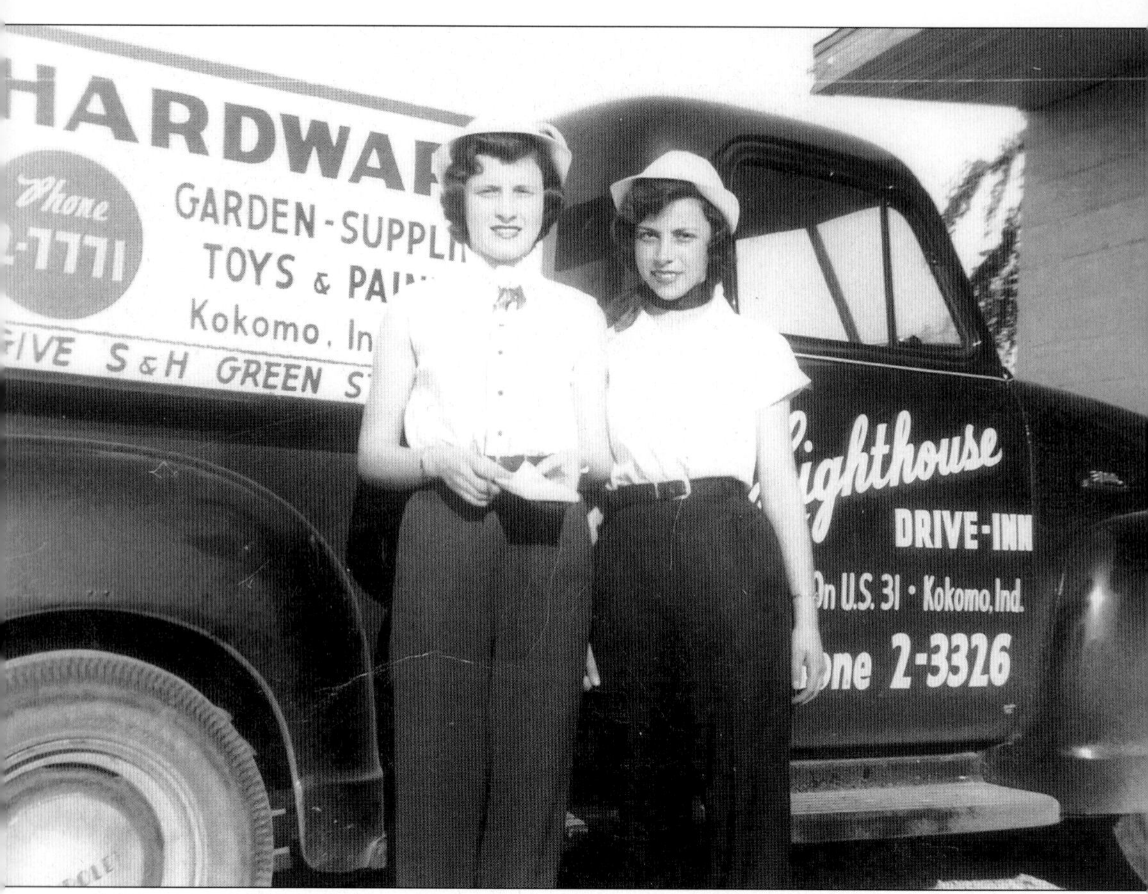

LIGHTHOUSE. The Lighthouse Drive-Inn was located at 3320 S. LaFountain. It looked like fun being a waitress, as these two sisters seem to have happy faces.

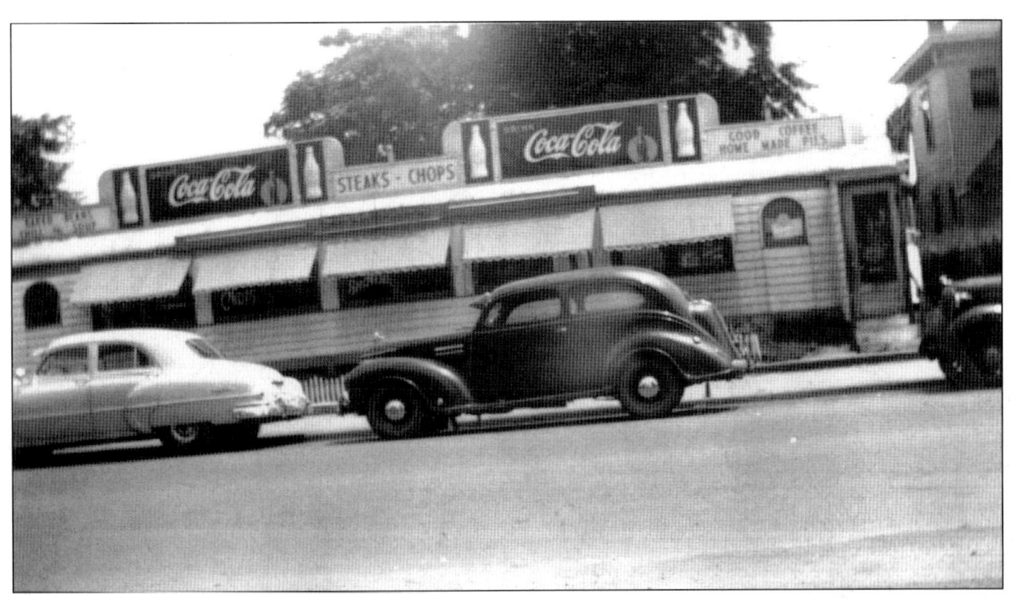

STEAK DINER. The Steak Diner was located at 620 N. Main. The Diner was owned by Dwight and Ann Fritz. They were wonderful people. The Salvation Army, located at 604 N. Main, would feed the transients who passed through Kokomo at the Steak Diner. This picture was taken in 1946.

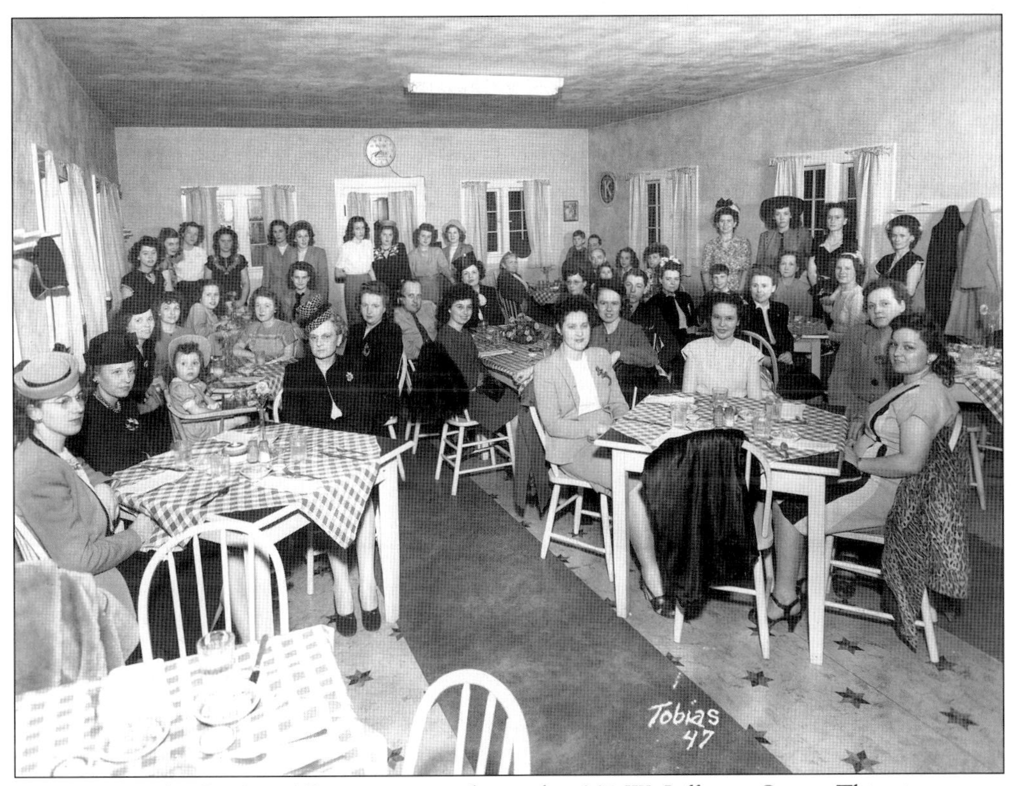

CUPBOARD. The Cupboard Restaurant was located at 901 W. Jefferson Street. This picture was taken in 1947. Perhaps you or someone you know is in this picture. (Photo courtesy of Tobias.)

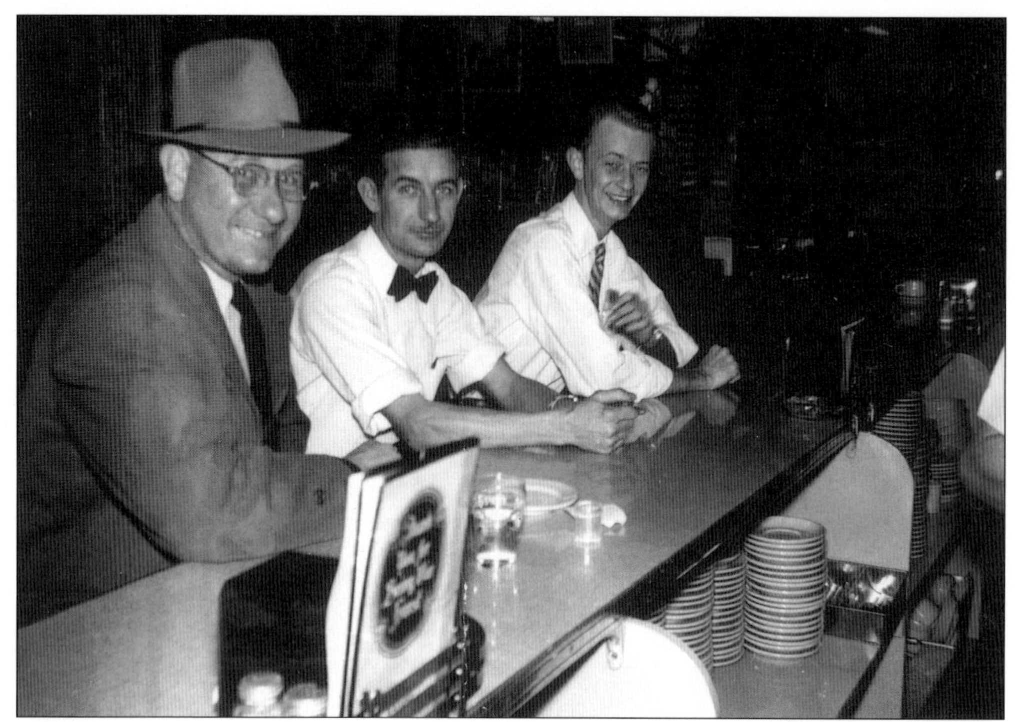

MUIR'S DRUGSTORE. Coffee drinkers from 1951 are pictured here. Does this face look familiar? One might have been a manager.

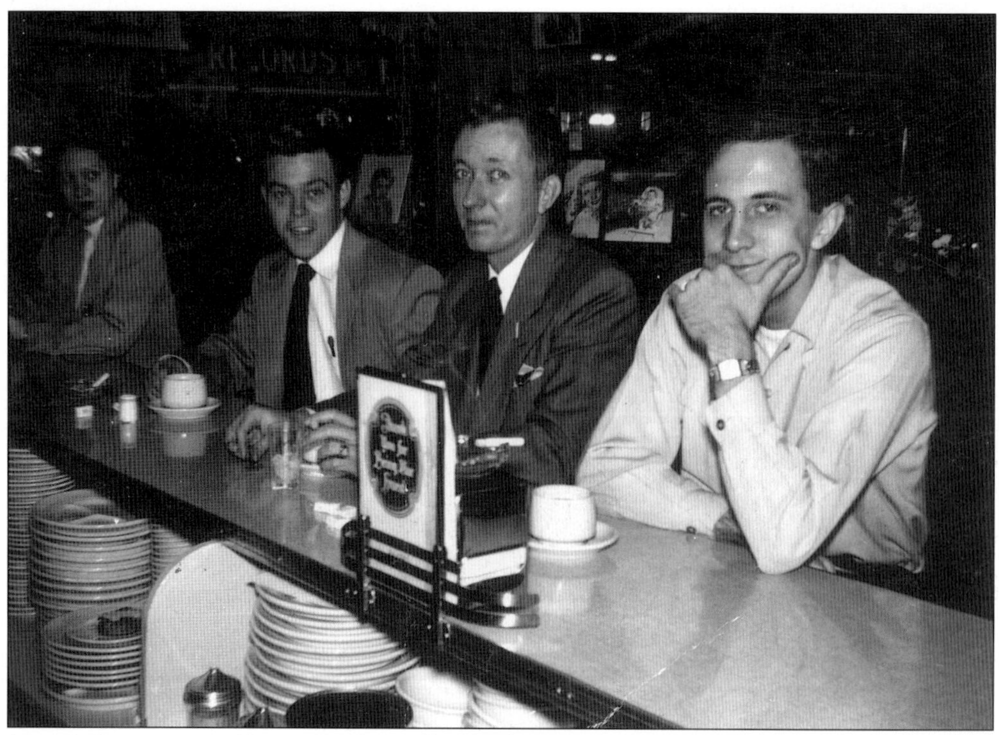

MUIR'S DRUGSTORE. Here are a few coffee drinkers in 1951. Do you know these men?

Five

FACTORIES

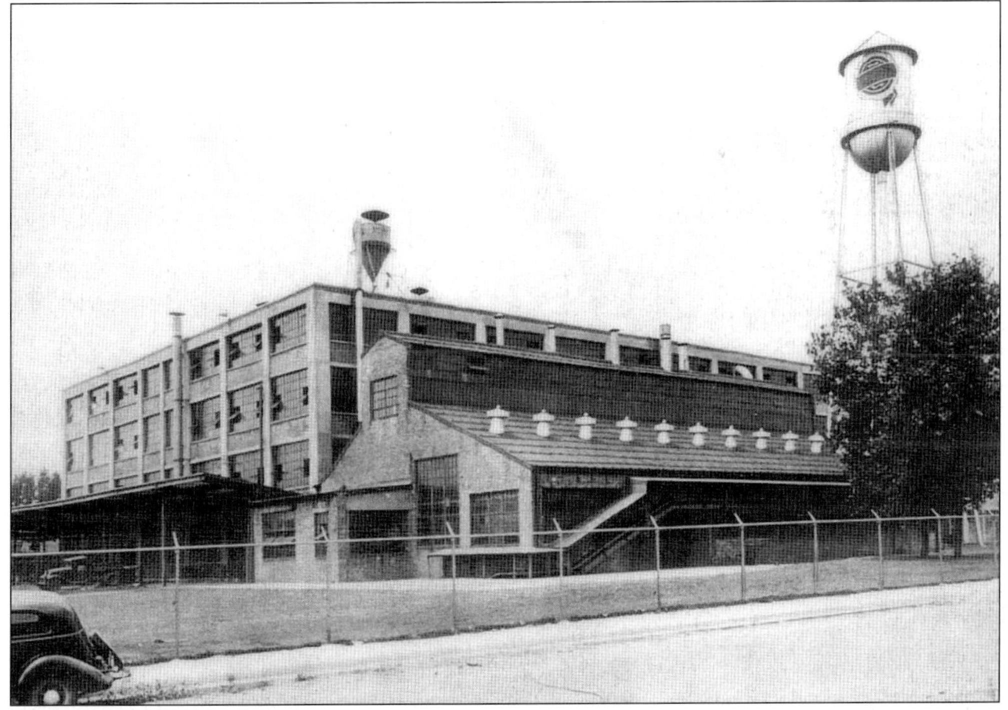

CHRYSLER. The Chrysler Corporation was located at 1103 S. Home Avenue. This was taken in the 1940s. It is now a building used for car parts. There are now two Chrysler plants in Kokomo.

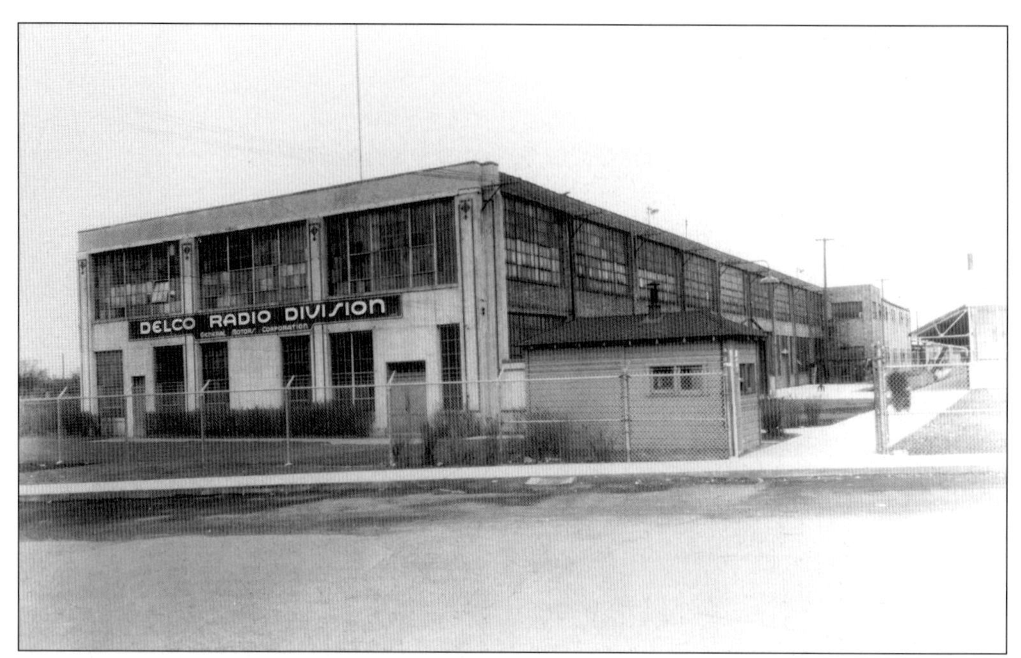

Delco Radio. Delco Radio was located on Home Avenue. It was started in 1937 and was torn down in 1999. A new building was built on Kokomo's bypass and is now called Delphi Division.

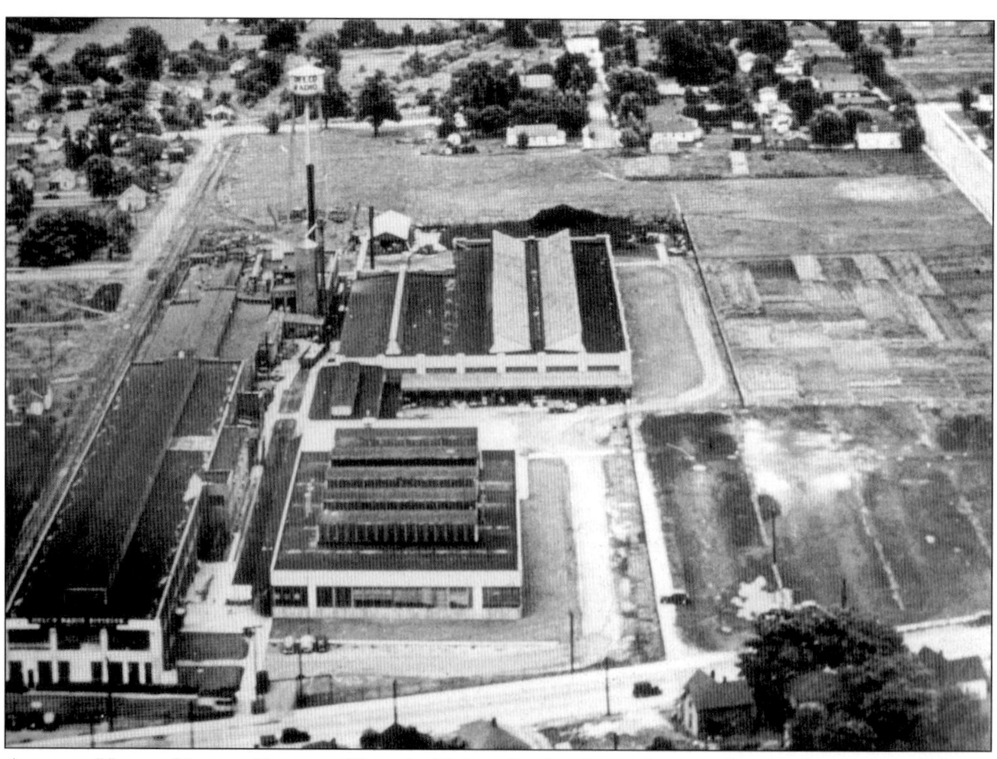

Aerial View, Delco Radio. Here is Delco Radio from the air. It was located on Home Avenue. This photograph was taken *c.* 1940. Gateway Gardens was also built in the 1940s.

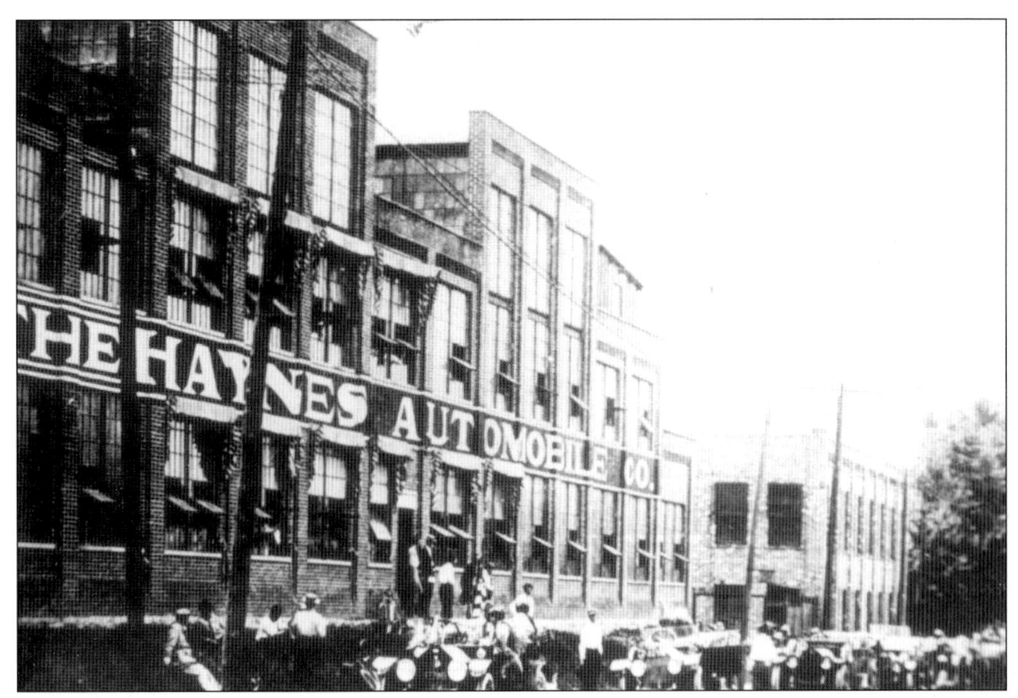

HAYNES AUTO. Here is the Haynes Auto Company on S. Union Street in the early 1900s. Take a look at these sharp cars.

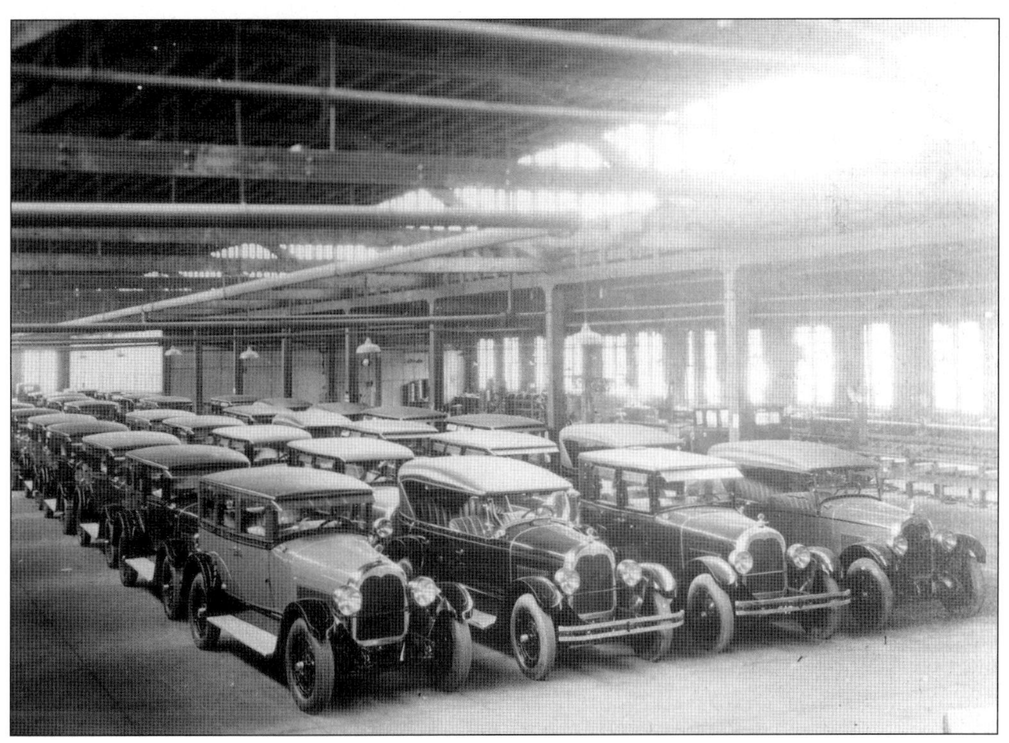

HAYNES AUTO. Here we have the finished product from the first Haynes automobile line. (Photo courtesy of the Ryan Archives.)

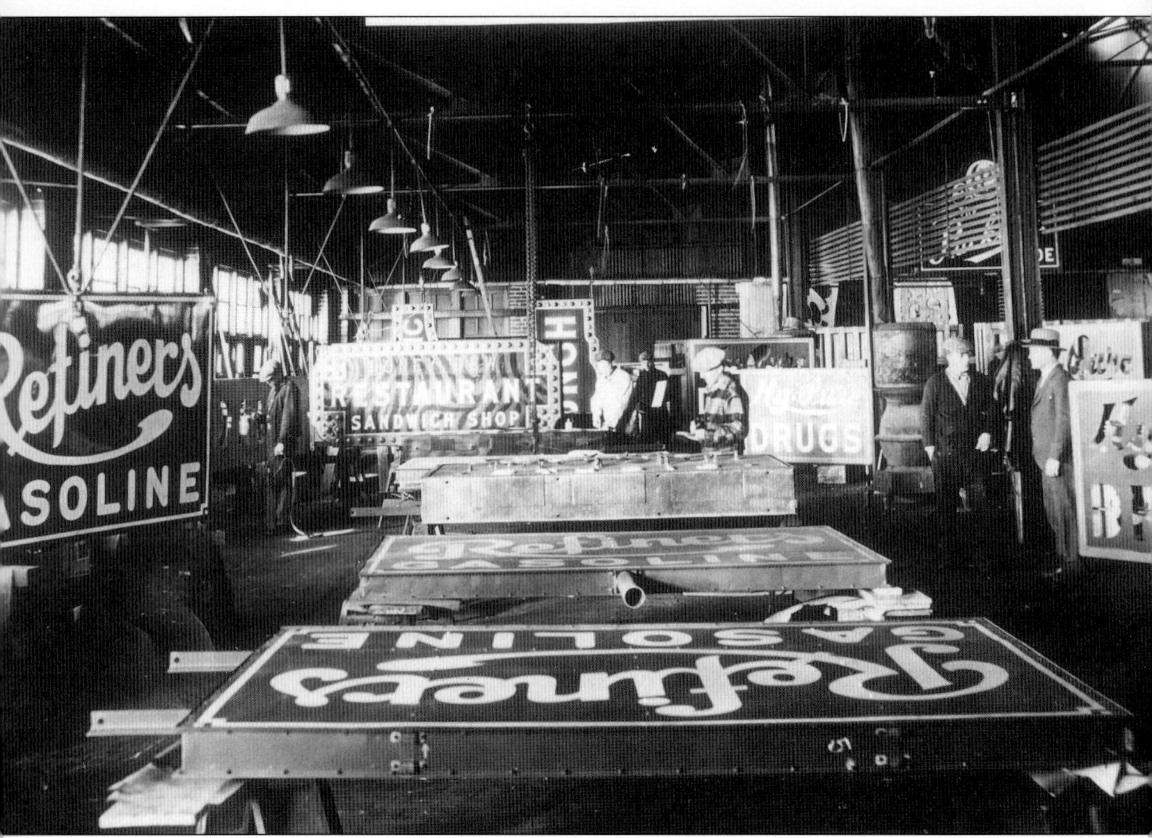

KOLUX. This is the inside of the Kolux Division in the early 1950s. It was located at 1064 S. Union Street. It is now an empty building.

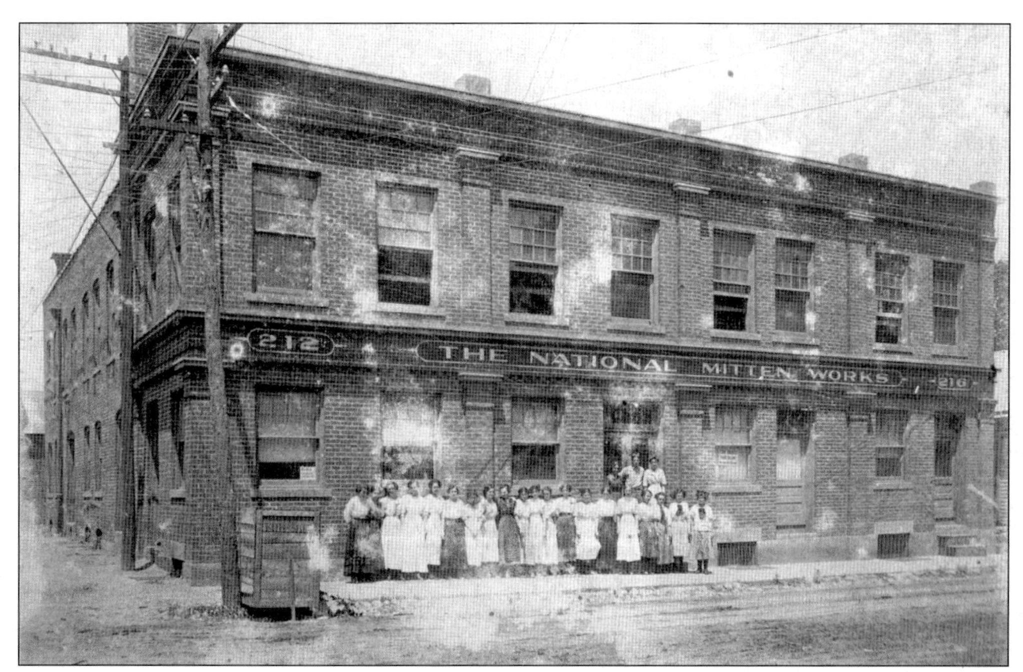

MITTEN WORKS. The Kokomo Mitten Works in the late 1800s. It was on E. Superior Street. The City Building is there now.

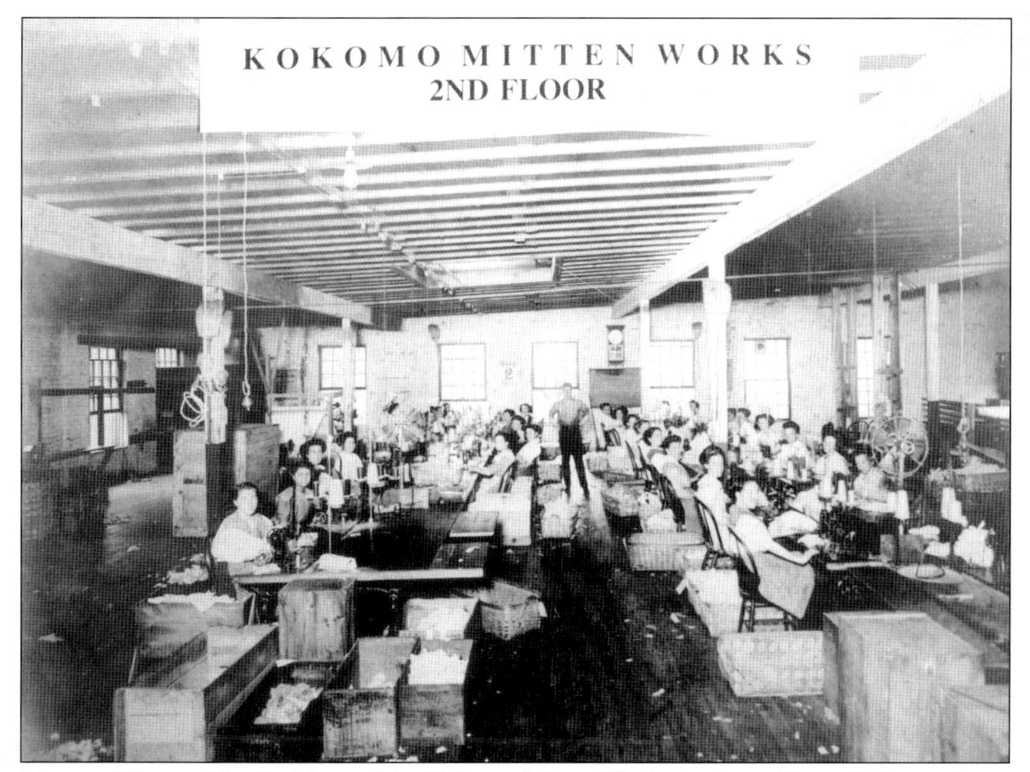

MITTEN WORKS. The 2nd floor of the Kokomo Mitten Works is pictured here. Did any of your family or friends work there?

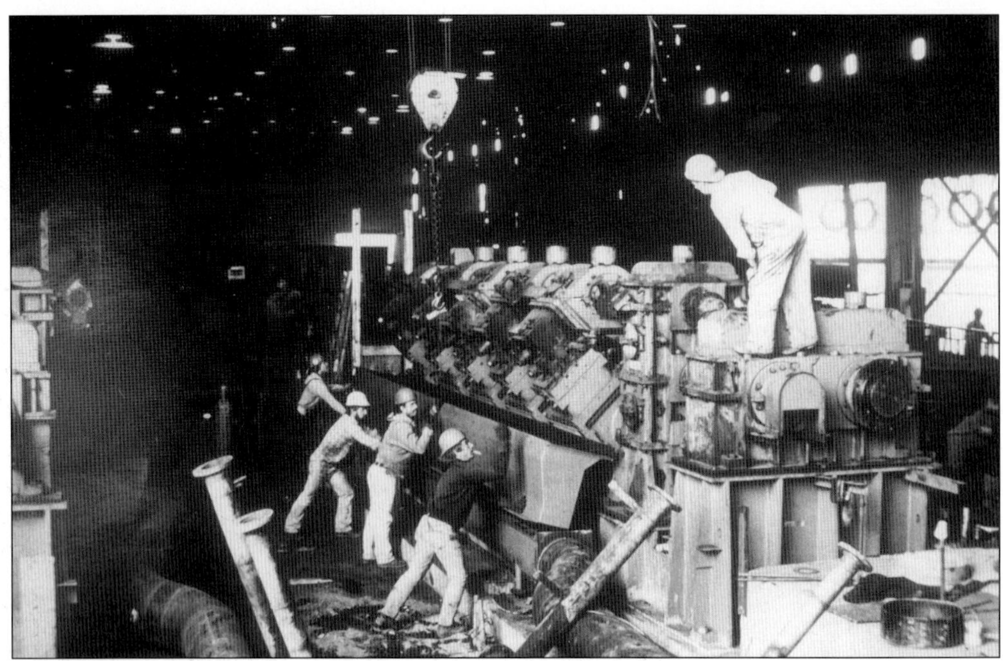

CONTINENTAL STEEL. The Rod Mill in 1982 is pictured here. Many people thought their children and grandchildren would work here someday.

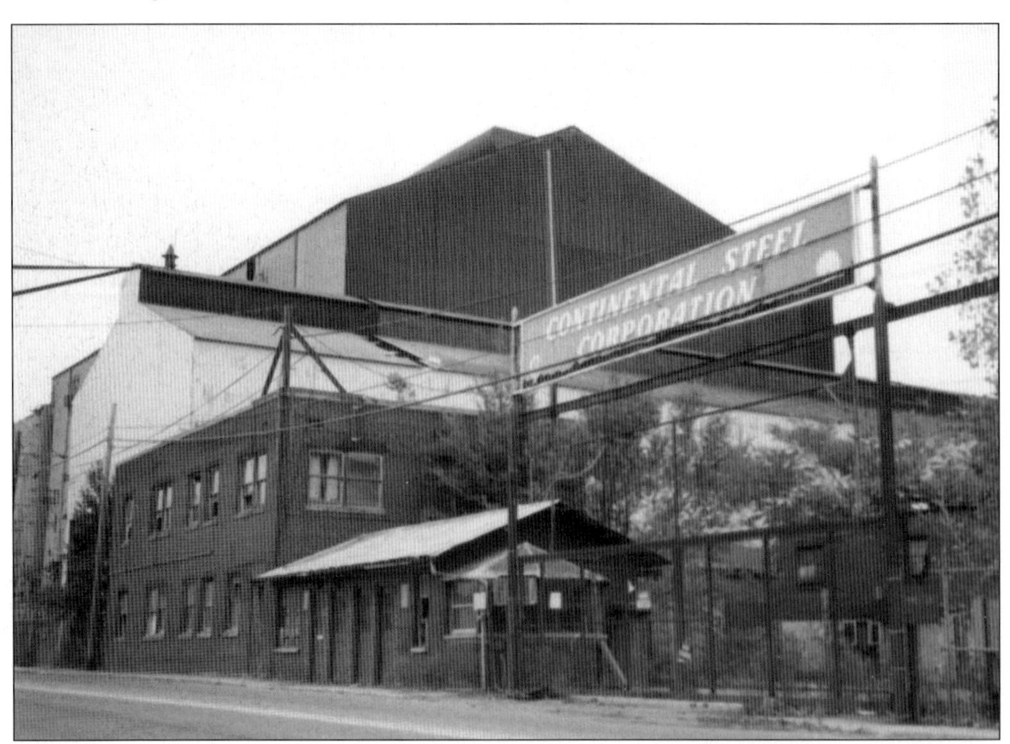

CONTINENTAL STEEL. Continental Steel was located on W. Markland Avenue and was the biggest steel plant at one time. They sold fence, nails, wire, and rods. They had a large wire and rod mill. They closed in 1985. It is now an empty lot.

Six
BAKERIES

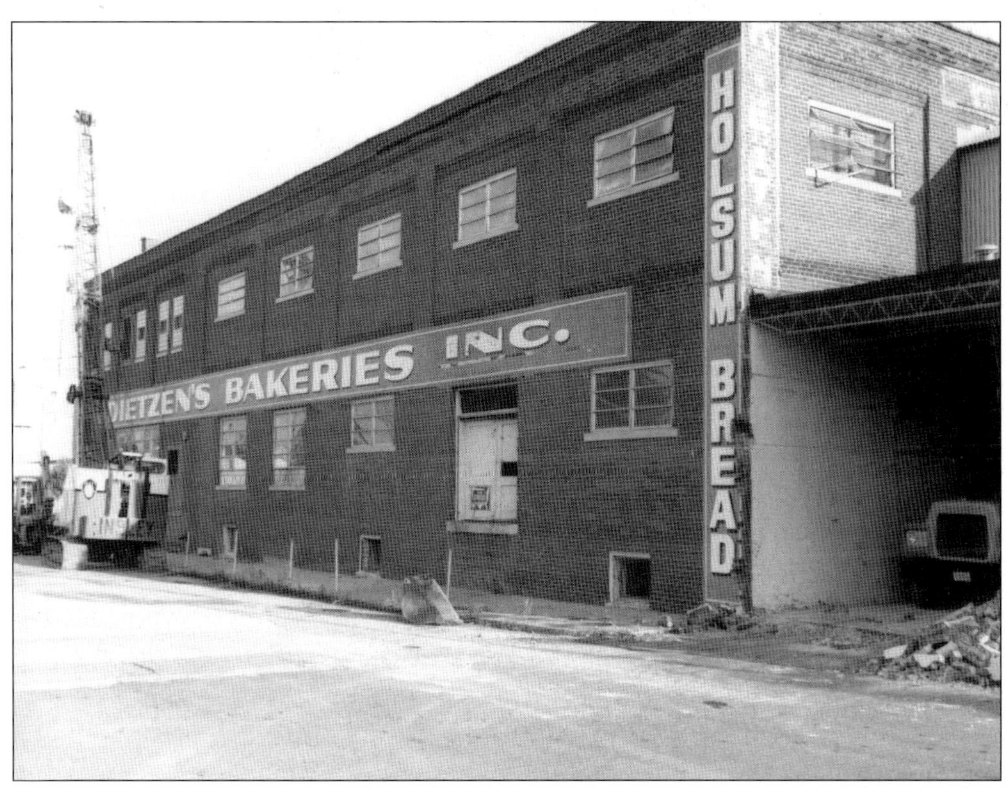

DIETZEN'S. Dietzen's Bakery was located at 113 W. Jackson. There were many bakeries such as Joy Ann, Schwenger's, Moores Pie Shop, and Maher's. Later in the 1960s and '70s, you couldn't beat a treat from Chuck's Donuts or anything from the Haworth Brothers' store. There are still some in Kokomo.

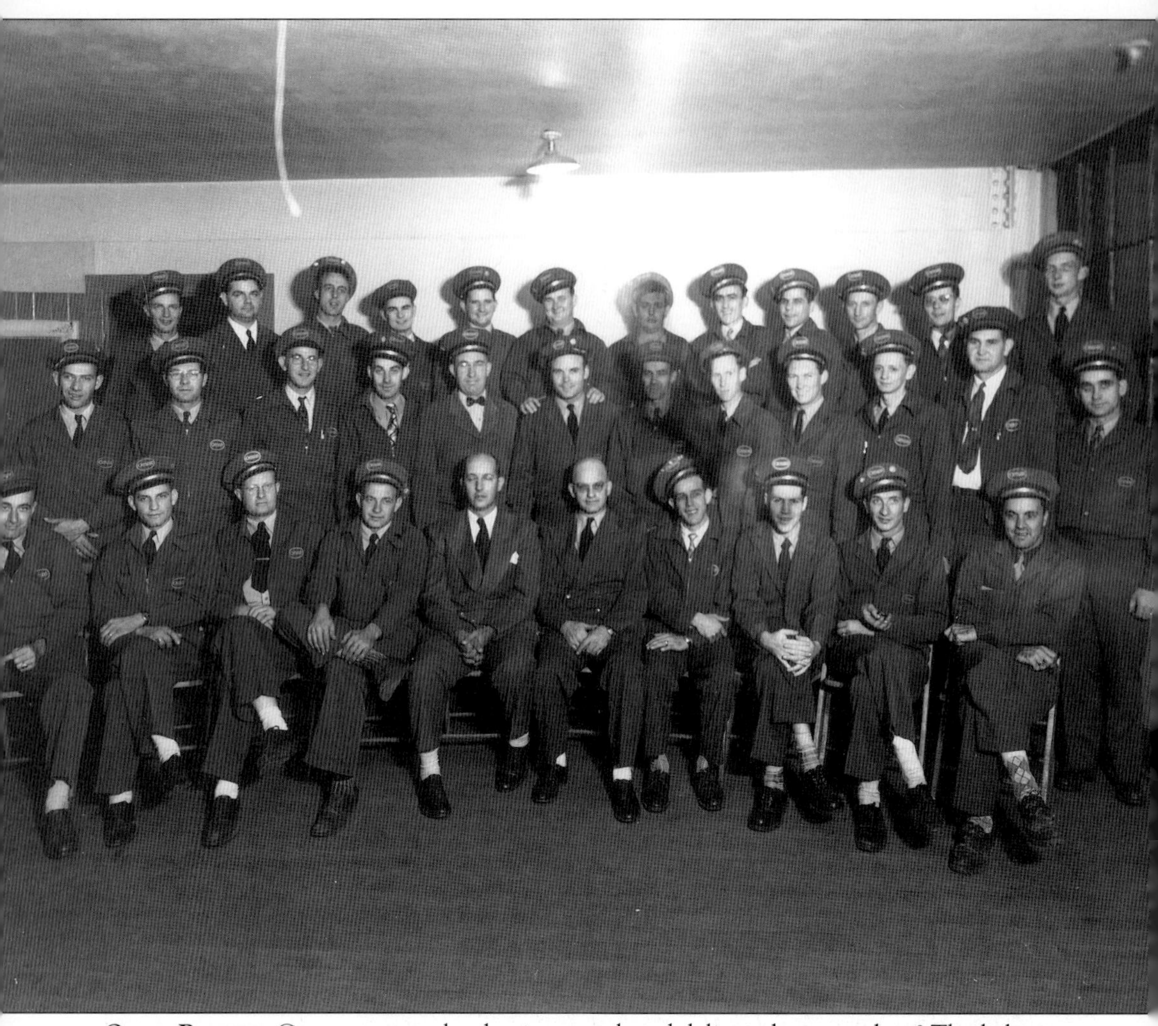

OMAR BAKERY. Can you remember having your bread delivered to your door? The bakery was located at 1200 Park Avenue. Was one of these men your route man? This picture was taken by John Ryan in 1948.

Seven

Hotels

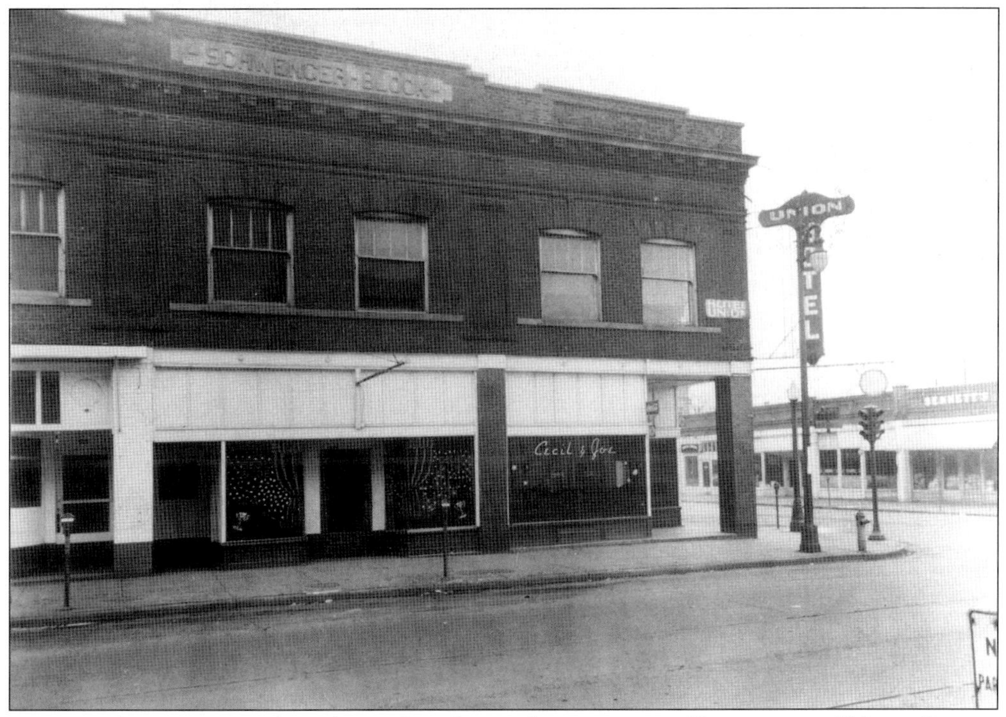

Union. The Union Hotel was located on the northwest corner of Sycamore and Union Streets. Cecil and Joe's Bar was also there. Back in the 1940s, Schwenger's Bakery was there. This photo was taken by John Ryan Photo in 1948.

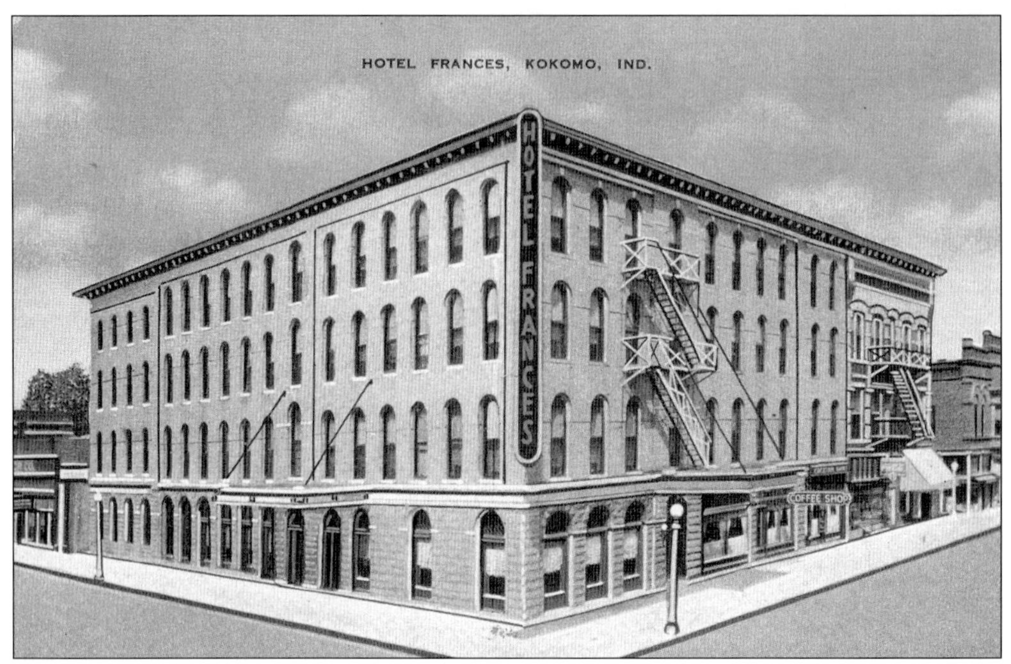

FRANCES HOTEL. Hotel Frances on the northeast corner of Buckeye and Mulberry. It had nice furnished rooms, a coffee shop, large bathrooms, private dining, and many club rooms for meetings.

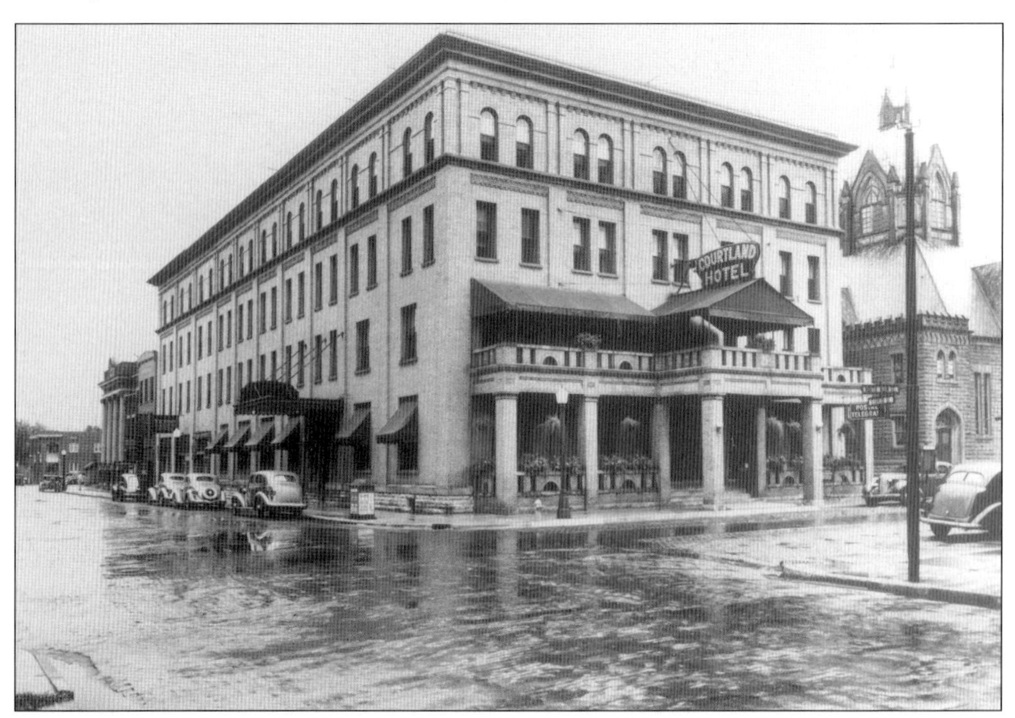

COURTLAND. Courtland Hotel was located on the northwest corner of Taylor and Main Streets. Remember when the streets were all brick? It is a bank drive-thru now. (Photo courtesy of the Ryan Archives.)

Eight
CHURCHES AND SCHOOLS

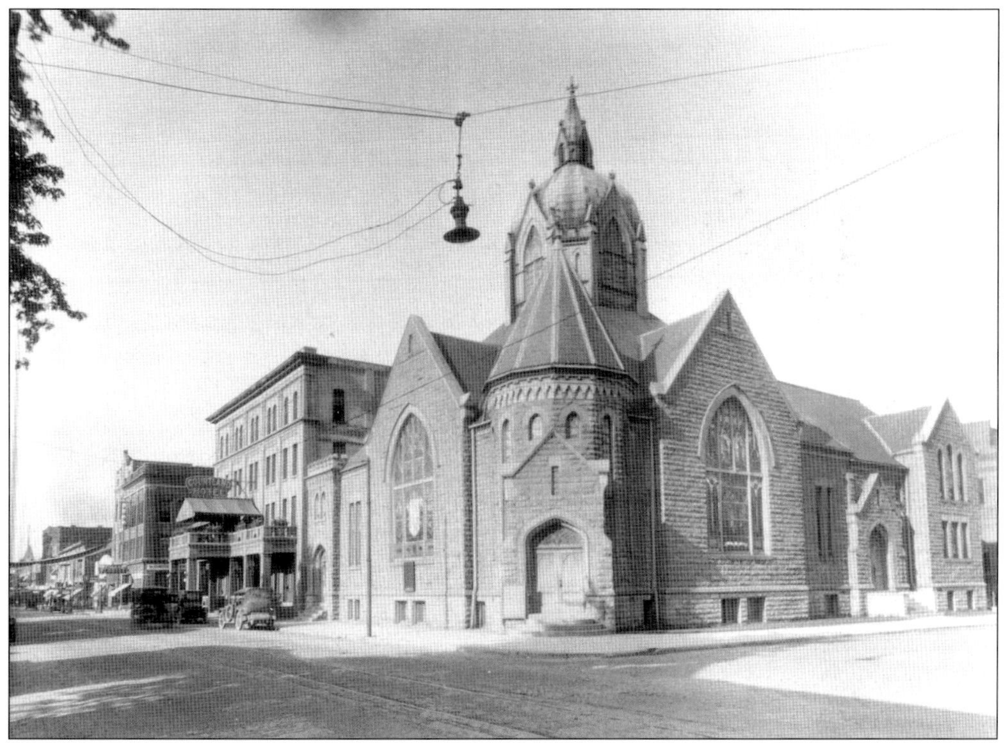

MAIN STREET CHRISTIAN. Main Street Christian Church was located at 415 N. Main. There were many different churches for all faiths. Nearly everyone in the 1940s and '50s sent or took their families to church. This is now a drive-thru bank. (Photo courtesy of the Ryan Archives.)

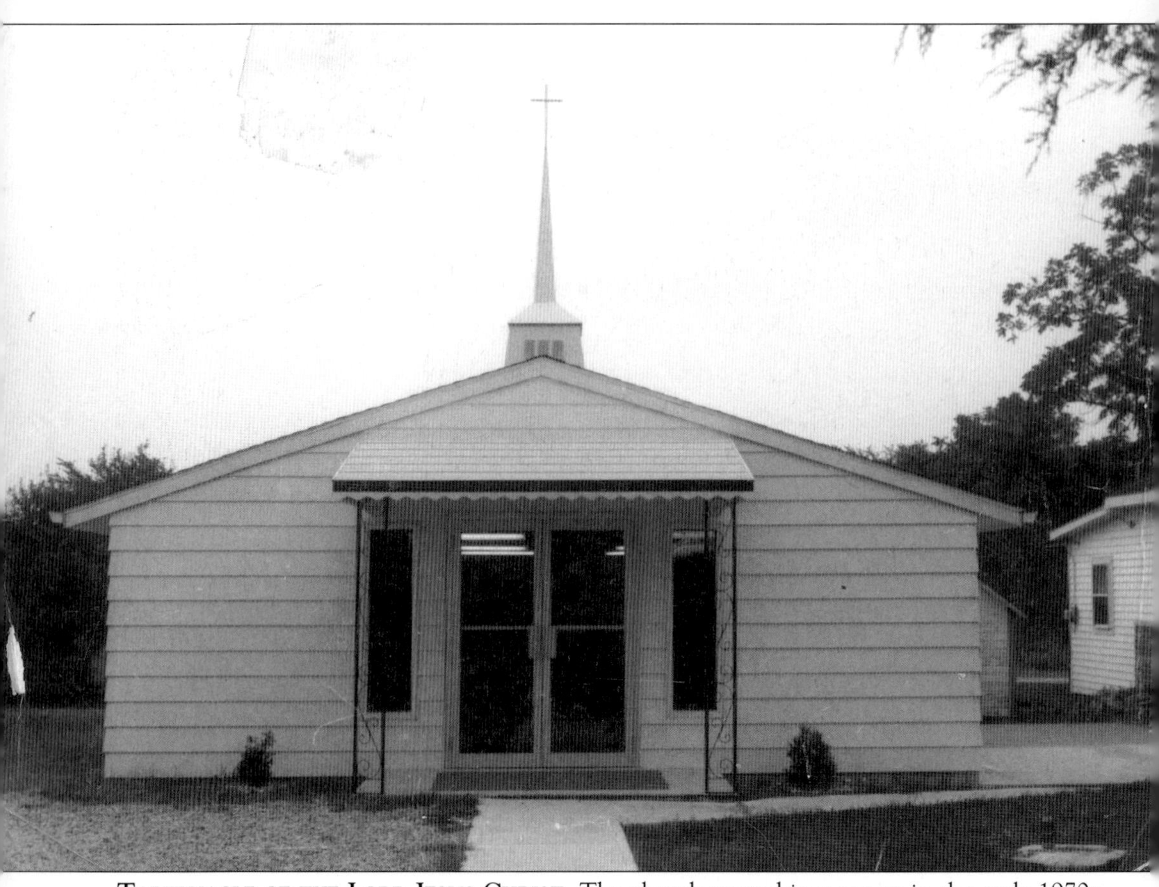

Tabernacle of the Lord Jesus Christ. The church started in a garage in the early 1970s. It started with the pastor and his family and later grew to 50 people in attendance. It was located in Greentown, Indiana, till 1993. The church moved to Kokomo, Indiana, till 2001. Tom Hamilton was the pastor until 2001, before moving to Florida. The people loved to praise the Lord.

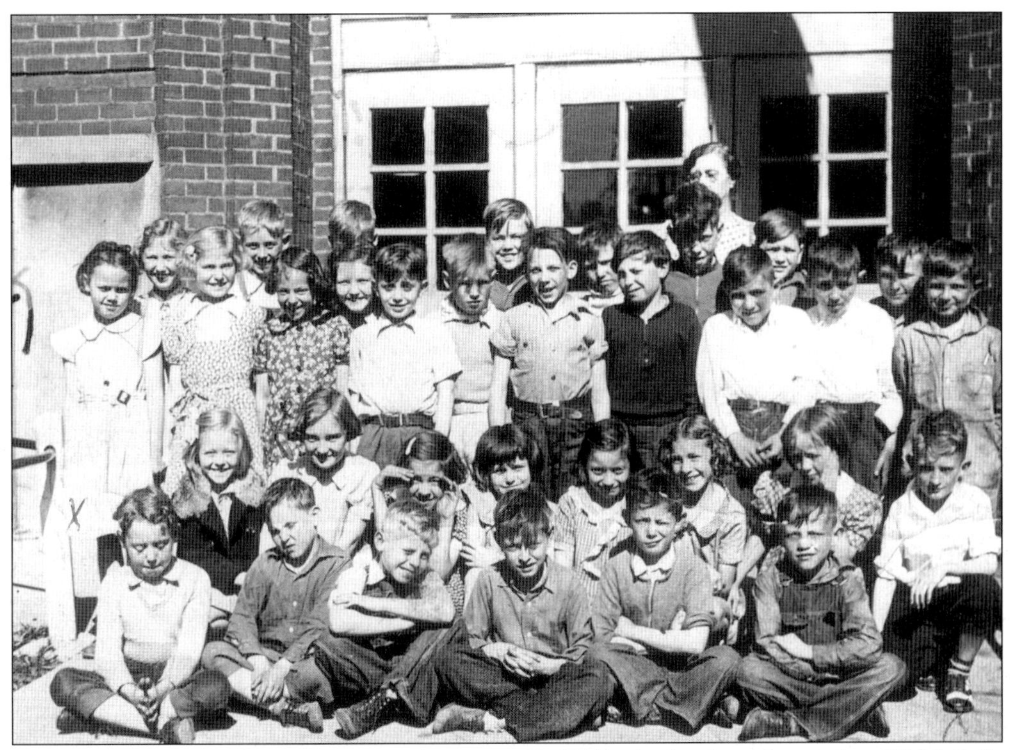

WILLARD SCHOOL. This picture was taken in 1937. Willard school was located at 628 N. Bell. Are you in this group of happy kids?

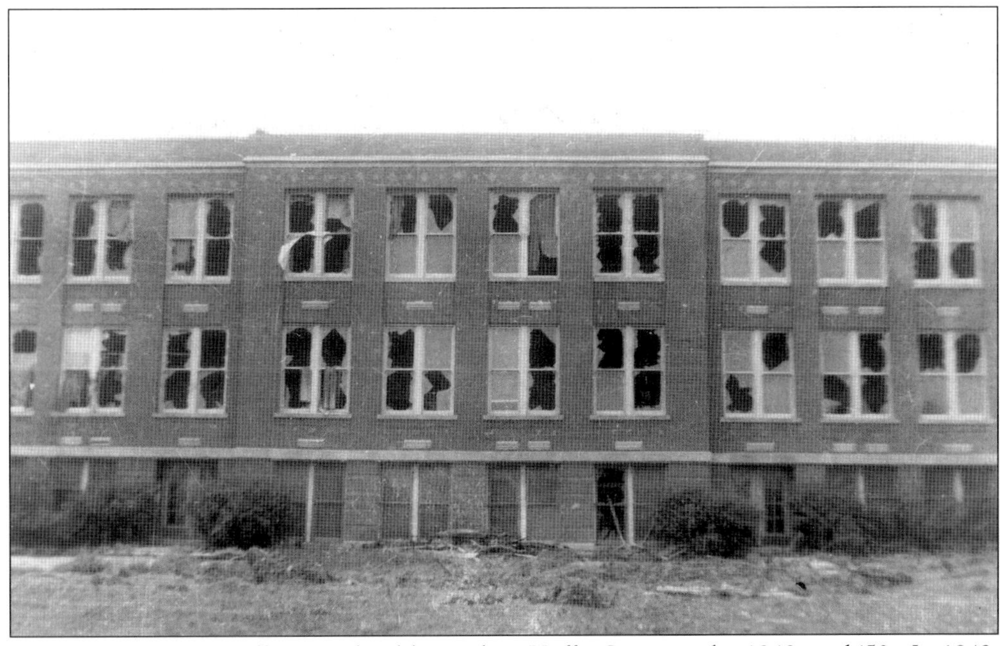

JEFFERSON SCHOOL. Jefferson School located on Hoffer Street in the 1940s and '50s. In 1942, a tornado came through and did a lot of damage. If you lived in the south end, you will never forget this school and all of the great teachers we had.

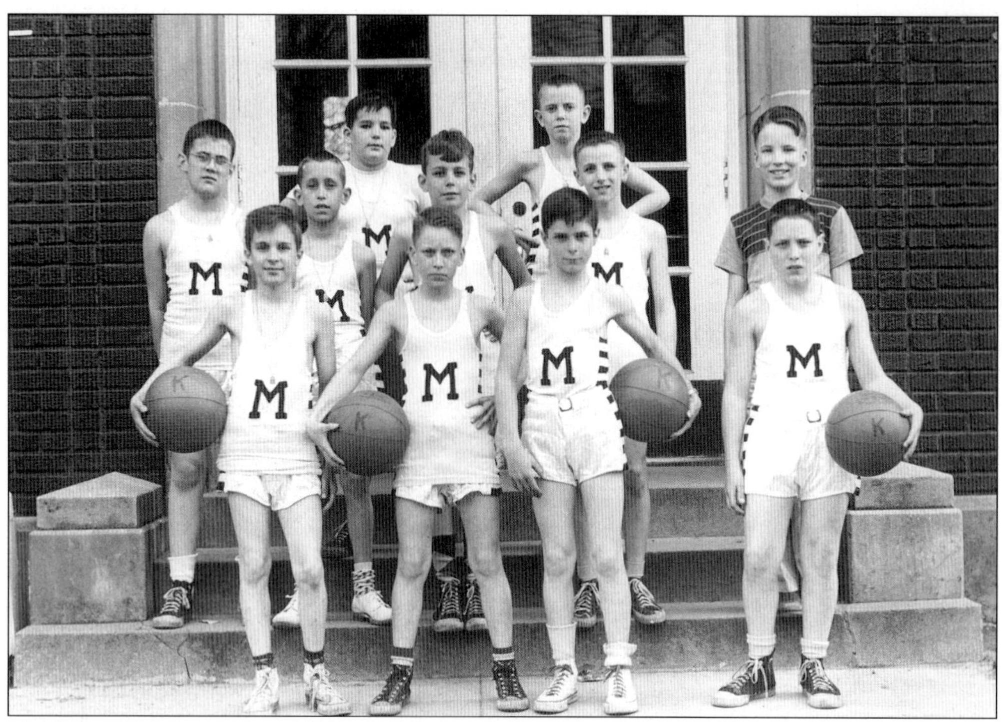

McKINLEY SCHOOL. McKinley School is pictured here in 1953. Is Jim Rayls really here? Jim was the most famous high school player in Kokomo. He later played for Indiana University.

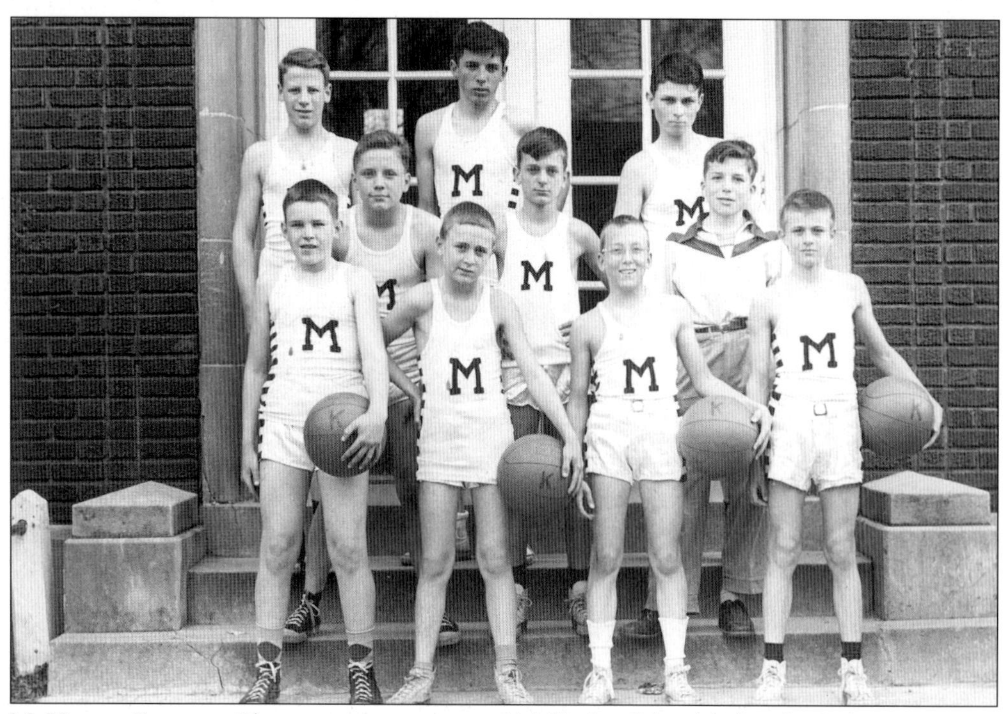

McKINLEY SCHOOL. This is another picture of McKinley School, taken by Robert Davies in 1953. Were you in this picture?

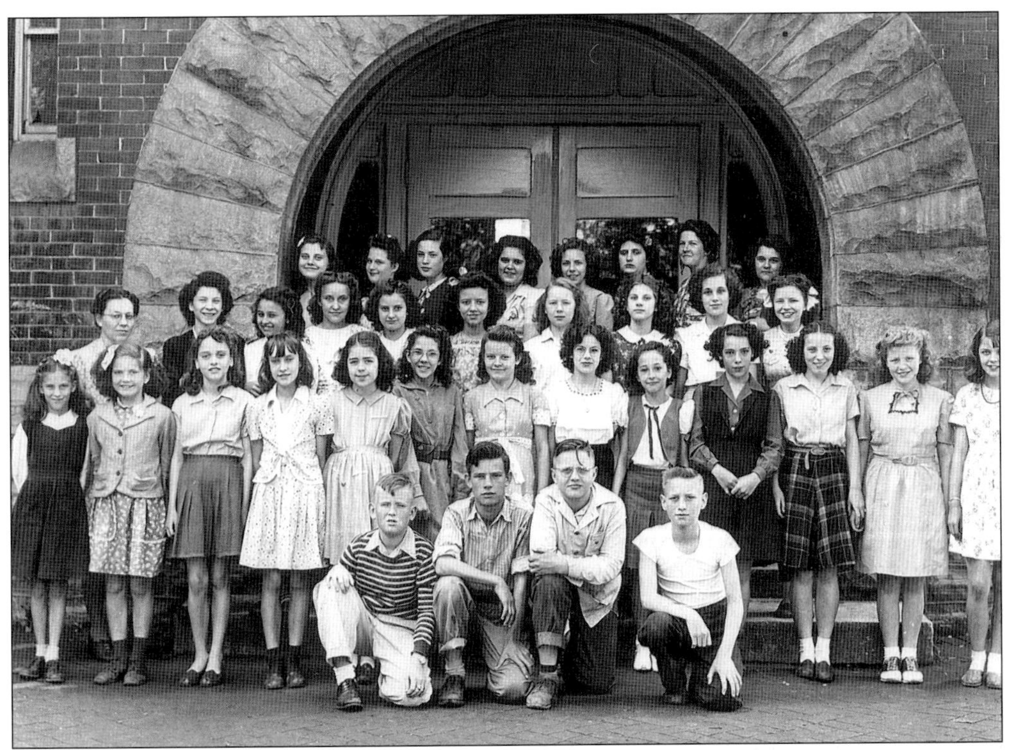

MERIDIAN SCHOOL. Here is a picture taken at Meridian School in the late 1940s. The school was located at the northwest corner of Bell and Harrison Streets. Are you in this picture? (Photo courtesy of Deloris Fipps Williams.)

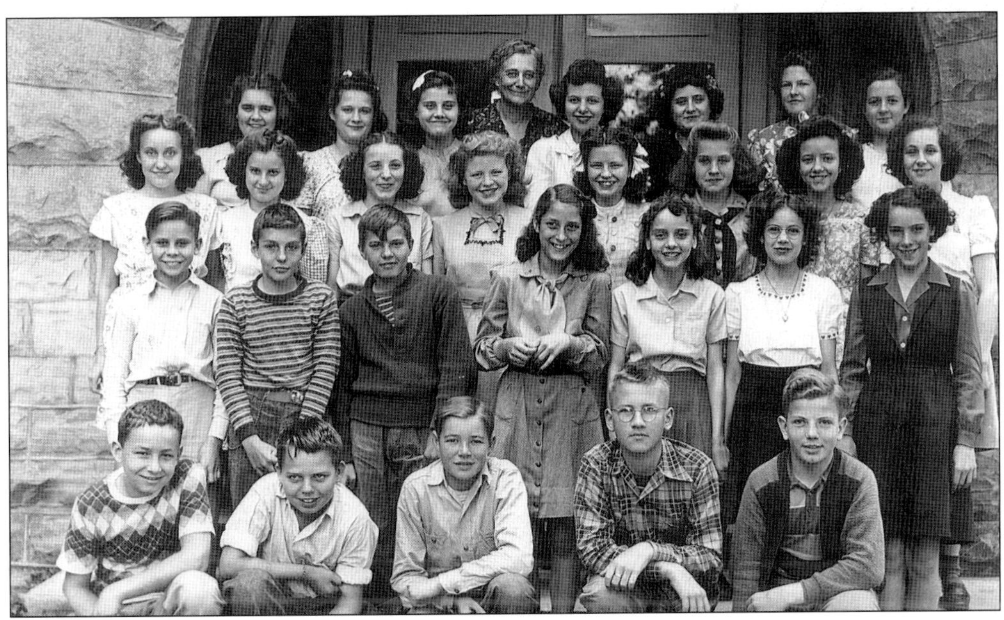

MERIDIAN SCHOOL. This photo at Meridian School was taken in the late 1940s.

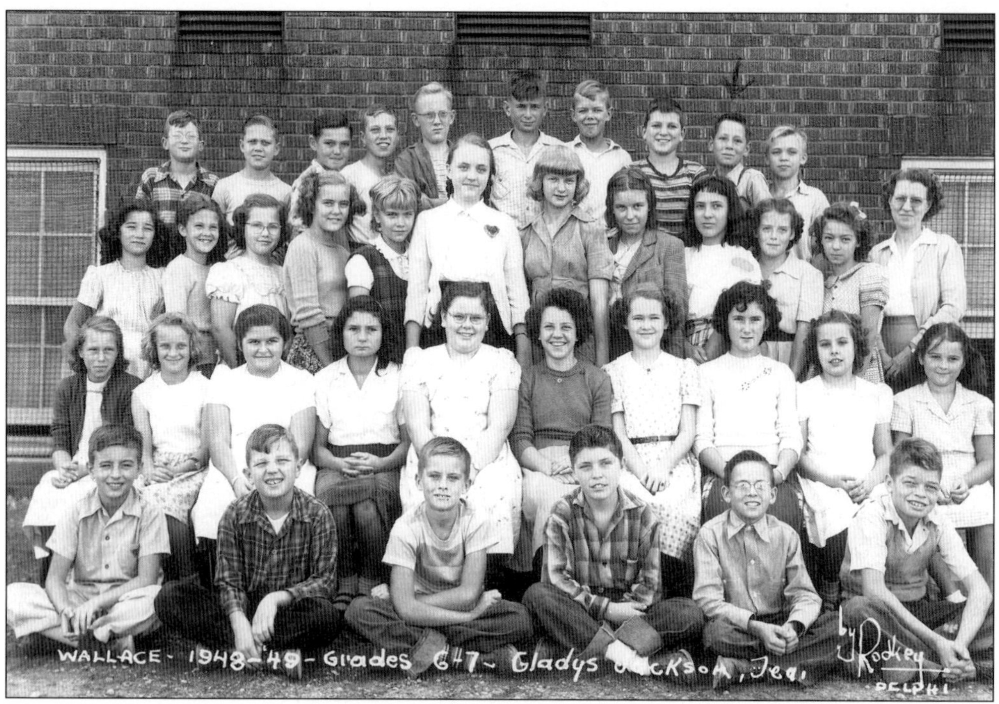

WALLACE SCHOOL. Here is a picture at Wallace School taken in 1949. The school was located on W. Jefferson Road. Gladis Jackson furnished the picture.

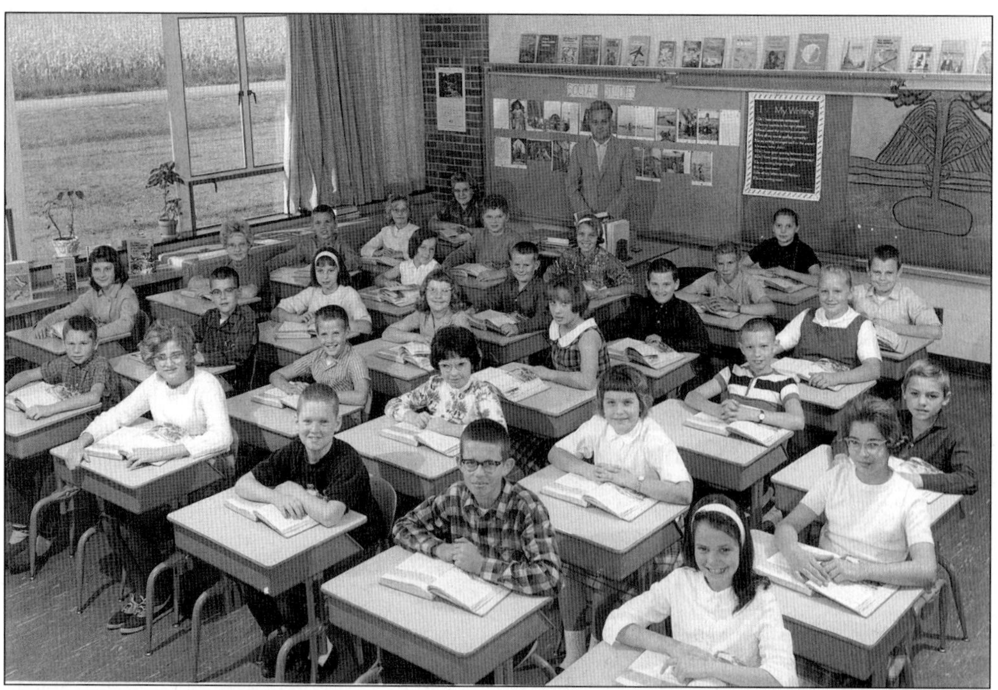

WALLACE SCHOOL. This is a photo at Wallace School, 1963-1964. The teacher was James Maddox and the principal was Joe Mullins. Are you in this picture? Remember the fingernails on the blackboards? There was always a class clown.

Nine
BUSINESSES

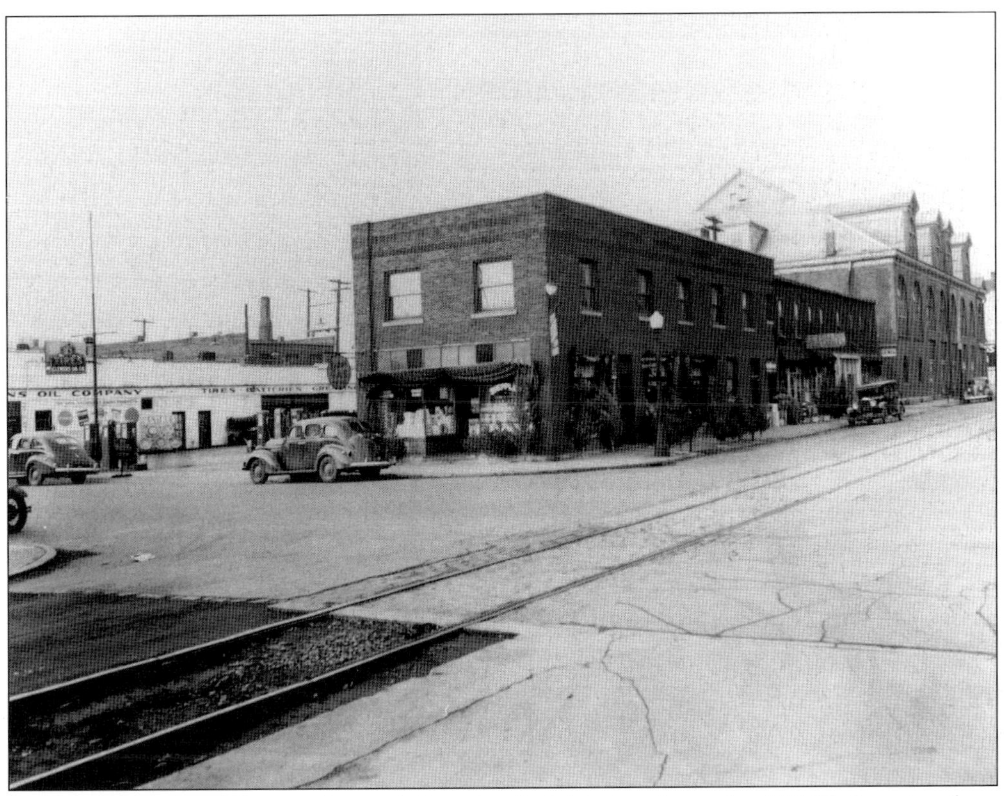

SHEPPLES MARKET. This is a photo of Shepples Cash Market, located at 200 W. Superior, from 1930.

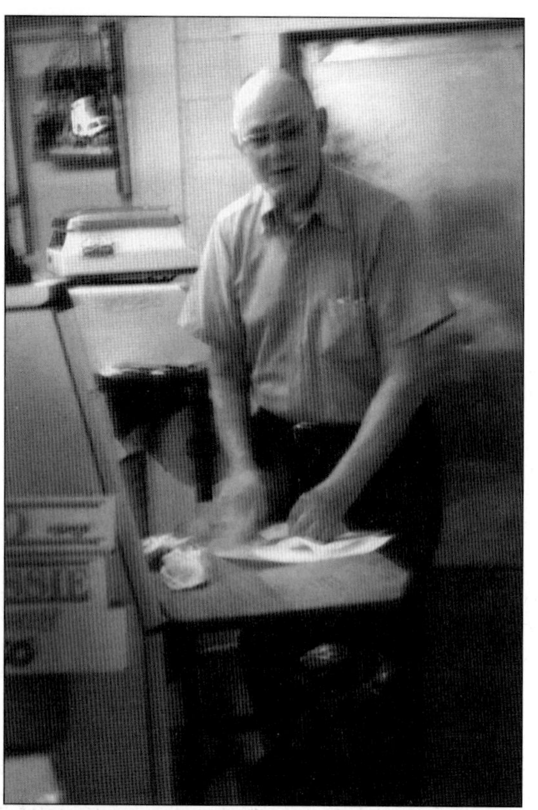

ART WEAVER—WEAVER'S MARKET. Weaver's Market was located on S. Delphos. The owners, Art and Mary Lou Weaver, were well-liked people. Gateway Gardens was very happy to have the store within walking distance. Art was known for his ham salad. If you had good ham salad it had to come from Weaver's Market. He was in the business for over 50 years.

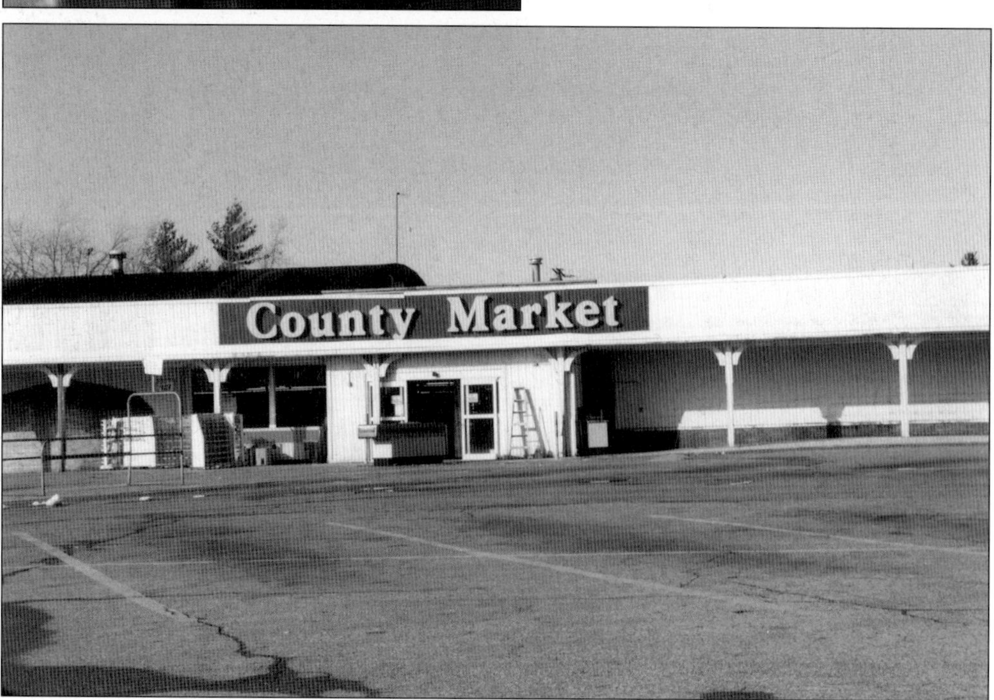

COUNTY MARKET. At one time, County Market was on S. Washington Street. The Indiana University Library is there now!

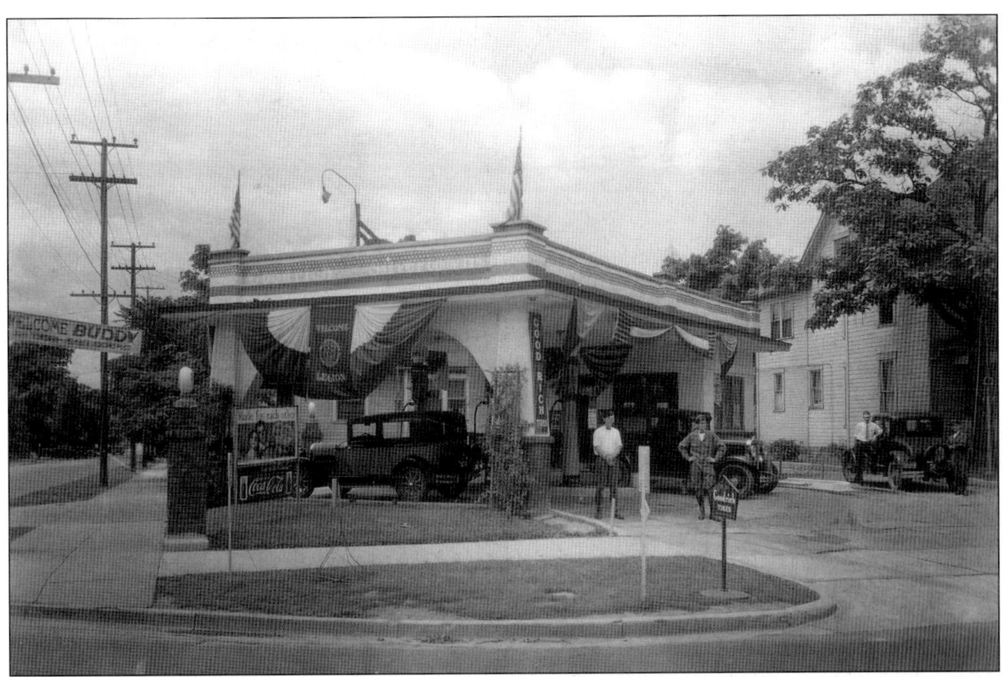

ZECK AND PETTY'S. Zeck and Petty's was started with family and friendly gas attendants.

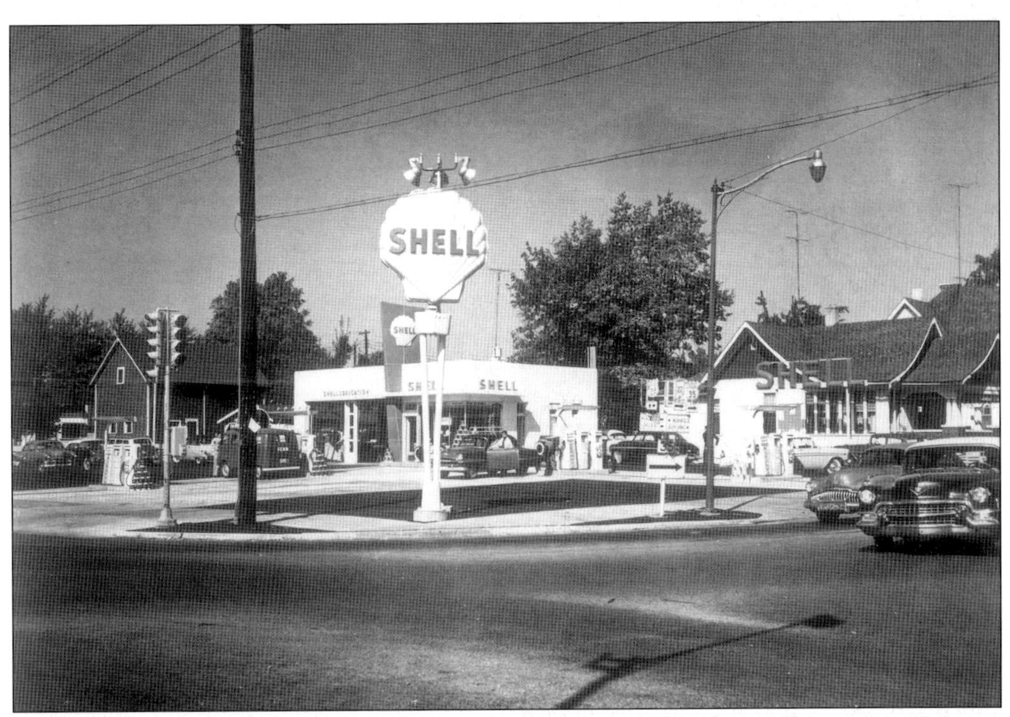

ZECK AND PETTY'S. Zeck and Petty's, started in the early 1930s, was well known in Kokomo because the proprietors were trustworthy. The station was located on the northwest corner of Markland and Washington. Here are two pictures. One was taken in the early1930s and the other in the mid-1950s.

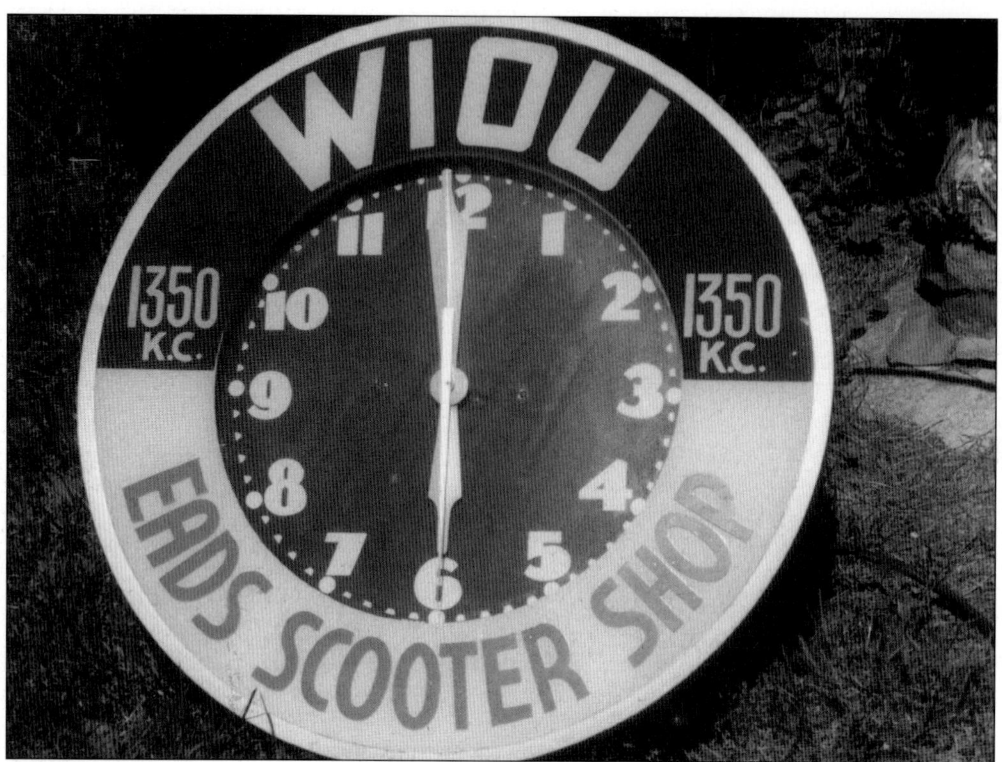

Eads Scooter. Eads Scooter Shop was located at 828 E. Markland. John Eads was the owner and his brother had an auto repair business. John and Thelma celebrated their 50th anniversary in February. They have three children.

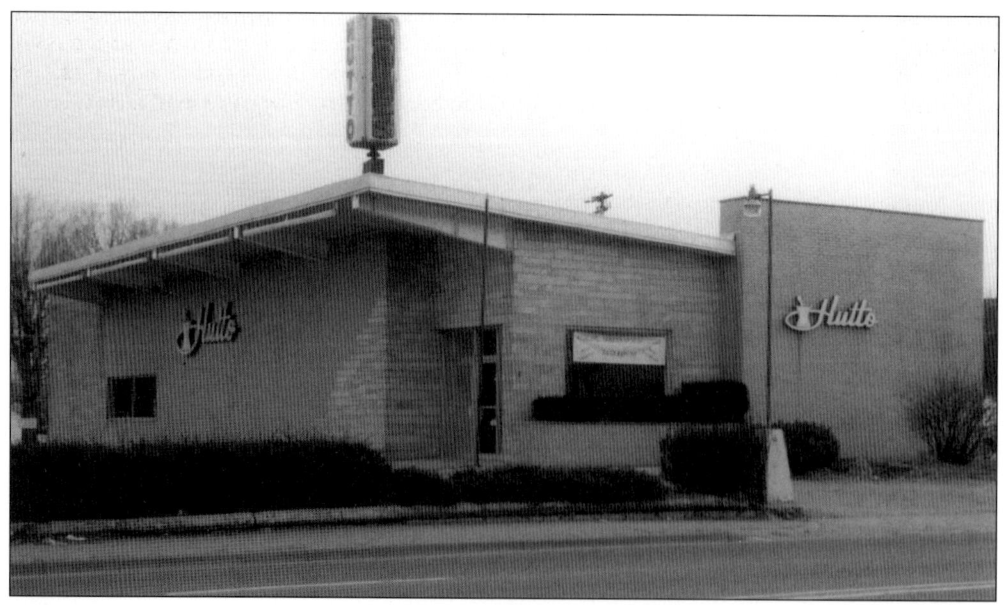

Hutto's Drugstore. Hutto's Drugstore was located at 119 E. Markland. This was a very friendly place with owners Bob and Eva Hutto. My wife and her two sisters worked there in the 1950s. They loved to make thick malts and shakes for all to enjoy.

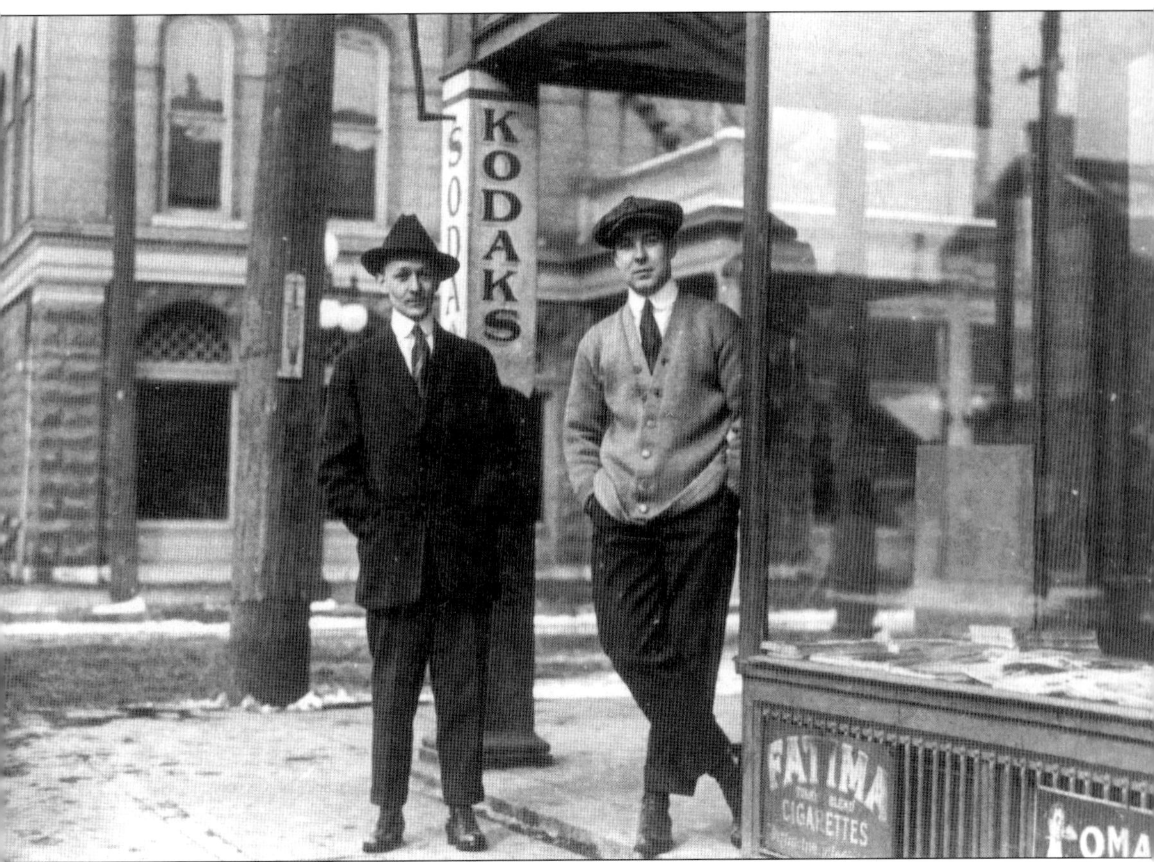

BLUE CROSS DRUGSTORE. Can you remember the Blue Cross Drugstore? It was located on the southeast corner of Buckeye and Mulberry. Here are two pictures. One was taken in the early 1930s. These two men who started the drugstore did not know that it would become one of Kokomo's best! Can you see the Hotel Frances in the background? The man on the left is Leroy Graff and the other is his brother, Doc.

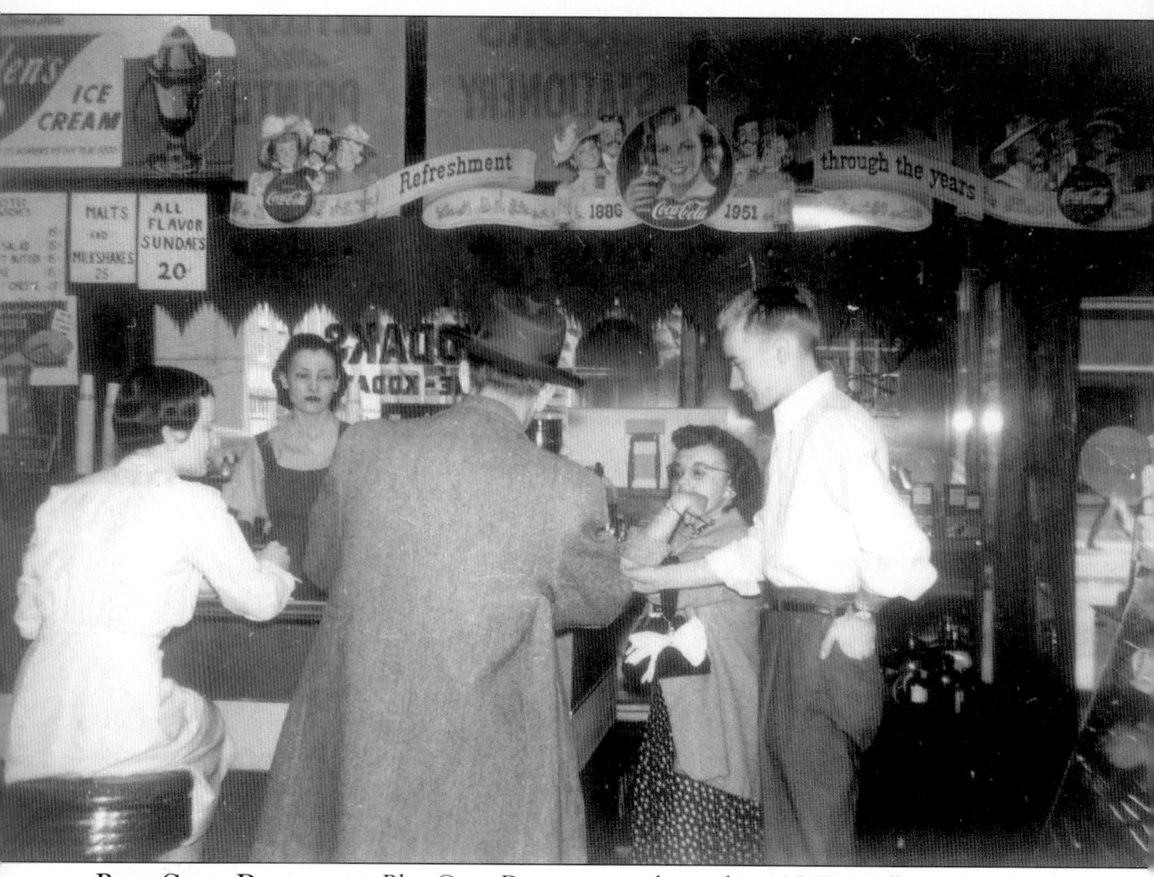

BLUE CROSS DRUGSTORE. Blue Cross Drugstore was located at 125 W. Mulberry. It started in the early 1900s and closed in the 1960s. The man in the white is Bob Graff, son of Leroy.

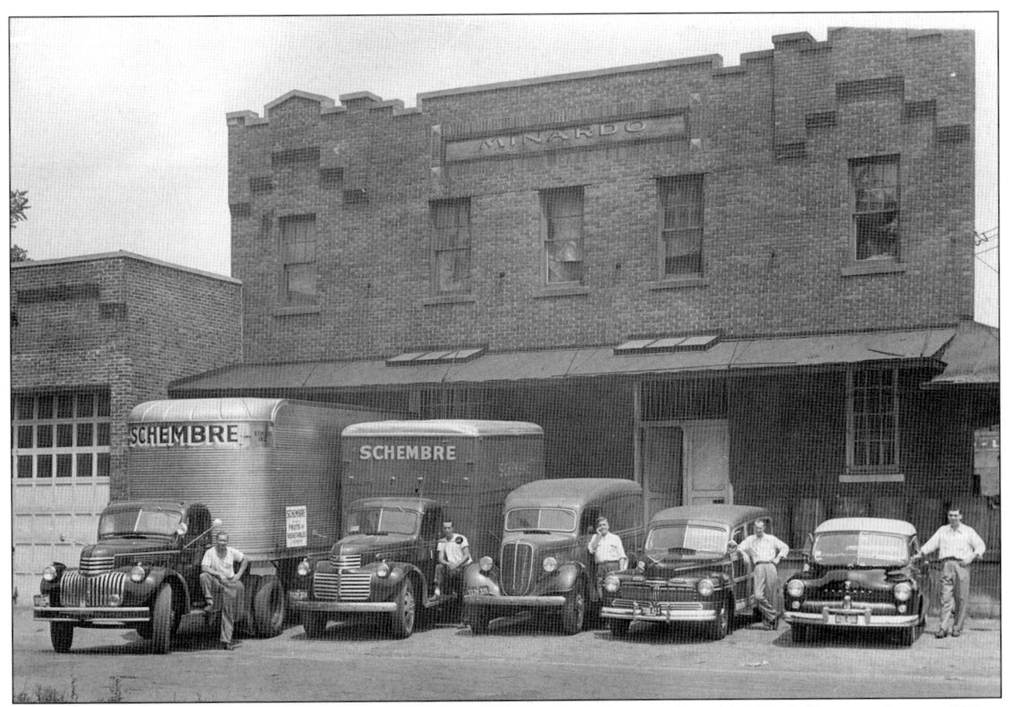

THE SCHEMBRE FRUIT CO. The Schembre Fruit Co. was located at 314 E. Jefferson Street. This picture was taken in 1948 by Robert Davies. Back in the late 1930s and early '40s it was called the Minardo Bros. Fruit Co. Did you buy fruit there?

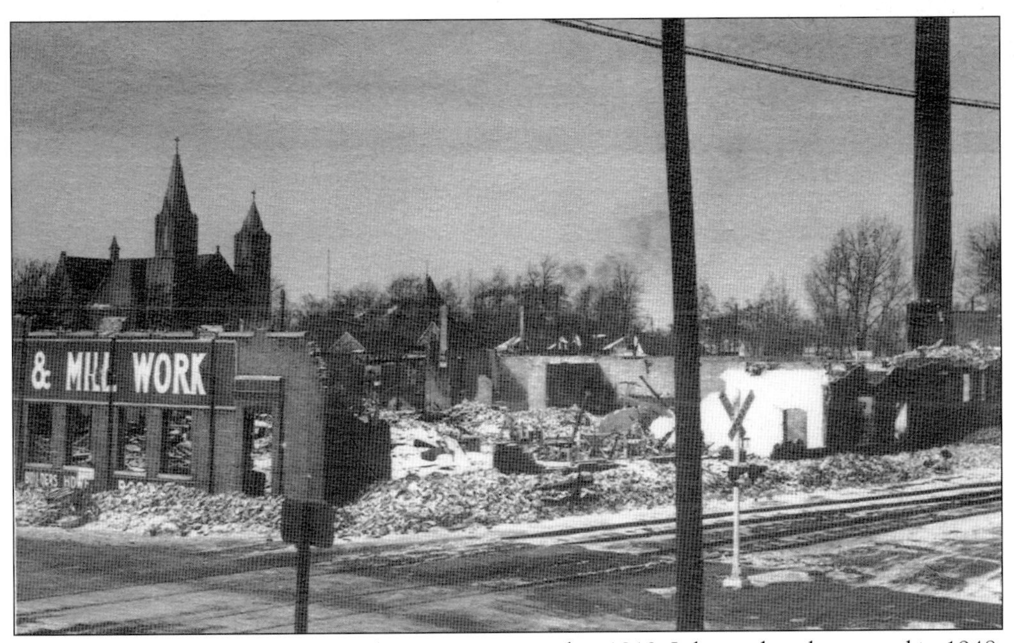

LUMBER YARD. The Kokomo Lumber Co. was started in 1912. It burned to the ground in 1948. It was rebuilt and in 1956 seemed to be going nowhere. Clifton Robinson took over in 1956 and turned things around. Today, it is a very formidable business. His daughter Lana Childress and the Robinson family still own Lumber Co.

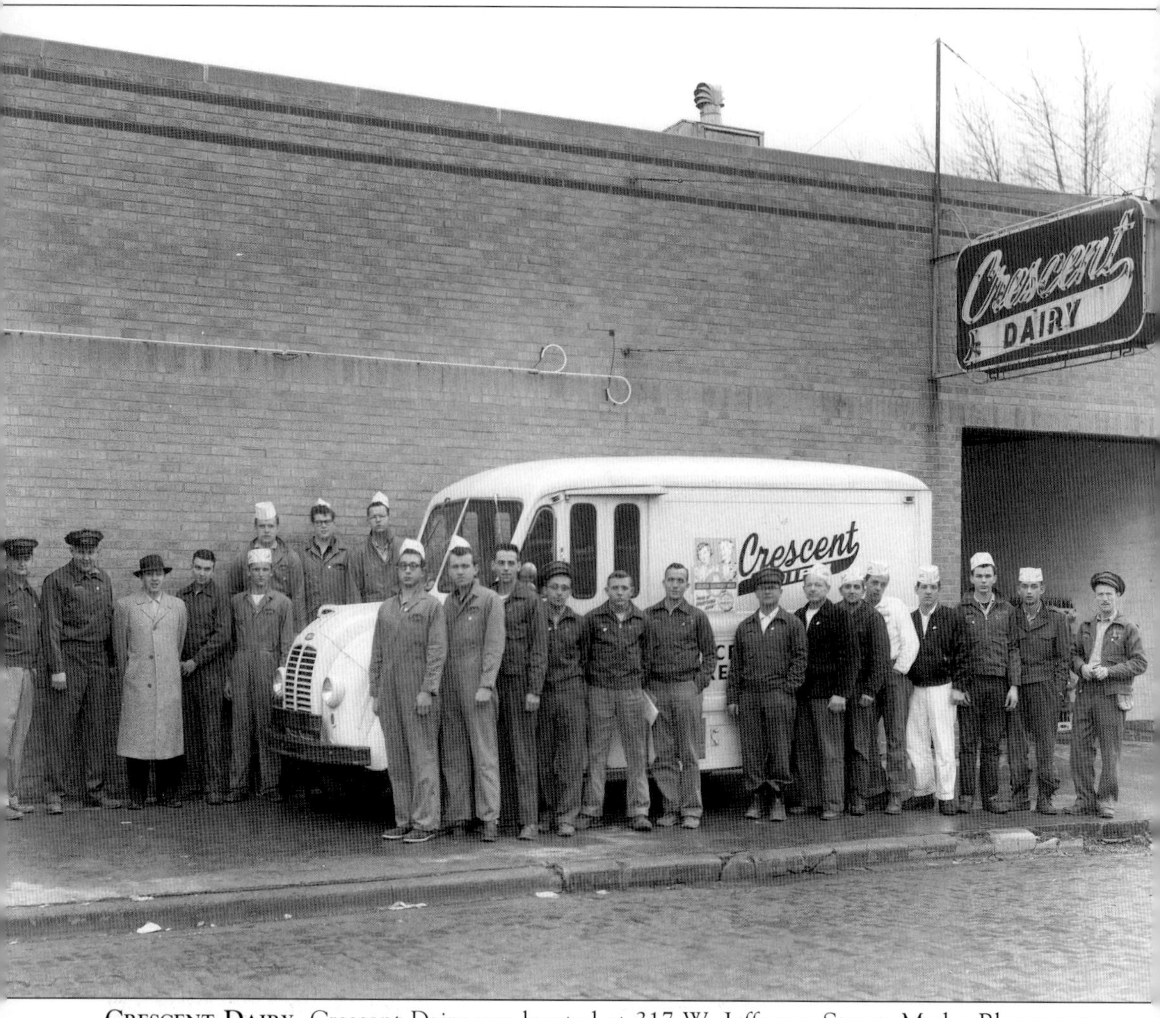

CRESCENT DAIRY. Crescent Dairy was located at 317 W. Jefferson Street. Med-o Bloom was also a home delivery. We put a note in the bottle and they would leave our order.

Ten
PEOPLE

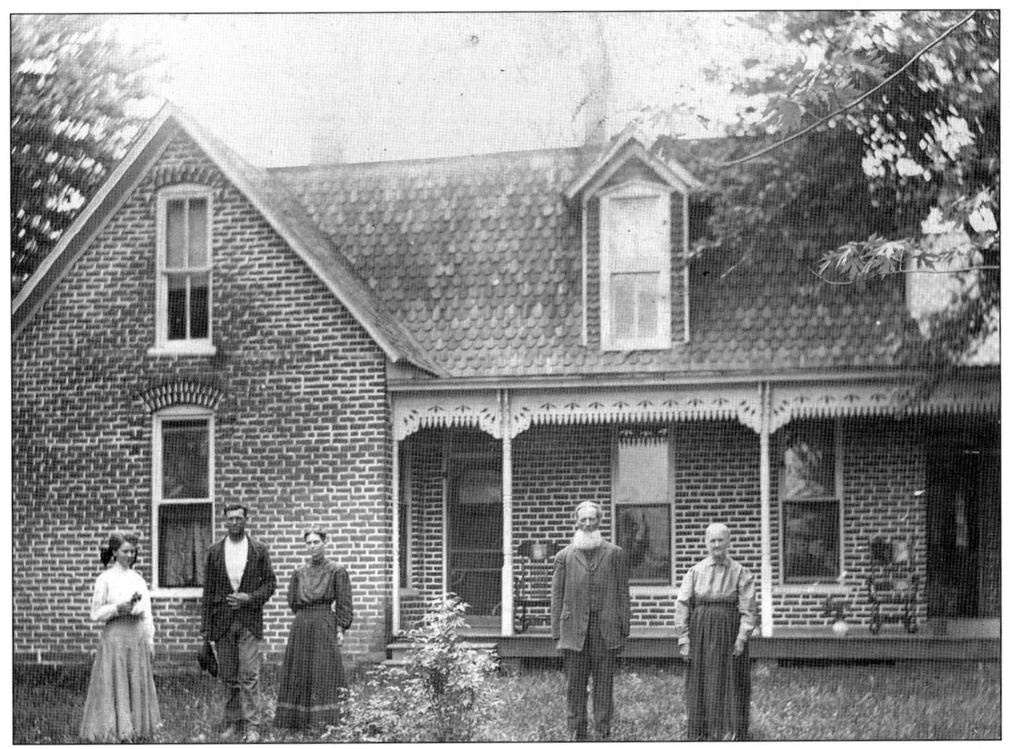

BOWMAN HOME. Bowman Home was located at 1424 S. Home Avenue. The couple to the right was Robert and Pauline Bowman, grandparents of Archie Bowman.

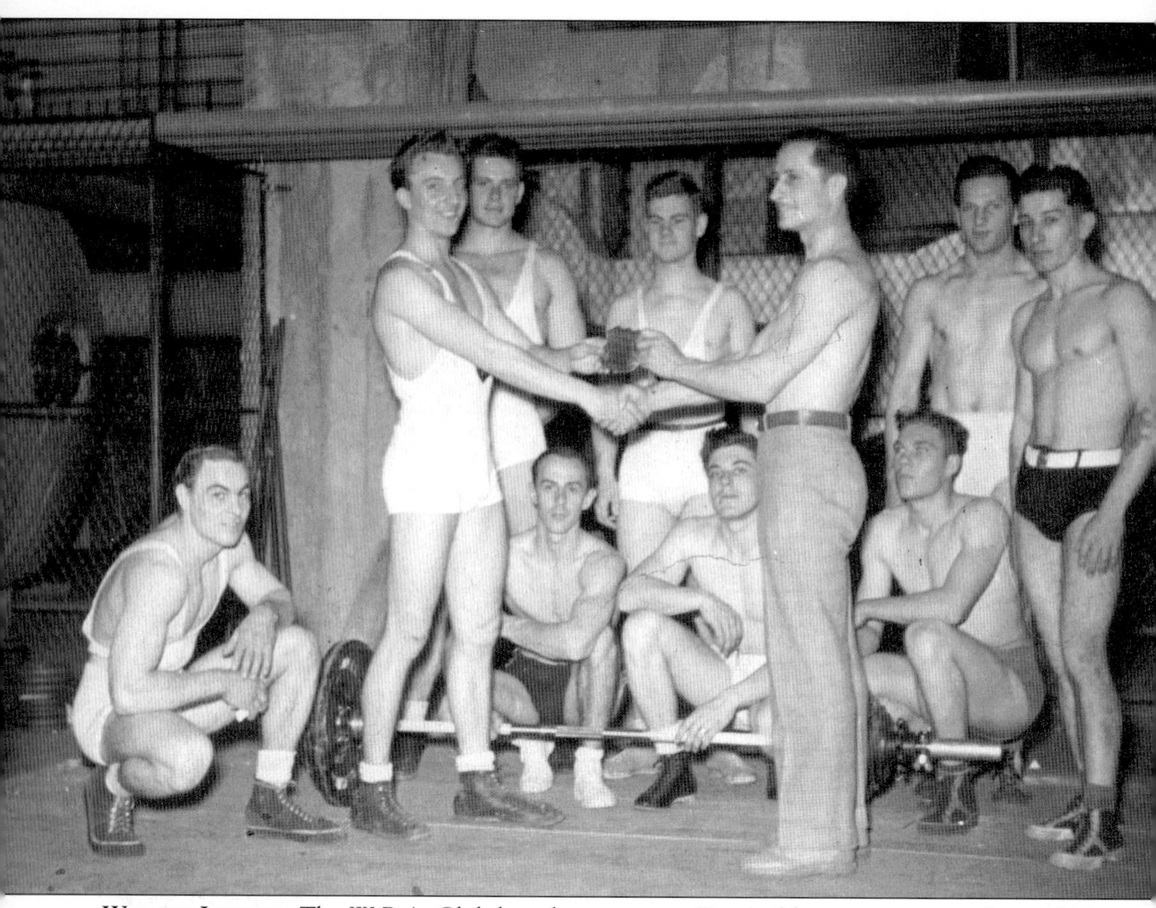

Weight Lifters. The W.B.A. Club lasted many years. Pictured here are a group of men, led by Andy Richards who won many weight lifting contests. Do you know any of these men?

TROLLEY CONDUCTOR. James R. Small was one of the first conductors on the trolley cars in the 1900s.

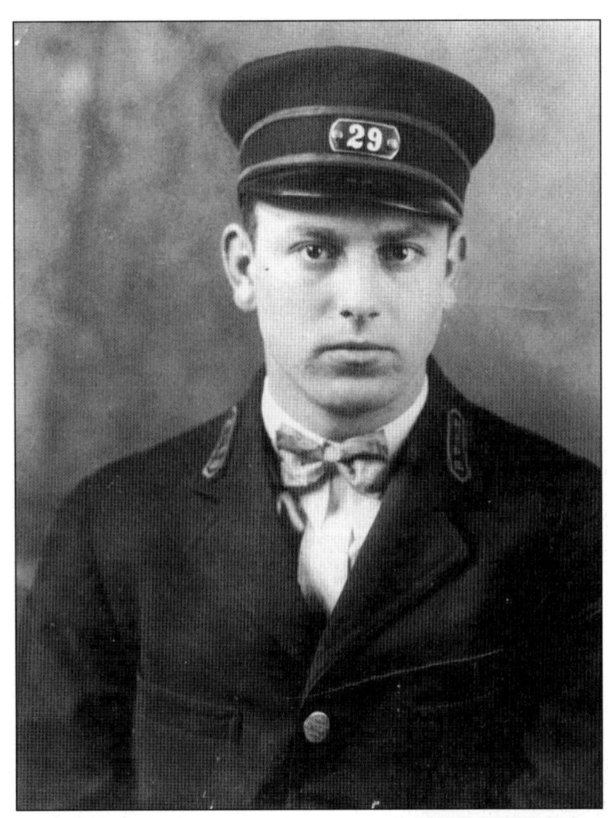

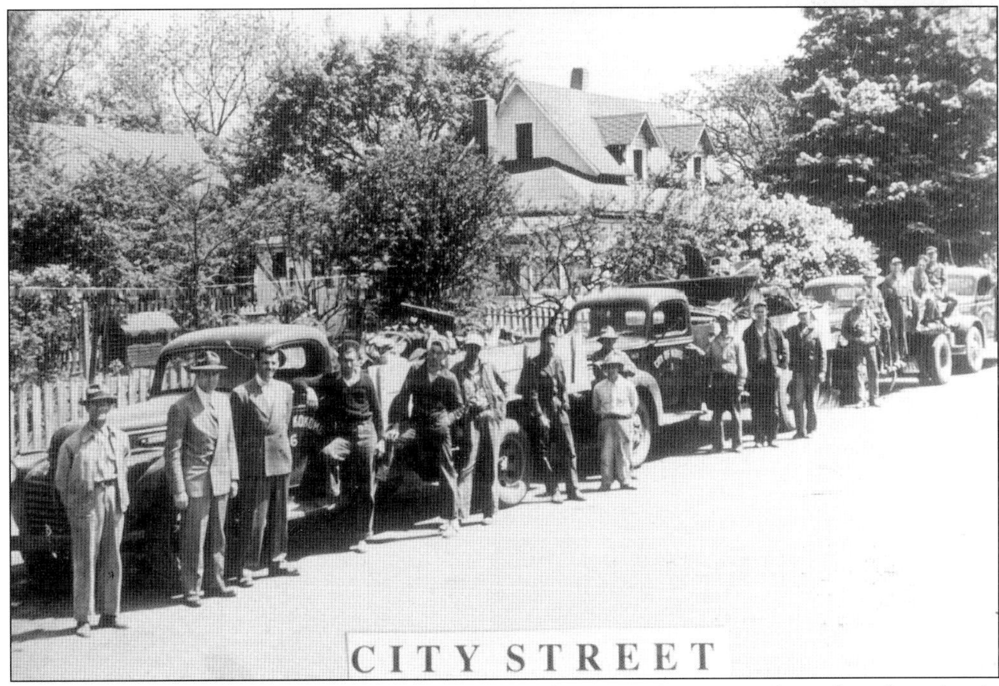

CITY WORKERS. Here is a picture of many city workers in 1950. Do you have friends or family here?

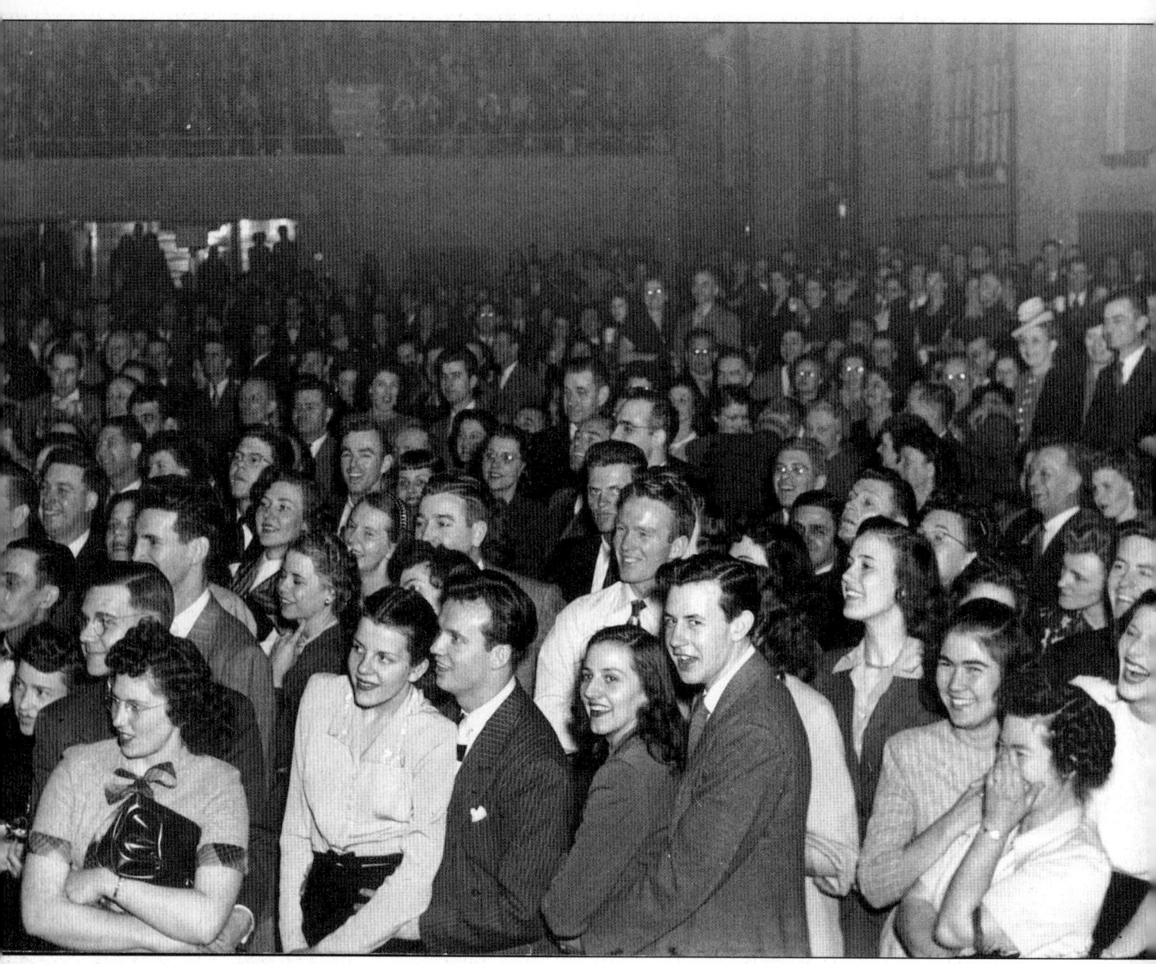

DANCE AT ARMORY. Here is another picture taken at the National Guard Armory in 1948. Perhaps you and your sweetheart are in this photo taken by Robert E. Davies. Or could your parents or a relative be in this picture?

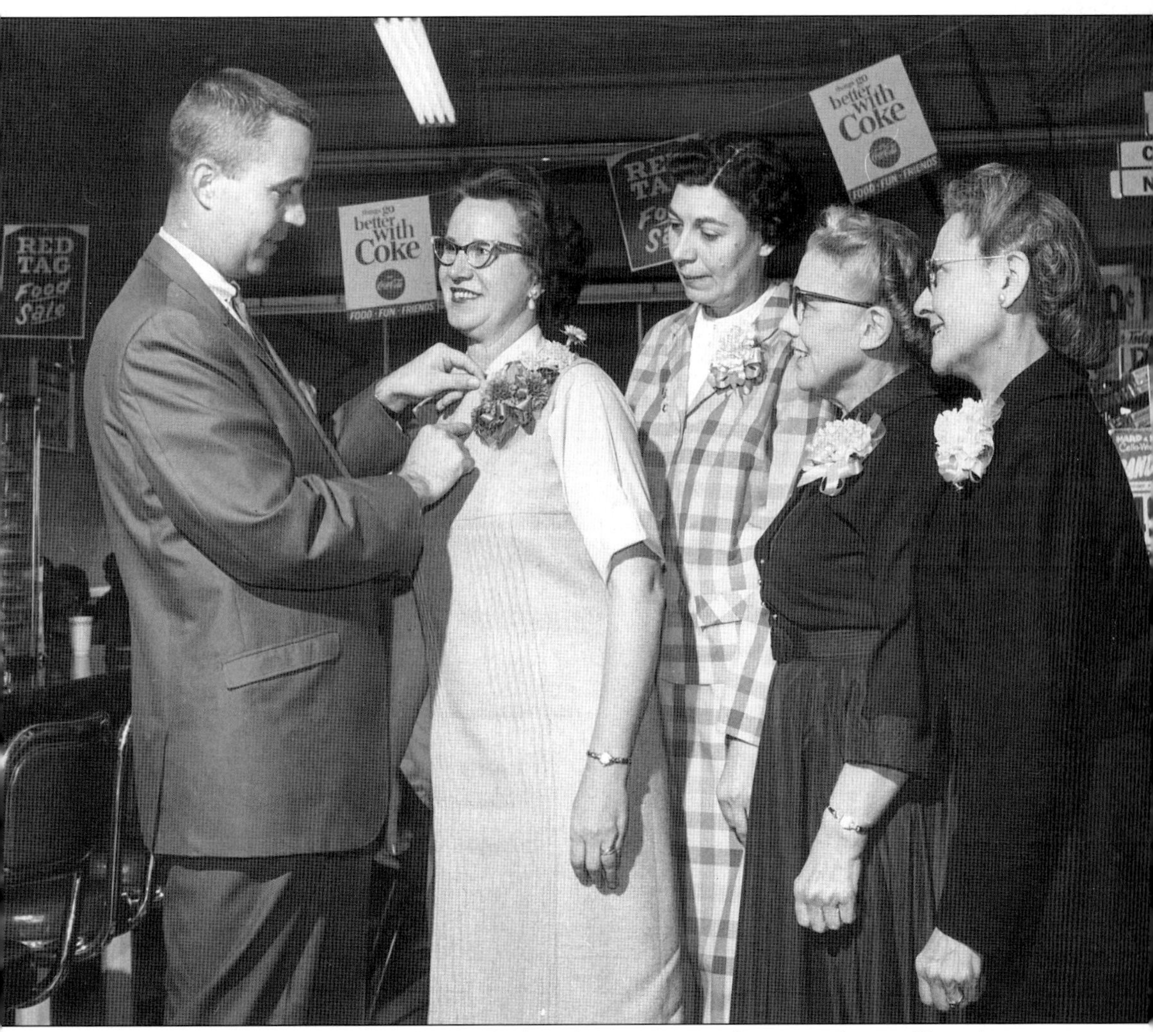

20TH ANNIVERSARY. Leanna Bolen worked at the S.S. Kresge for over 25 years. Here she is in 1966 on her 20th anniversary. Pictured left to right in picture are Clayton Doran, manager; Leanna Bolen; Emma Heath; Freda Gore; and Vera Billam.

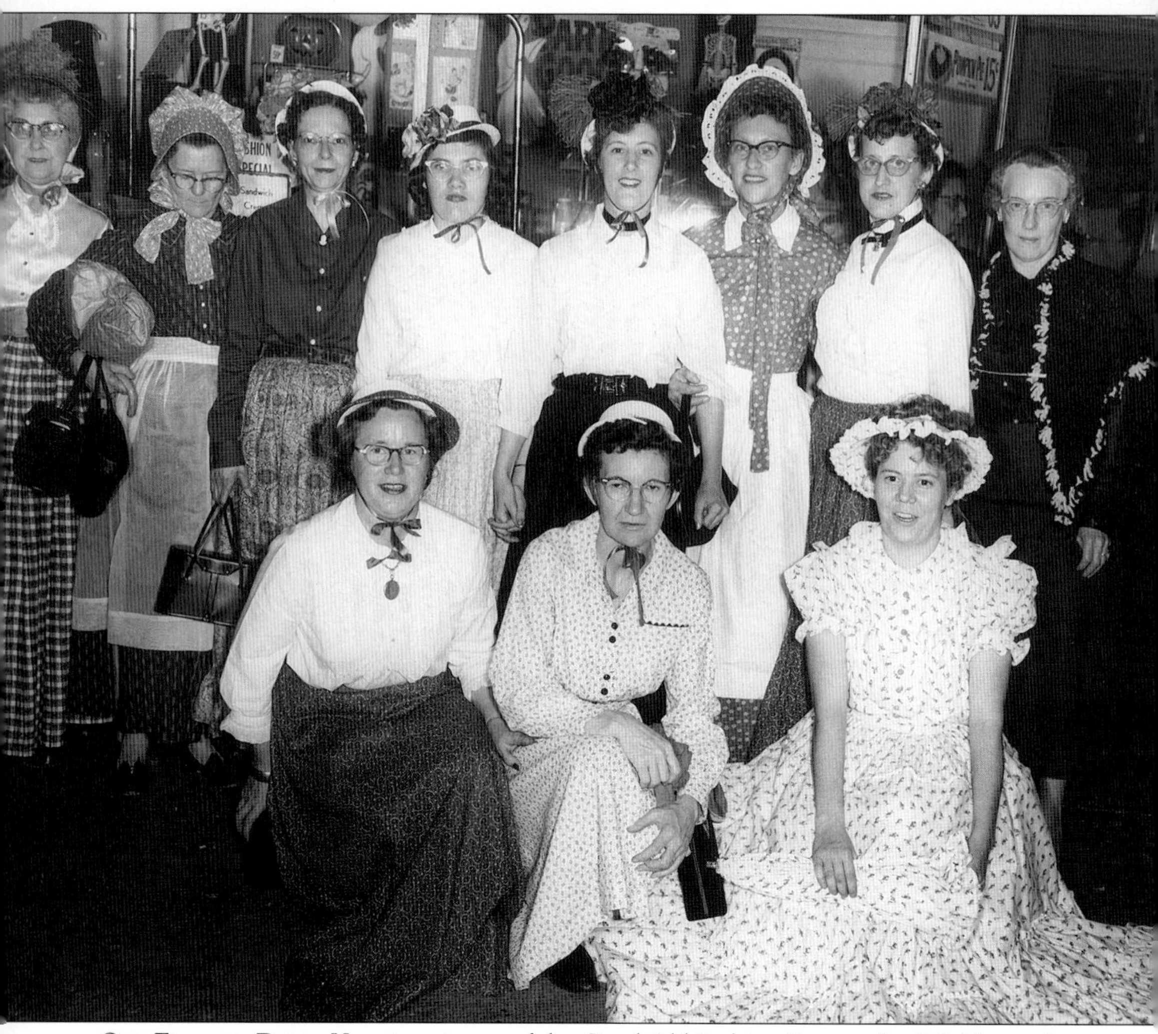

OLD FASHION DAYS. Here is a picture of the Good Old Fashion Days at the S.S. Kresge from 1966. Are you in this picture?

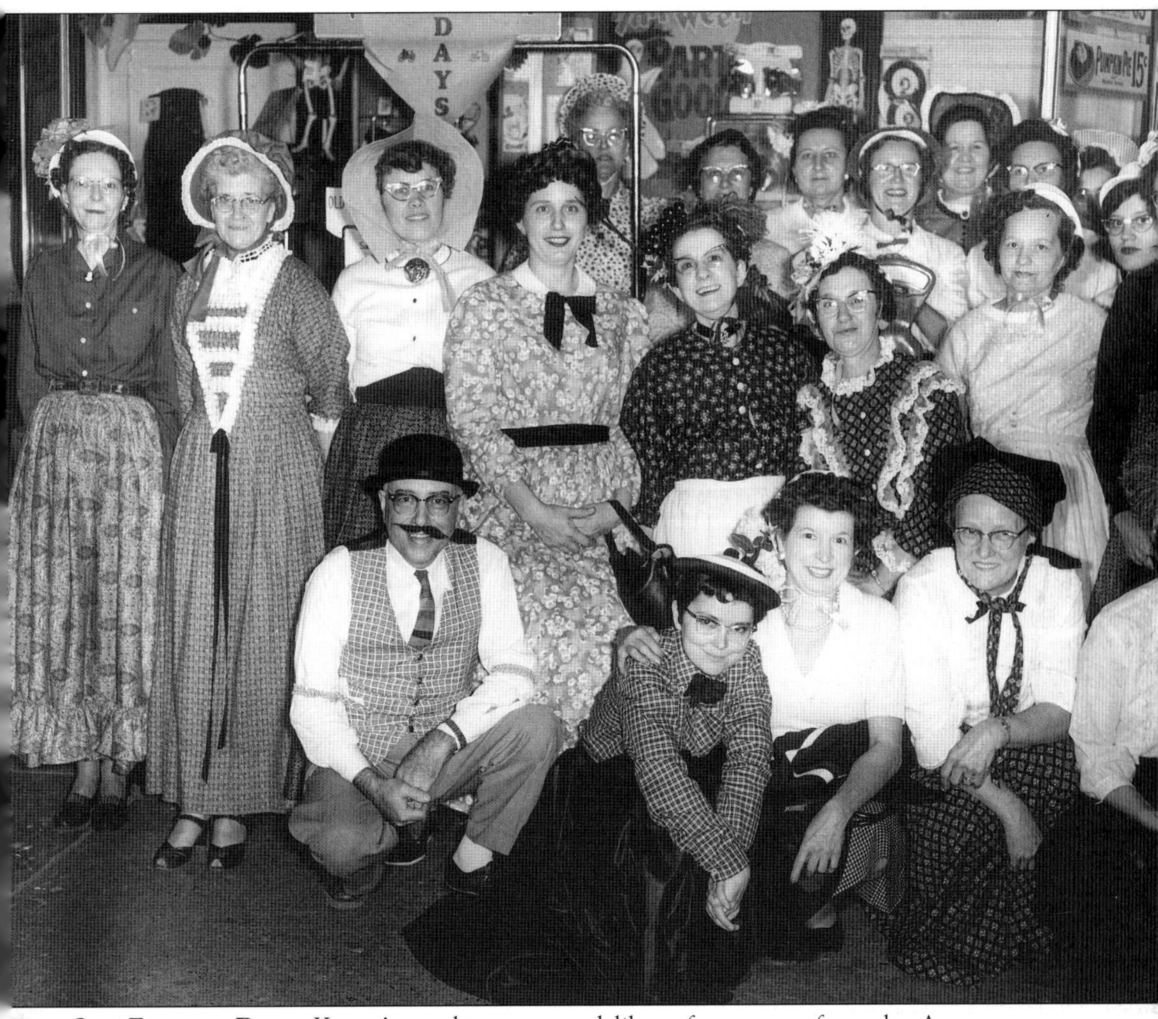

OLD FASHION DAYS. Kresge's employees seemed like a fun group of people. Are you or a relative in this picture?

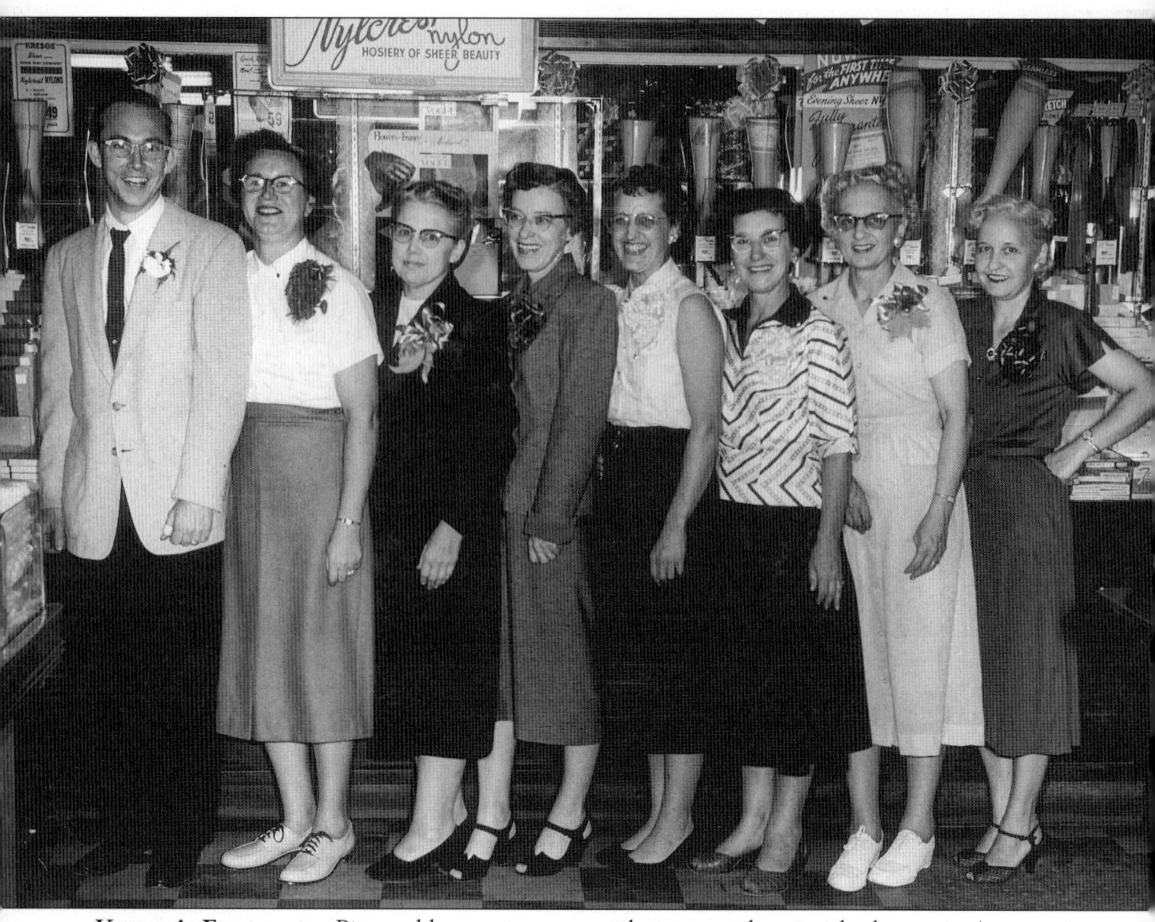

KRESGE'S EMPLOYEES. Pictured here are more employees standing inside the store. Are you or a relative in this picture? It was taken in the 1950s.

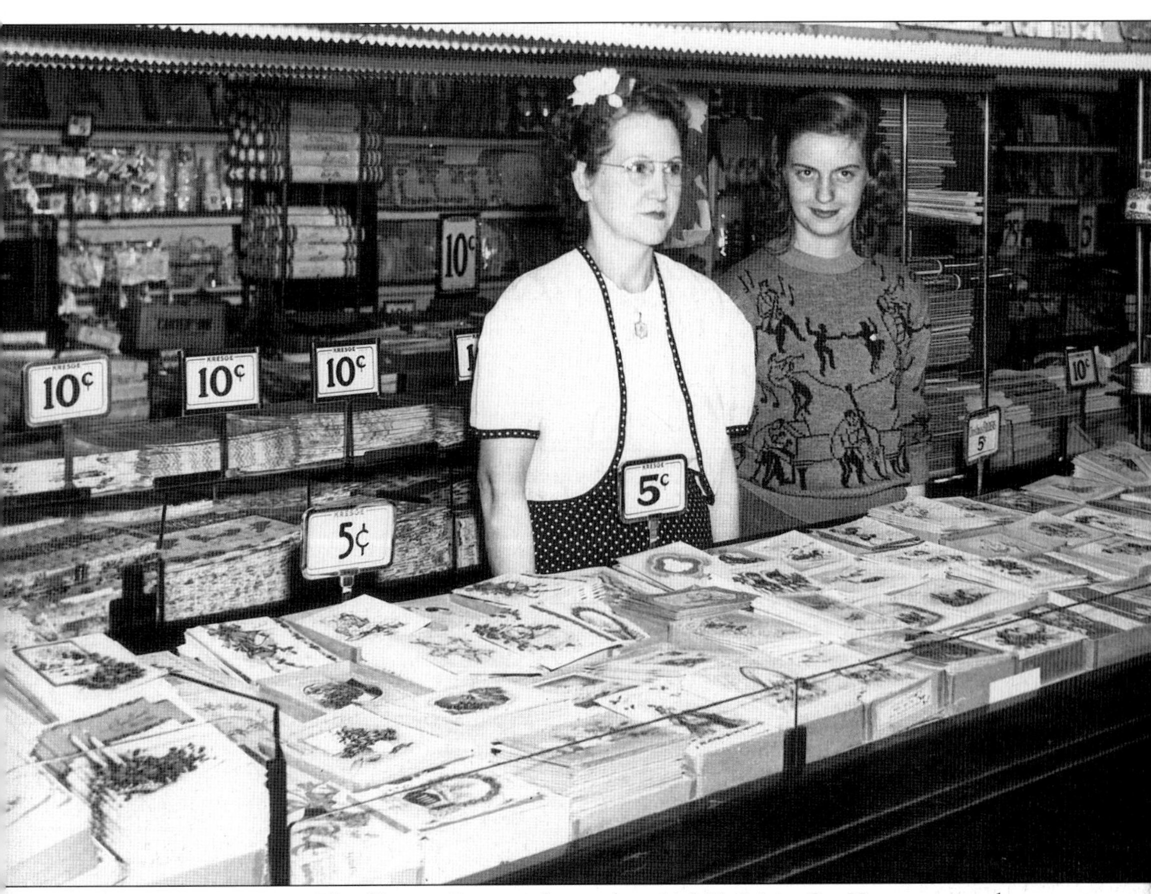

KRESGE'S EMPLOYEES. The Kresge Co. was located at 116 N. Main St. Here are two happy employees. Look at the nickel and dime signs! Those were the days, my friend. The 1950s were great!

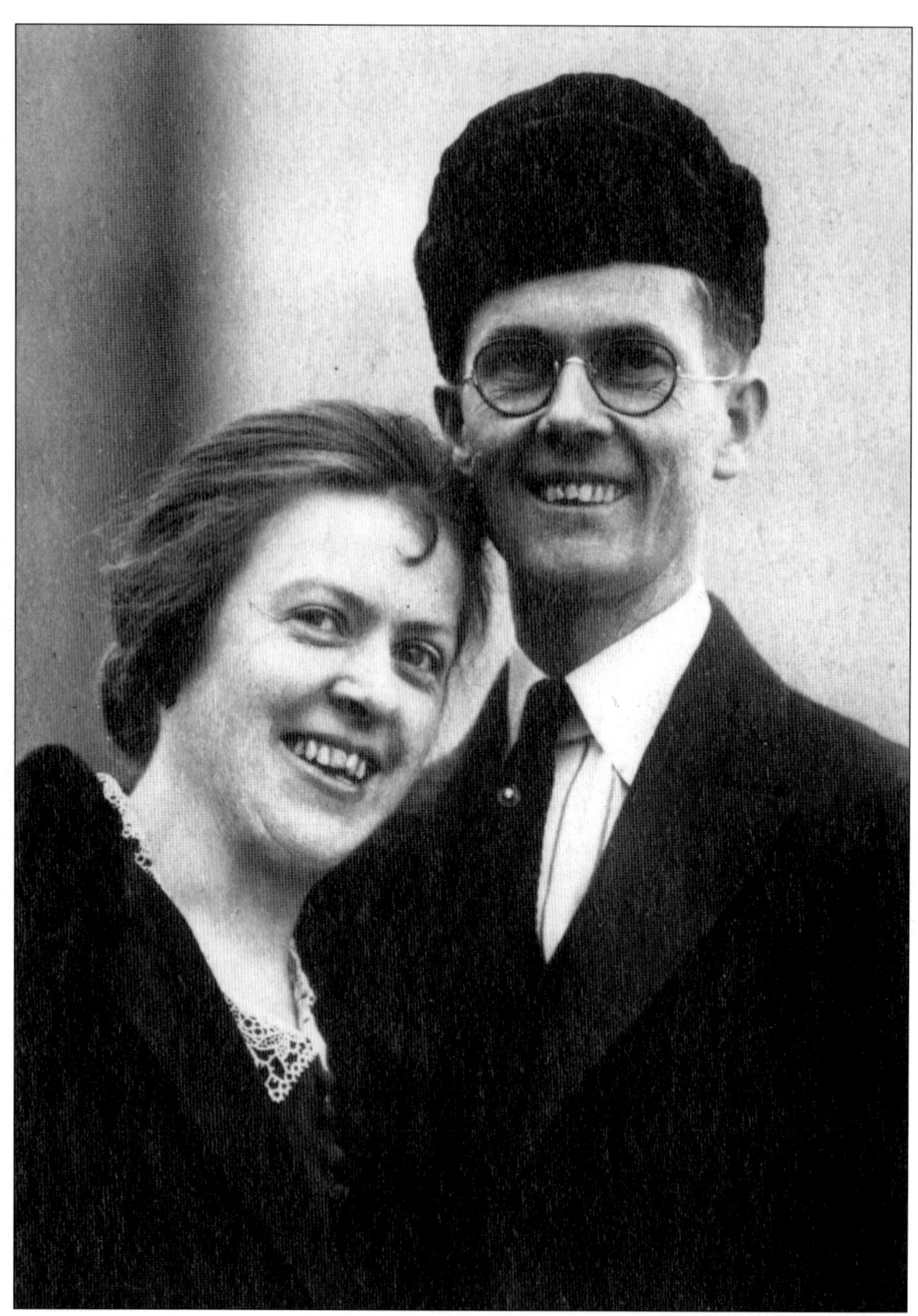

JOHN AND JEANETTE RYAN. John Ryan (1885–1996) and his wife, Jeanette, are pictured here. Ryan was voted the best-dressed man in Kokomo for many years. His motto was: "We will still shoot anything, anywhere, anytime." He was without doubt the best photographer to ever come to Kokomo. His pictures speak for themselves.

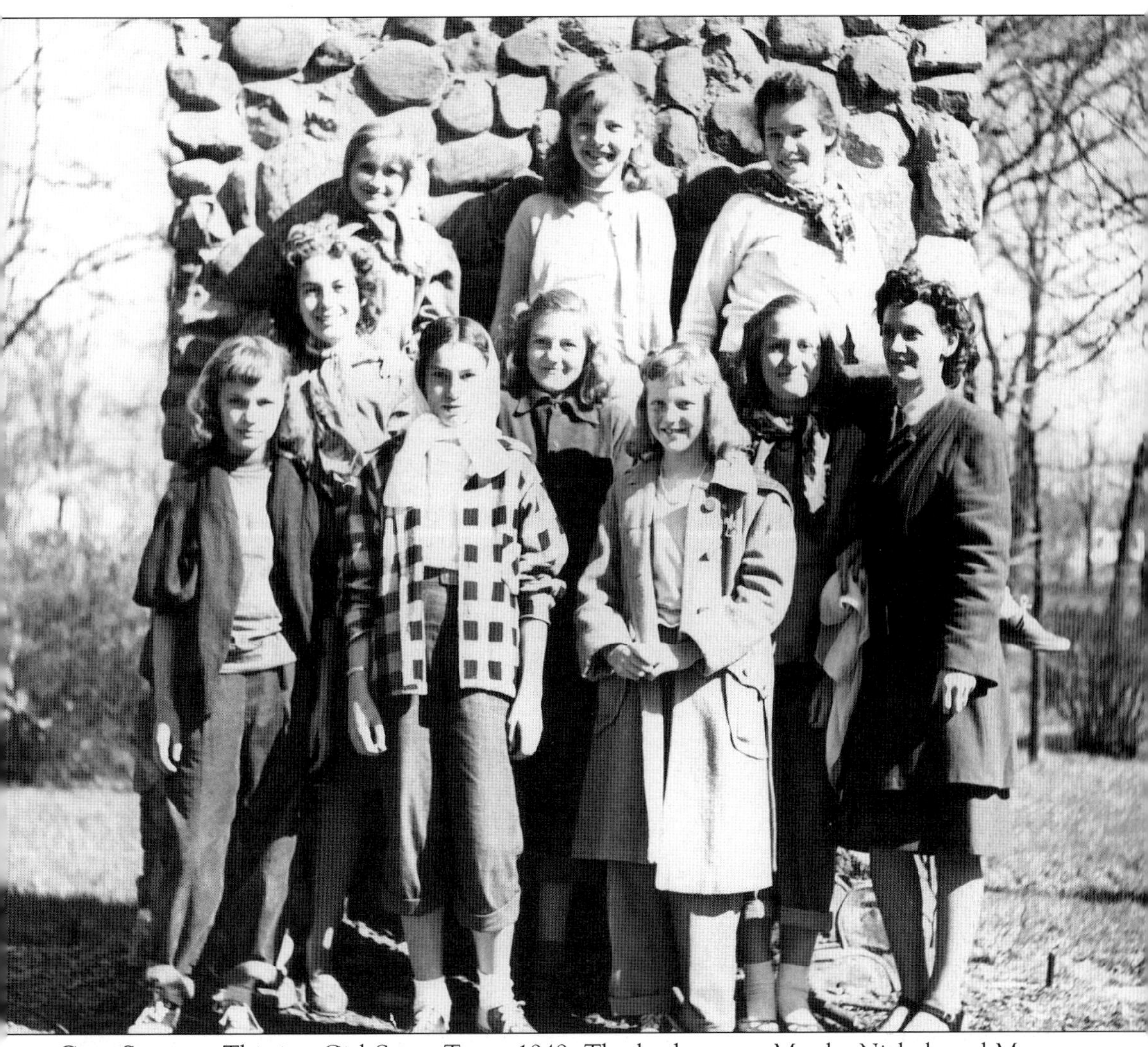

GIRL SCOUTS. This is a Girl Scout Troop 1949. The leaders were Martha Nichols and Mrs. James Harris. The girls were Jean Stanley, Rose Mary Wright, Joan Federspill, Jacque Kunau, Marietta Scherich, Rochelle Shook, Becky Harris, and Lana.

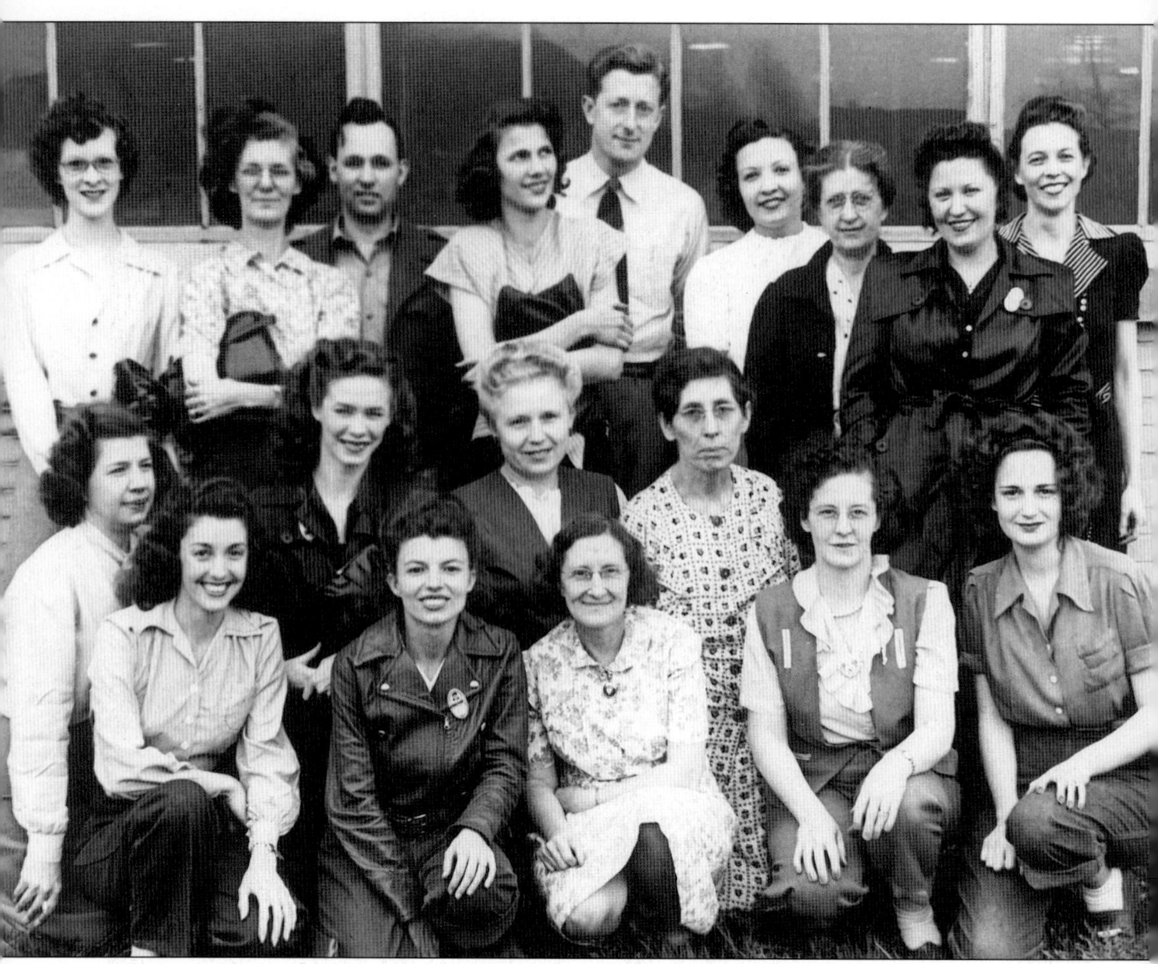

DELCO EMPLOYEES. This picture was taken outside the Delco Radio in April of 1947. (Photo courtesy of Robert Davies.)

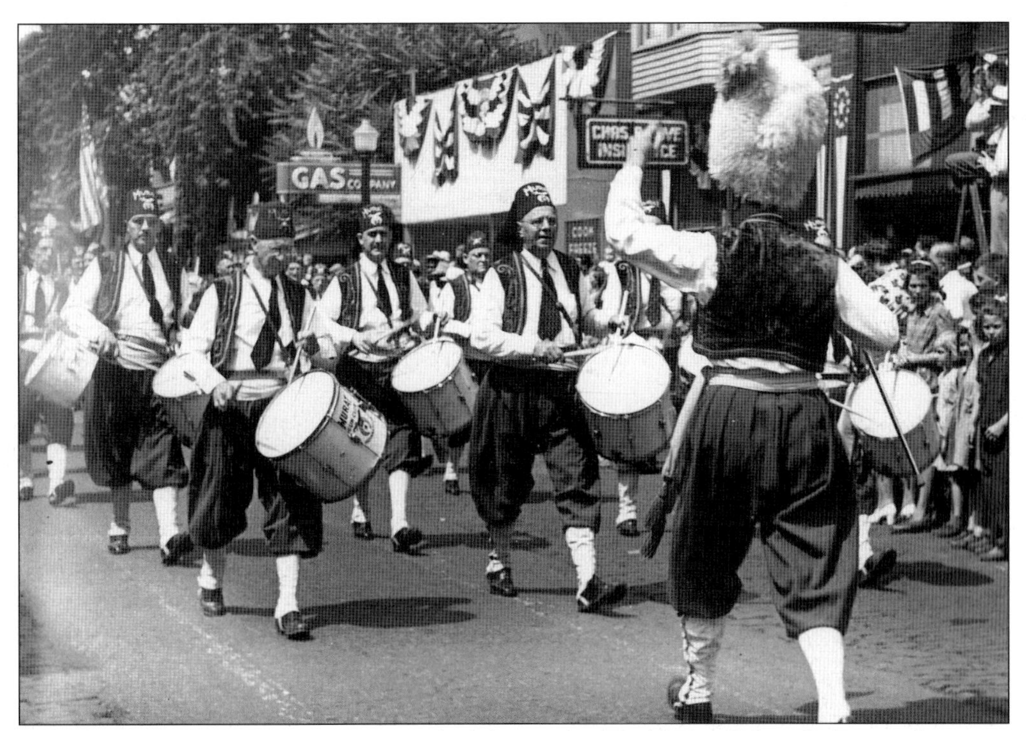

PARADE. The Murat Organization marched during the World War II Parade. Do you have any friends or family here?

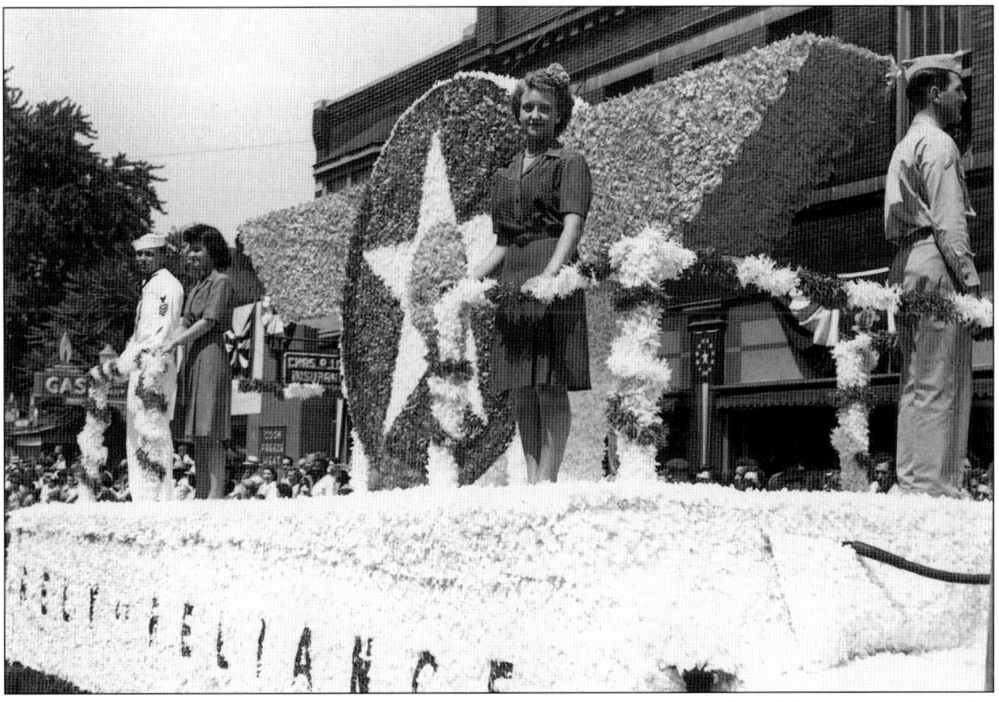

PARADE. This is the Felt of Reliance Float during the World War II Celebration Parade. Do you know who these people are?

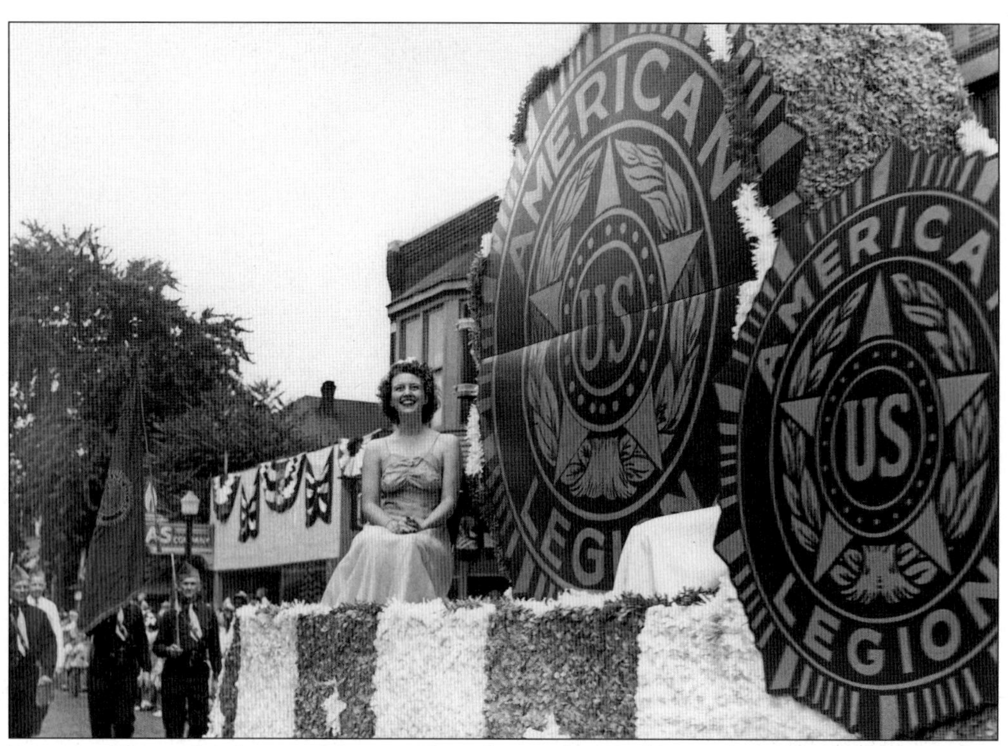

PARADE. This is the American Legion Float during the World War II Parade.

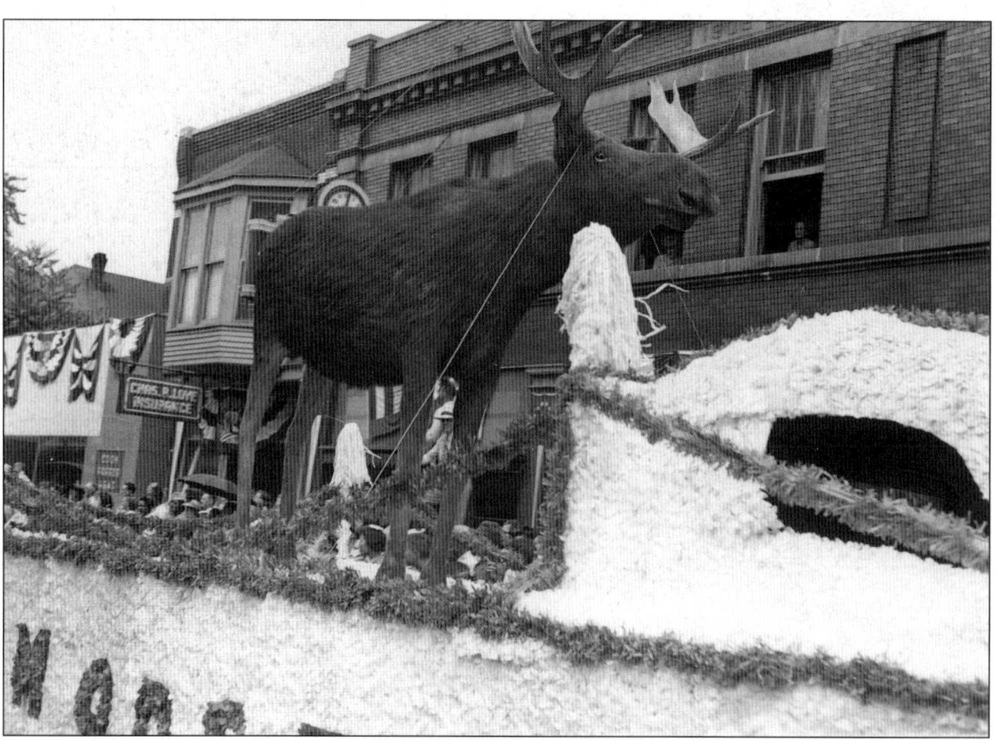

PARADE. Pictured here is the World War II Parade with the Moose Lodge represented.

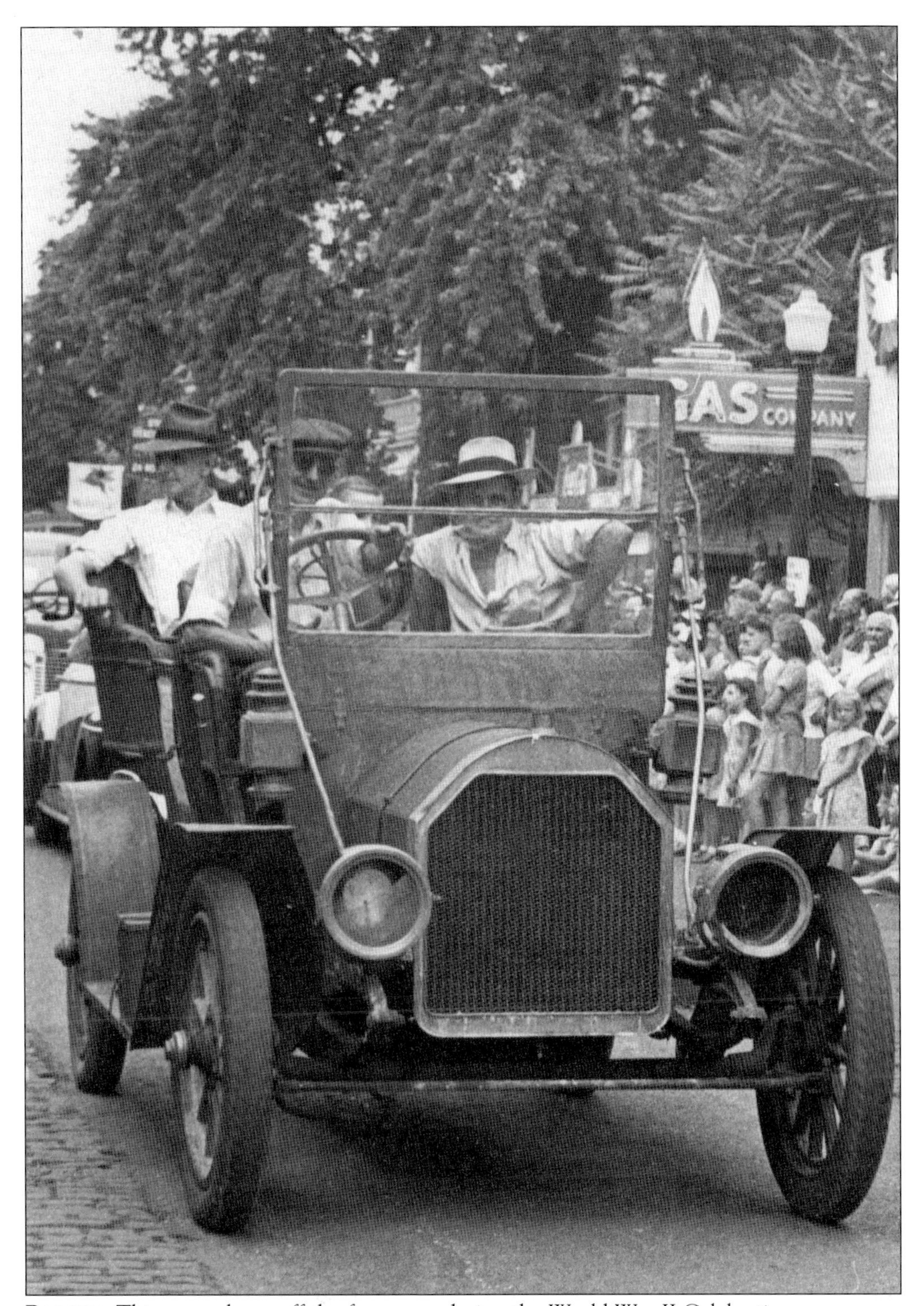

PARADE. This entry shows off the fancy cars during the World War II Celebration.

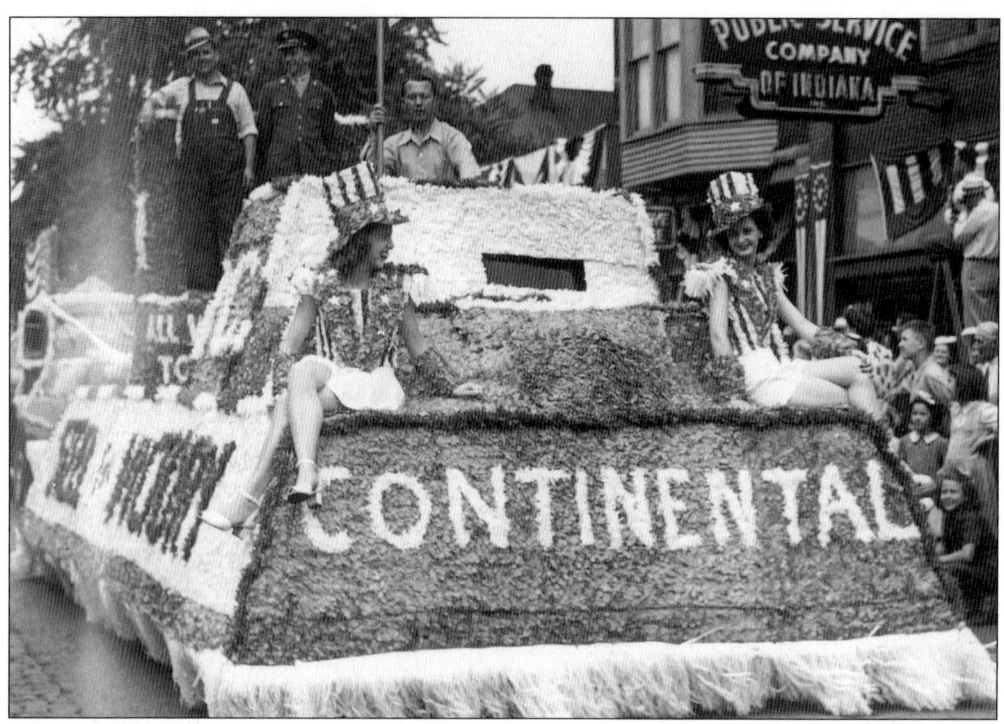

PARADE. This is the Continental Steel Float from the 1942 parade. Do you know anyone here?

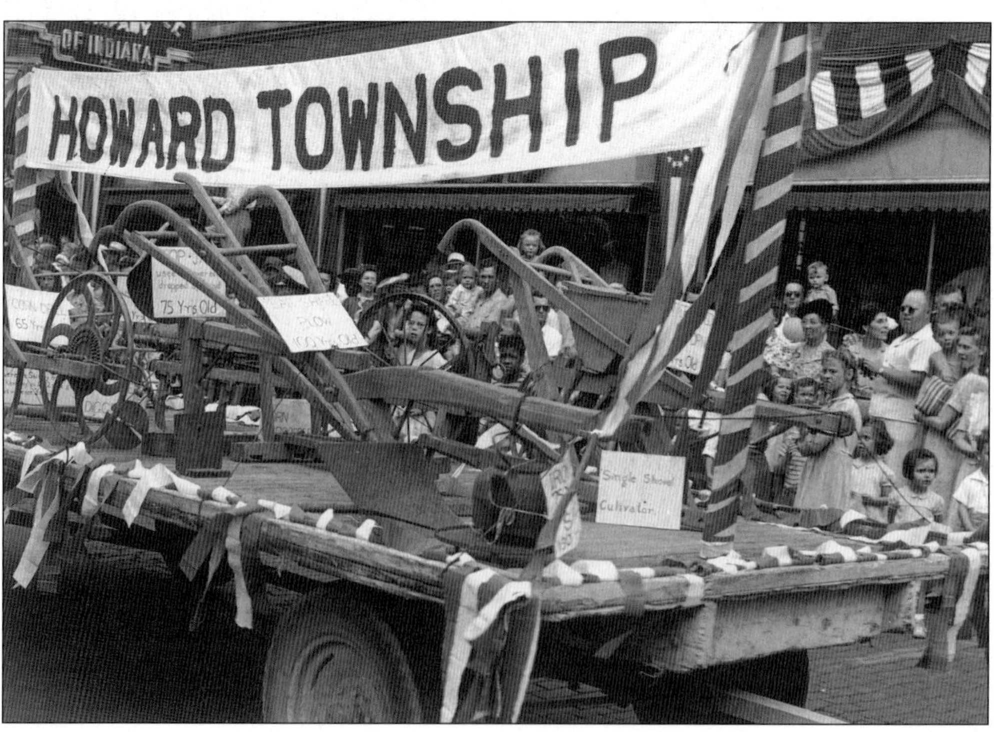

PARADE. The Howard Township Float was showed off at the World War II Celebration.

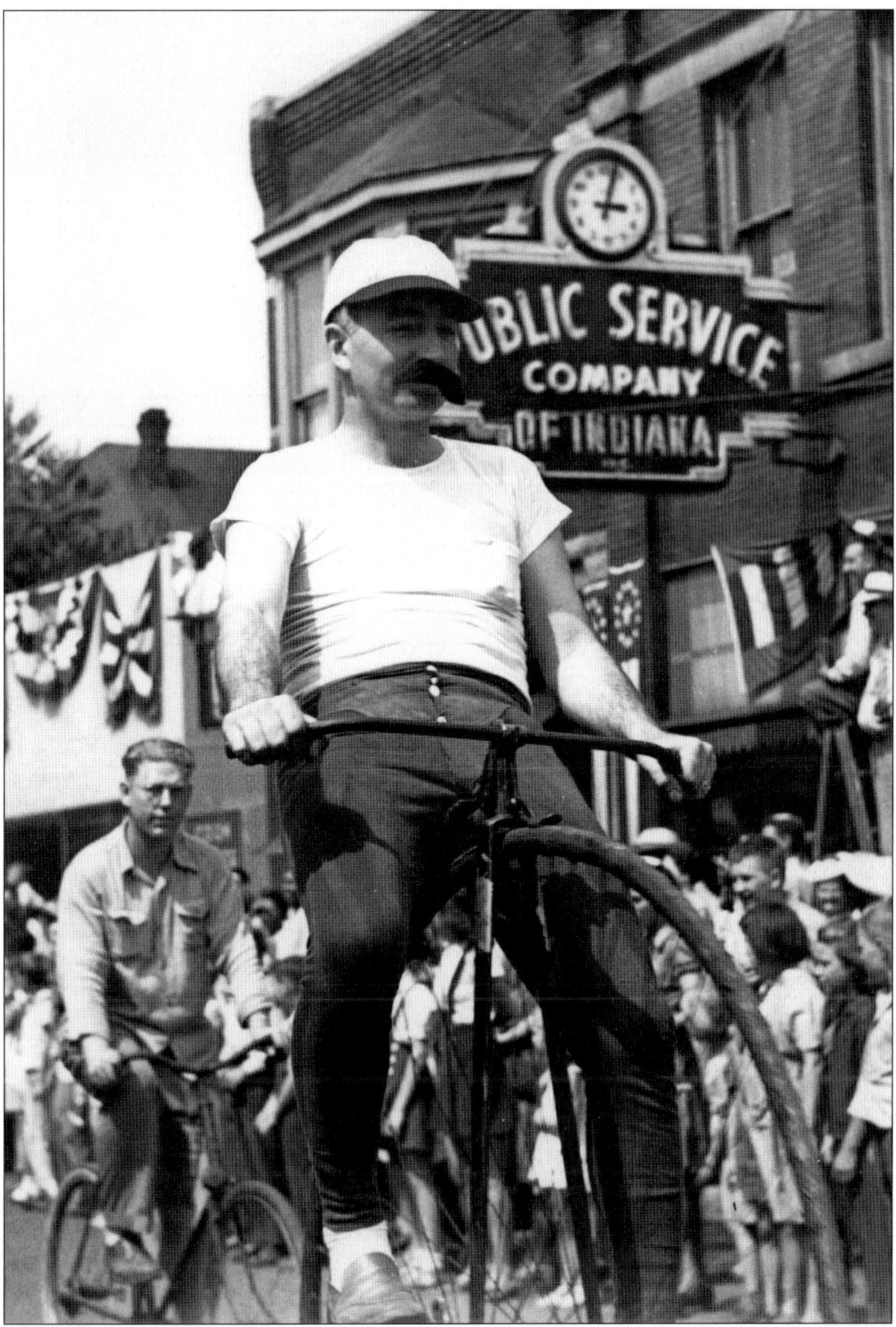

PARADE. Local bicyclists are pictured here during the World War II Celebration Parade. Who are they?

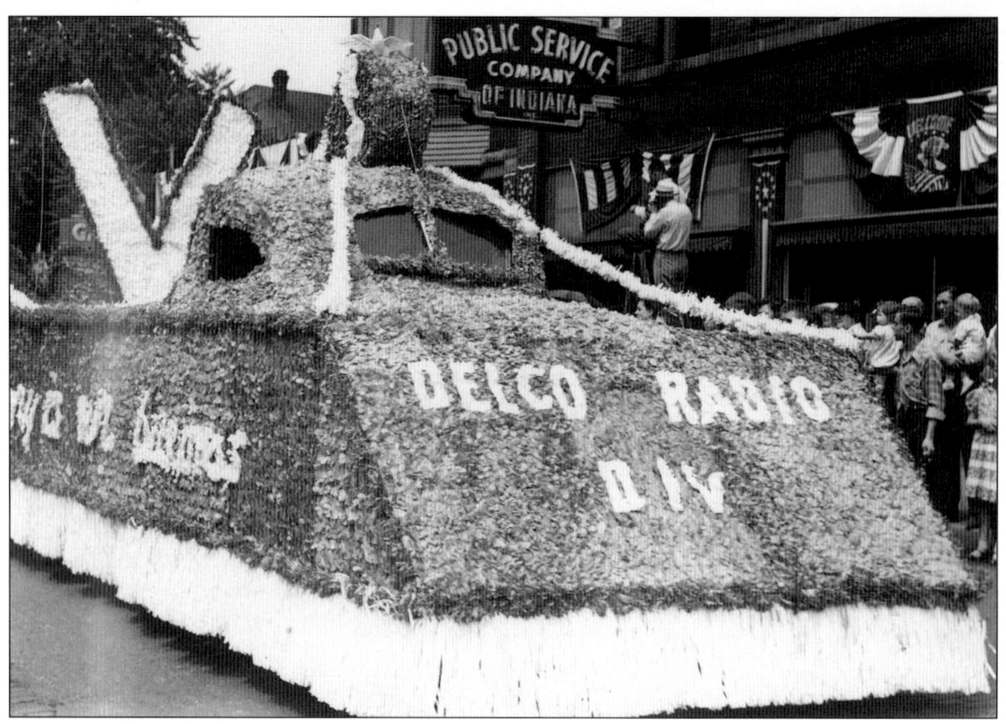

PARADE. Here is a Delco Float from the World War II Celebration Parade. Do you know anyone in this picture?

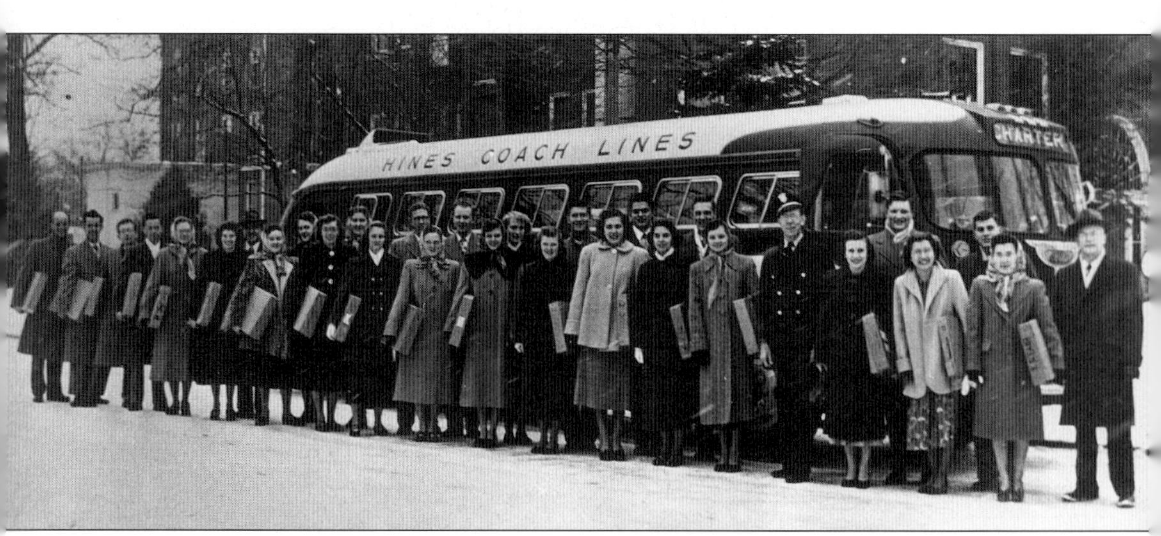

HINES COACH LINE. Can you remember the Hines Coach Lines? This picture was taken in the early 1950s, outside of McKinley School. Was someone you know in this picture?

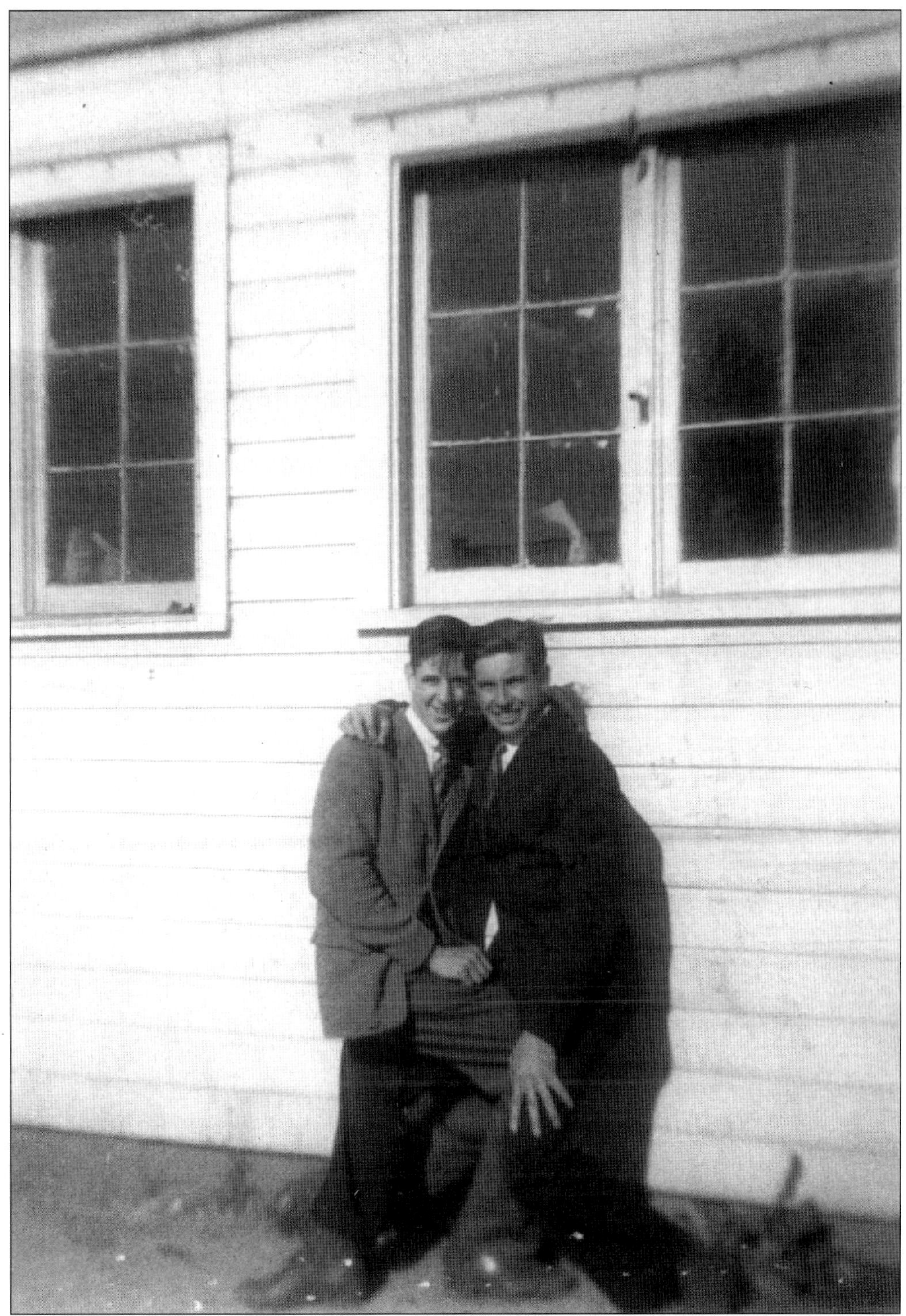

SKATERS DELIGHT. Here is a picture taken in 1946 outside the Skaters Delight. The skating rink was located at 2446 N. Washington. On the left is Jack Carter and Walter Baldwin is on the right. Remember how the spotlight would flicker on the floor?

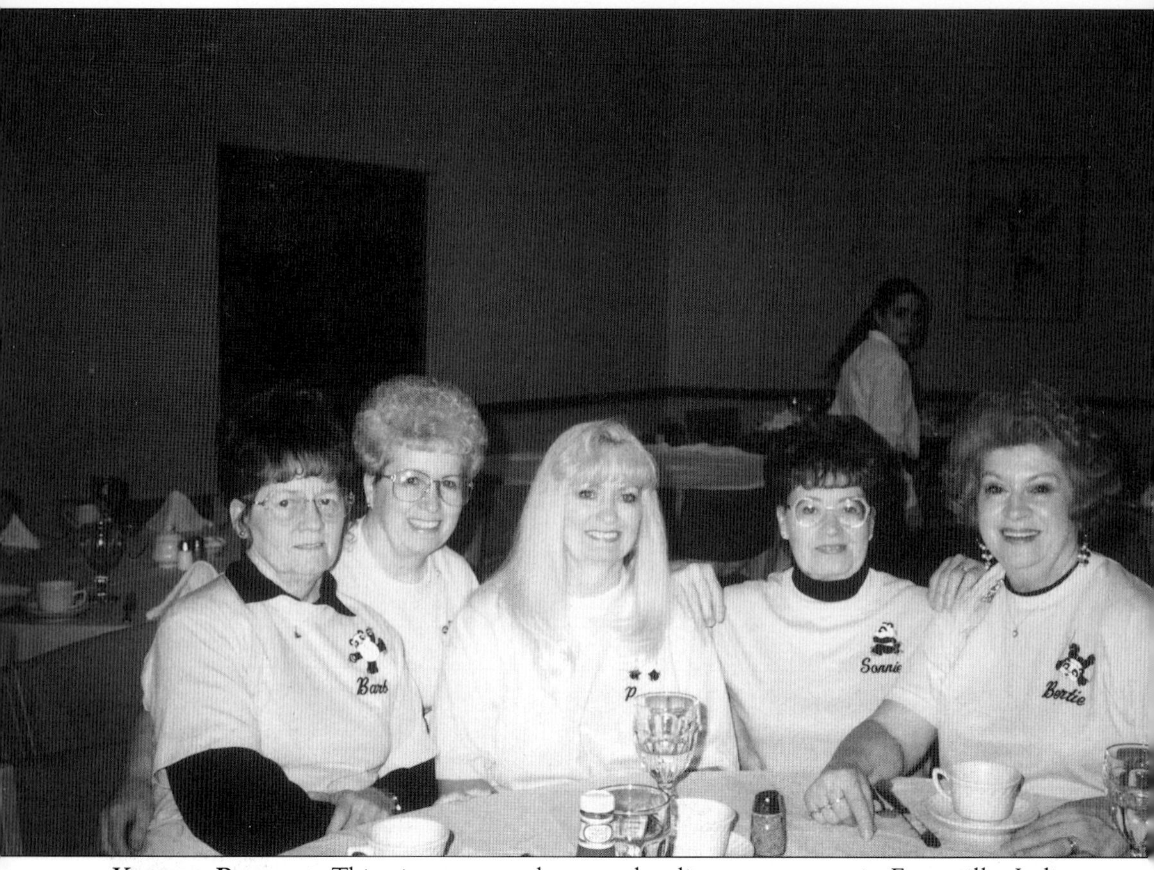

KOKOMO BOWLERS. This picture was taken at a bowling tournament in Evansville, Indiana. The sisters are from Kokomo, Indiana, and have bowled more than 30 years. They didn't win, but had lots of fun. Barb Hamilton, Wanita Luttrell, Patty Collier, Sondra Kemper, and Bertie Russell are the former Richards girls.

Eleven
SPECIAL

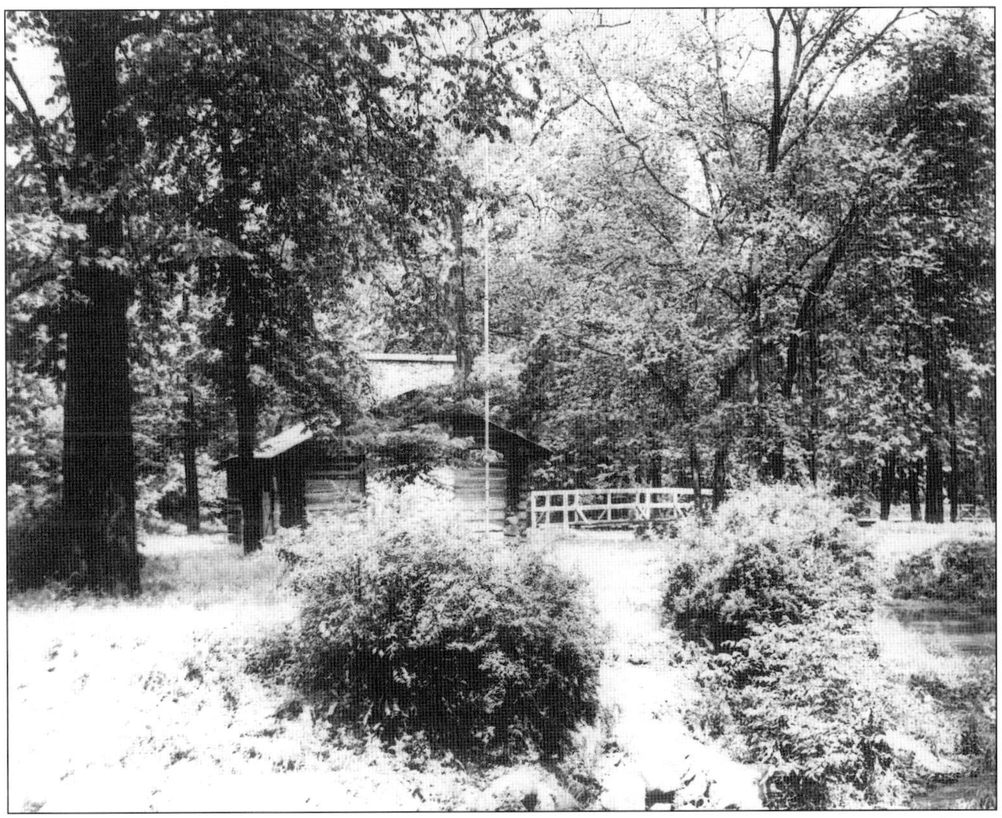

HIGHLAND PARK. This picture of Highland Park was taken in the early 1940s. Wasn't it fun to wade in the creek and walk through this summer wonderland?

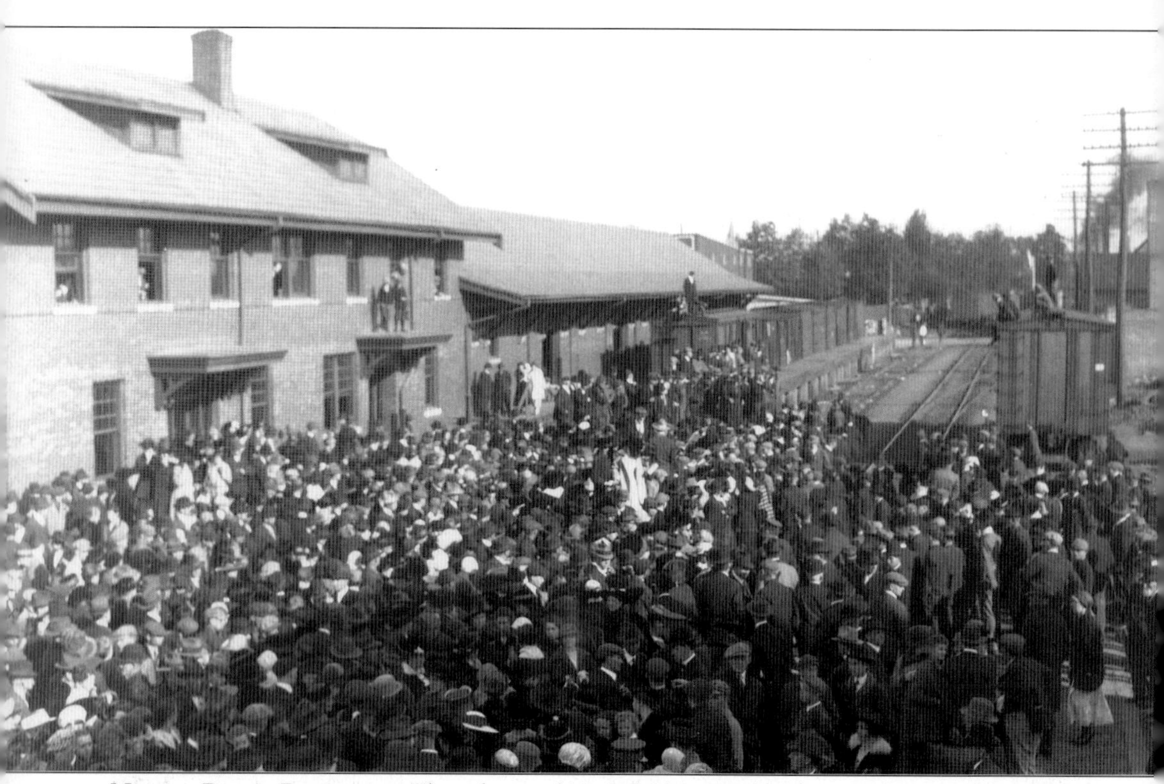

NICKEL PLATE RAILROAD. This photo of Nickel Plate Railroad was taken in the 1900s. It shows the boys coming home from World War I.

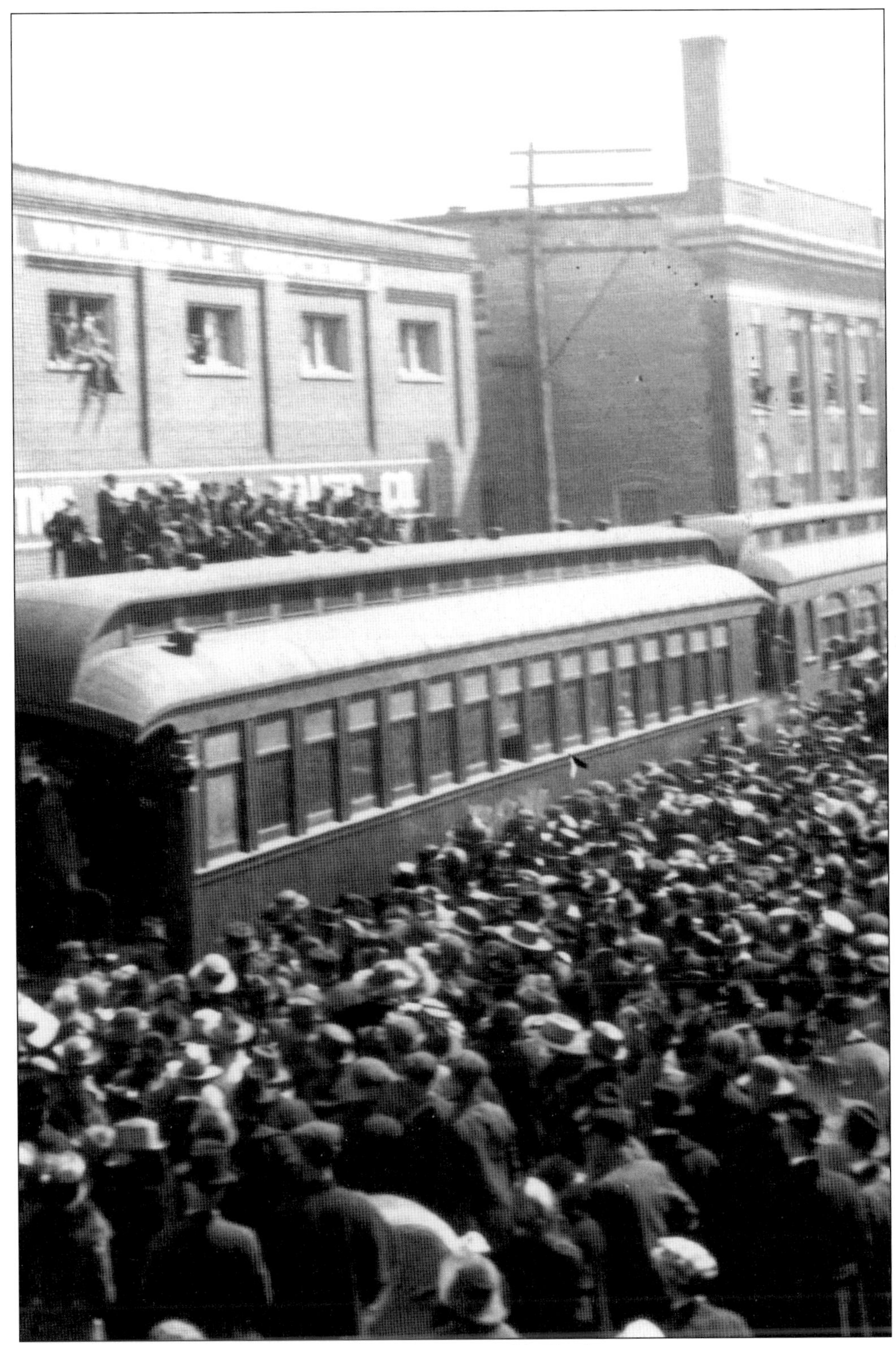

RAILROAD. The railroad is pictured here during World War I.

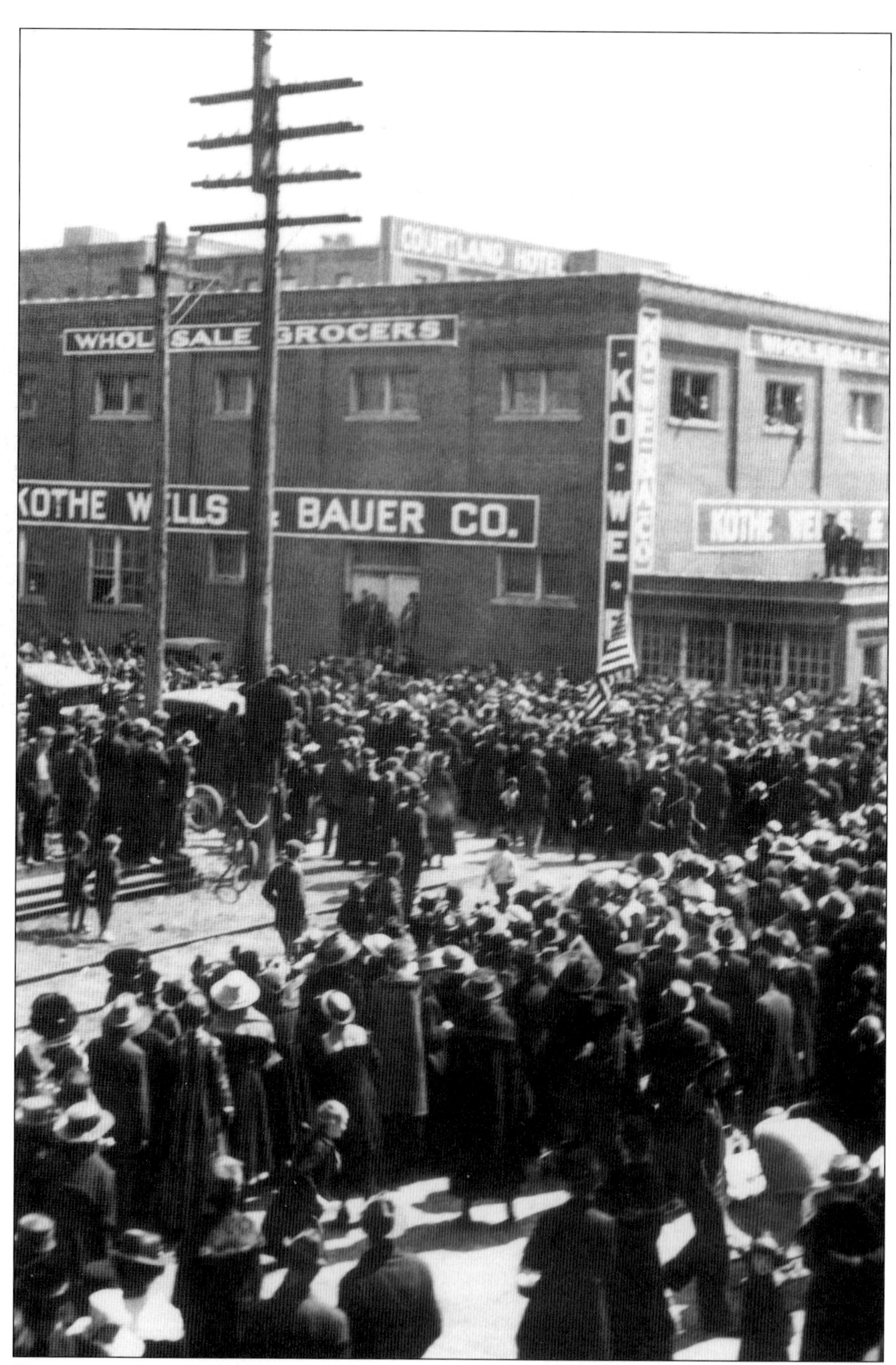

KOTHE, WELLS AND BAUER CO.

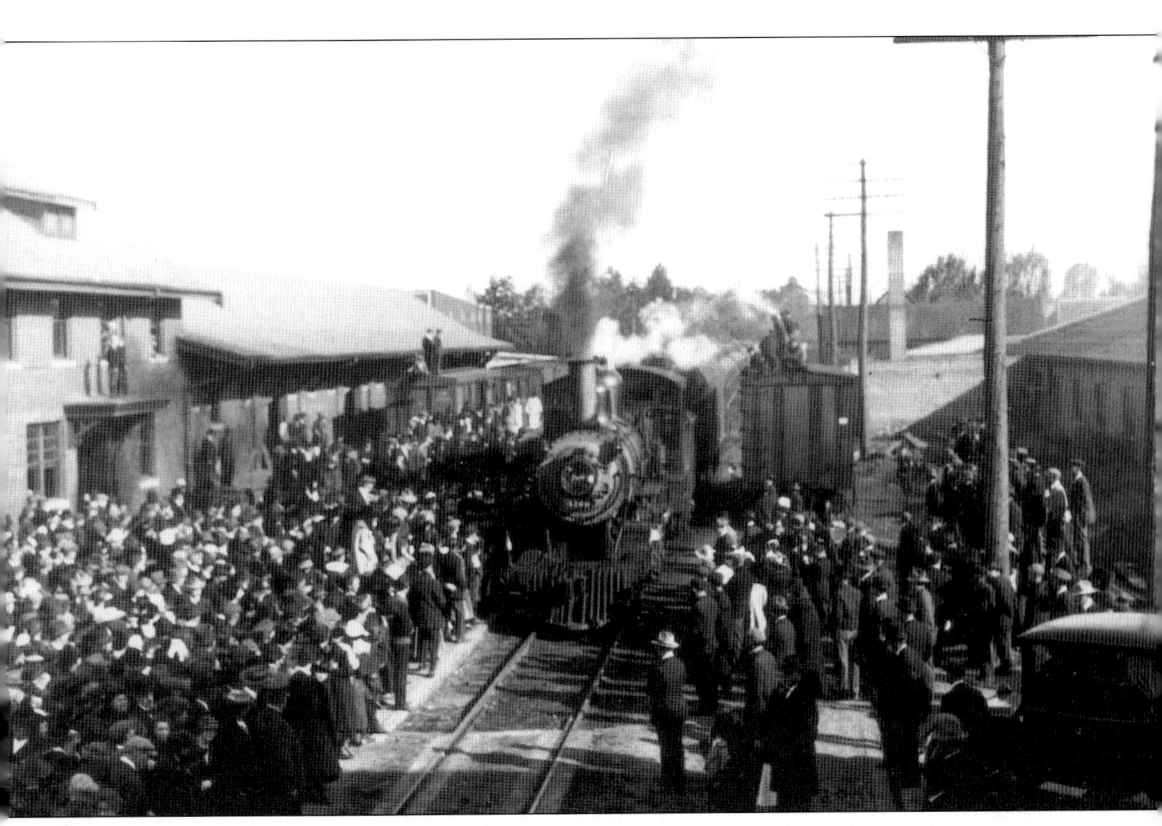

RAILROAD.

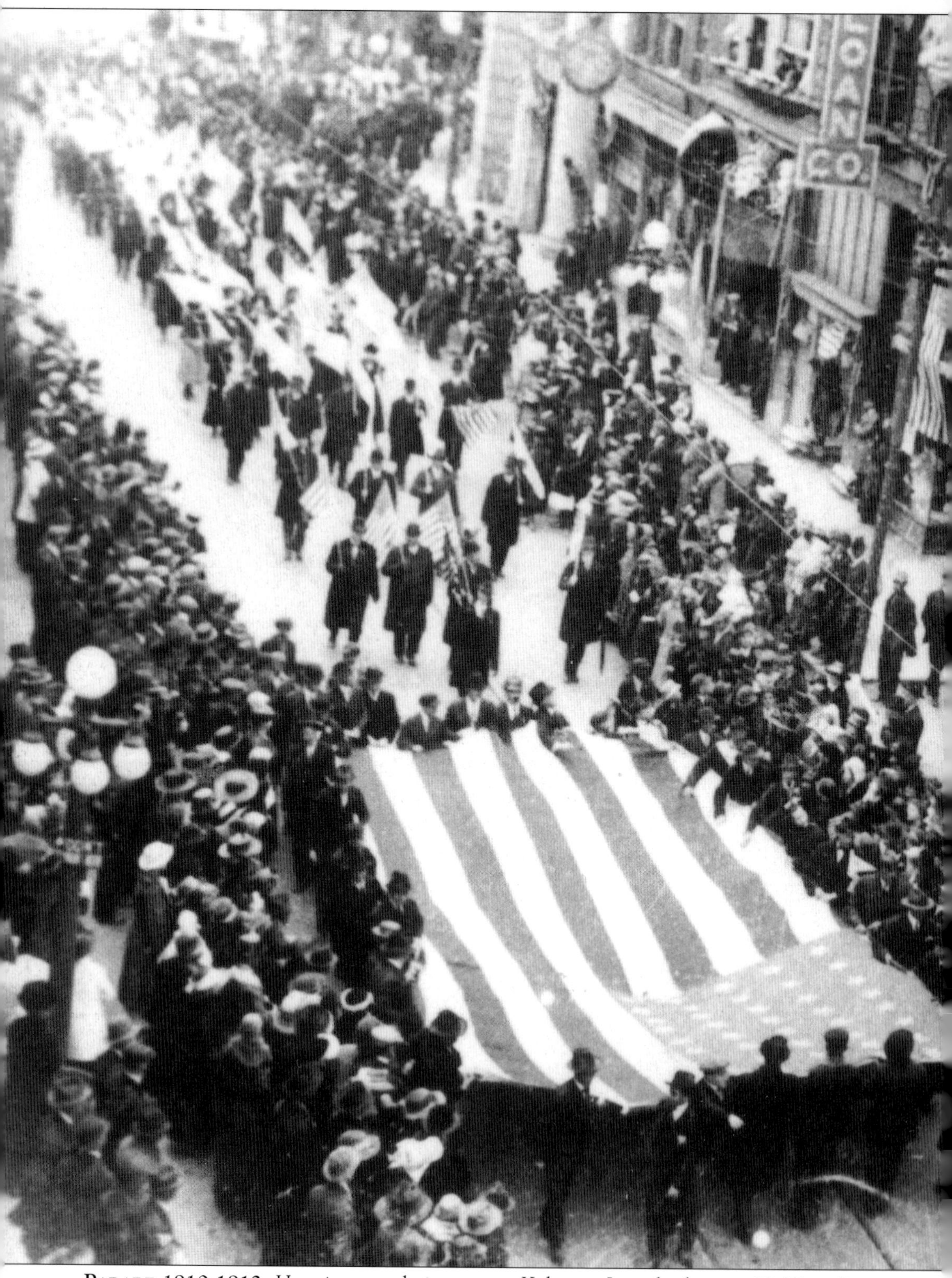

PARADE 1910-1912. Here is a parade in uptown Kokomo. It took place on N. Main Street,

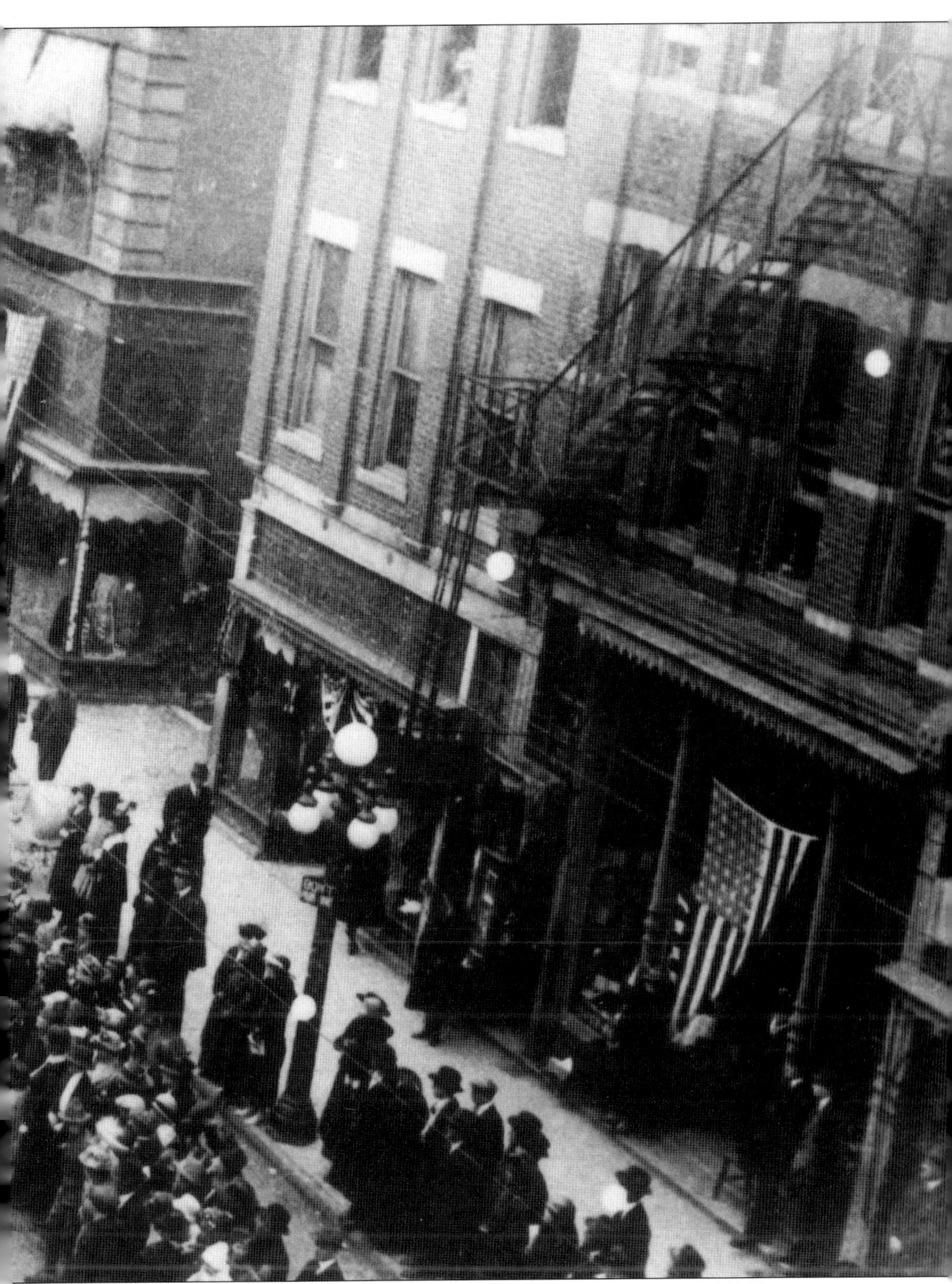

between Walnut and Mulberry. The year was 1910-1912. Look at the size of the flag.

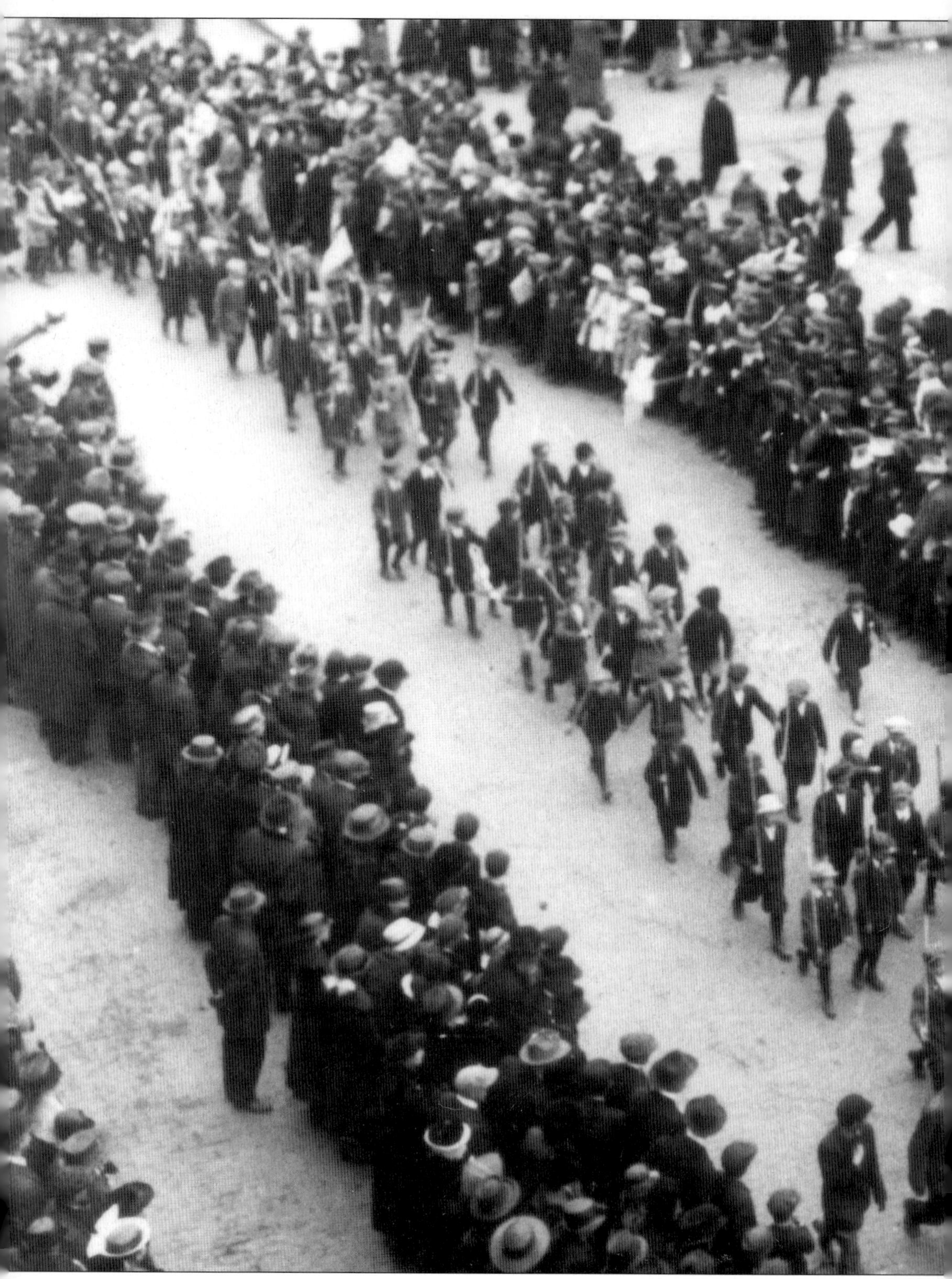

Parade. This picture was taken on the southwest corner of Walnut and Main Streets. In the

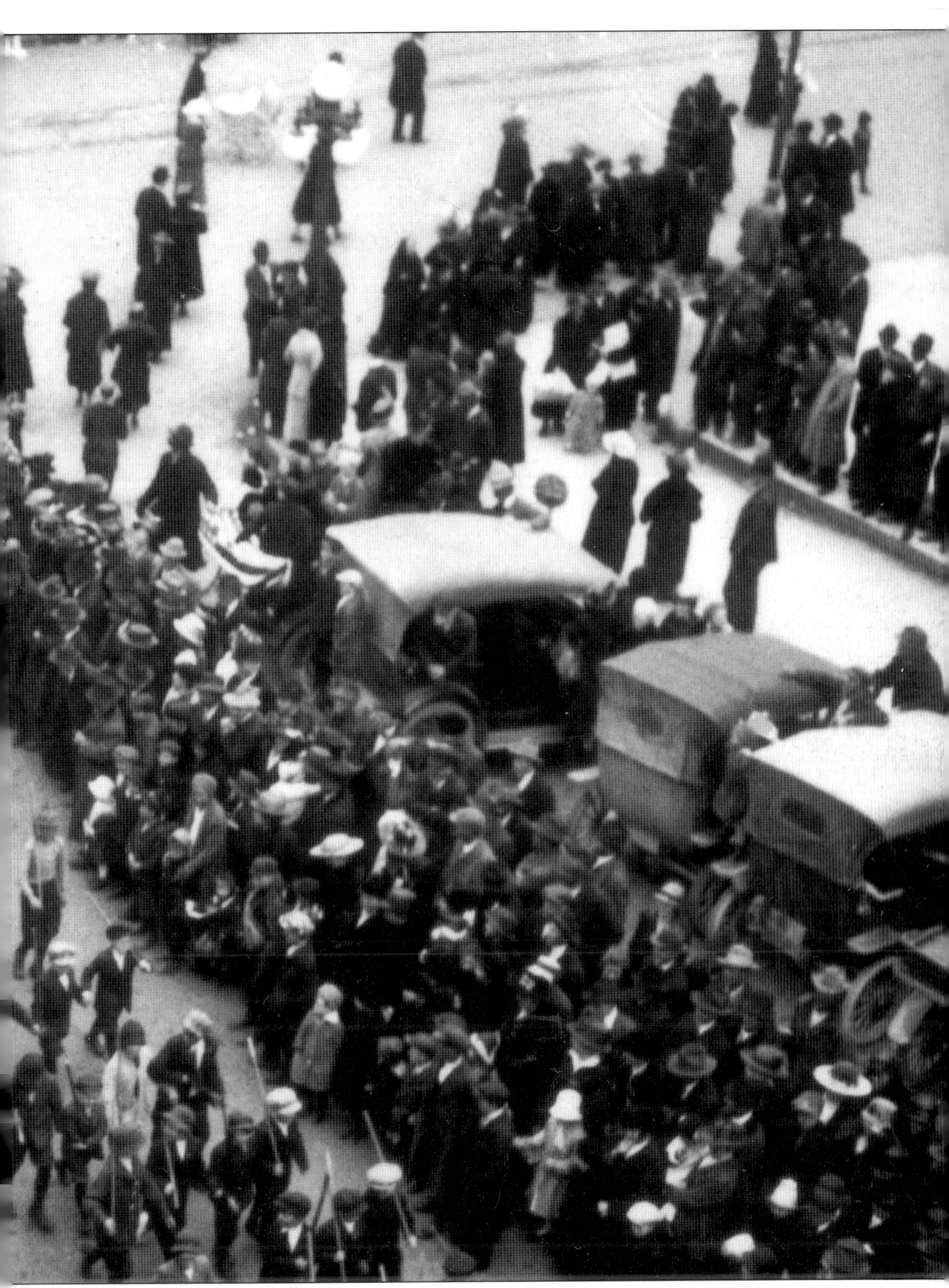

year 1918, World War I ended.

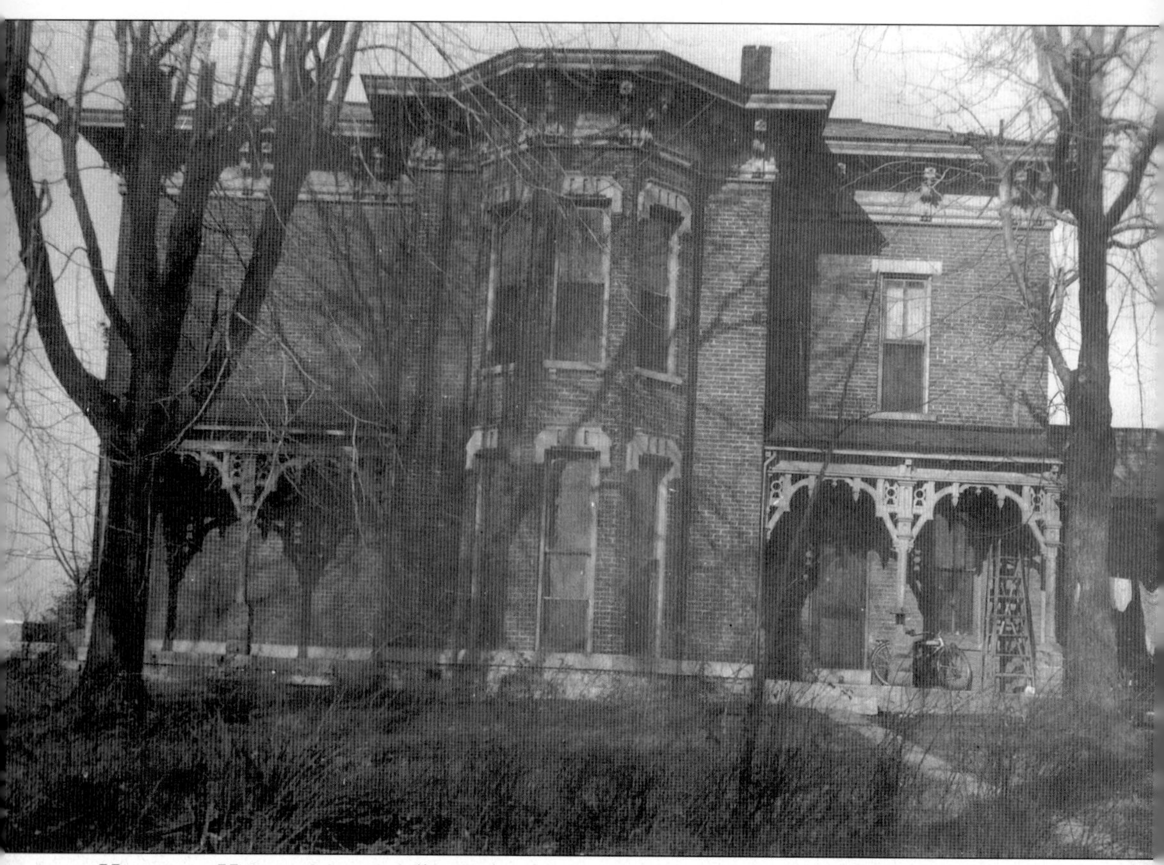

HAUNTED HOUSE. Mary Lindley Bolinger gave us this picture of the haunted house on the northeast corner of Home Avenue and Wheeler. At night time, we kids would dare each other to go near the porch. As I neared the porch she held my hand and said, "Tom should we go back?" All at one the light came on upstairs. The owl from the tree went "Hoot! Hoot!" If no one lived there, how did the light come on and off? She was scared and so was I! We turned and saw that the other kids had left! We ran and got out of there fast! Was it really haunted? Two young kids, a boy and a girl, thought it was.

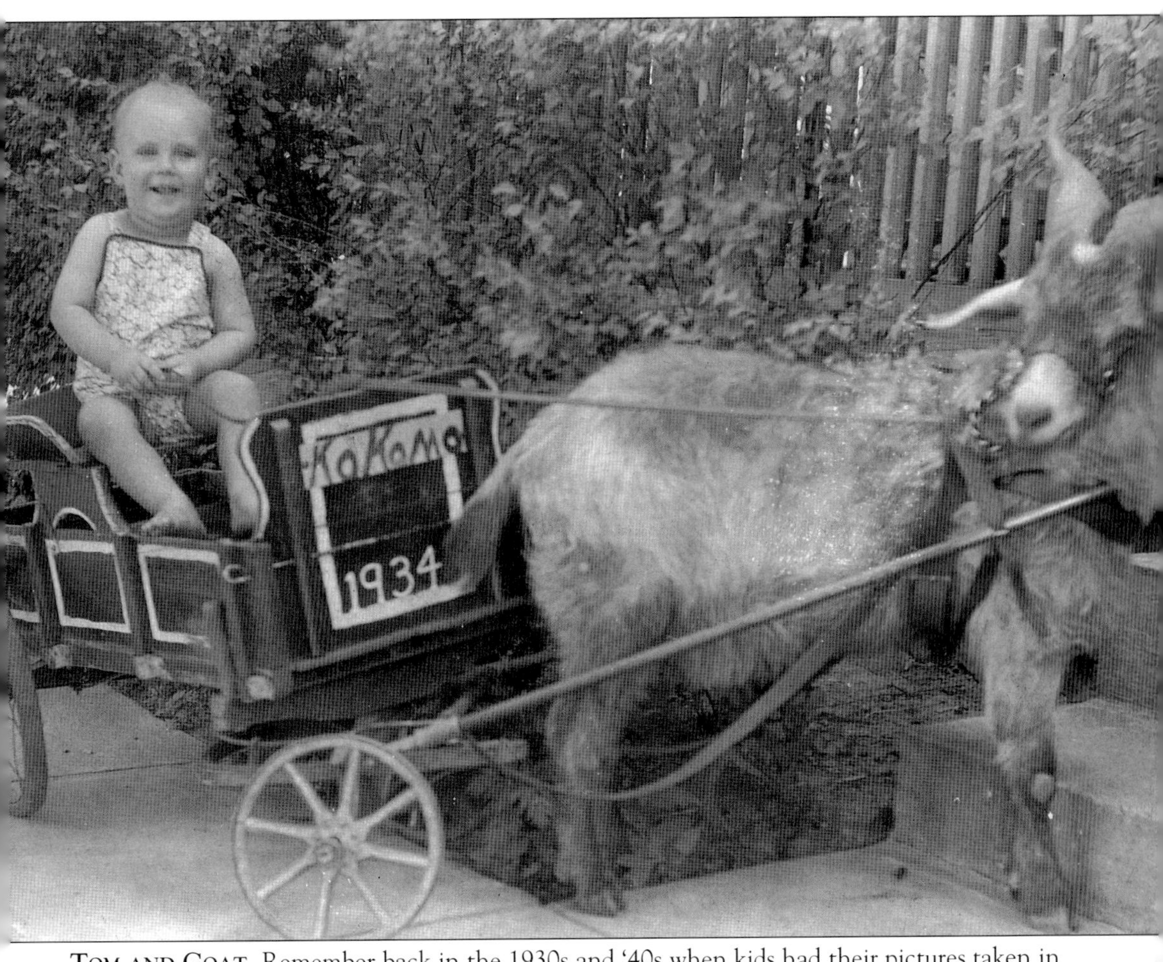

TOM AND GOAT. Remember back in the 1930s and '40s when kids had their pictures taken in a horse and buggy by a traveling camera man? All I got was a billy goat!

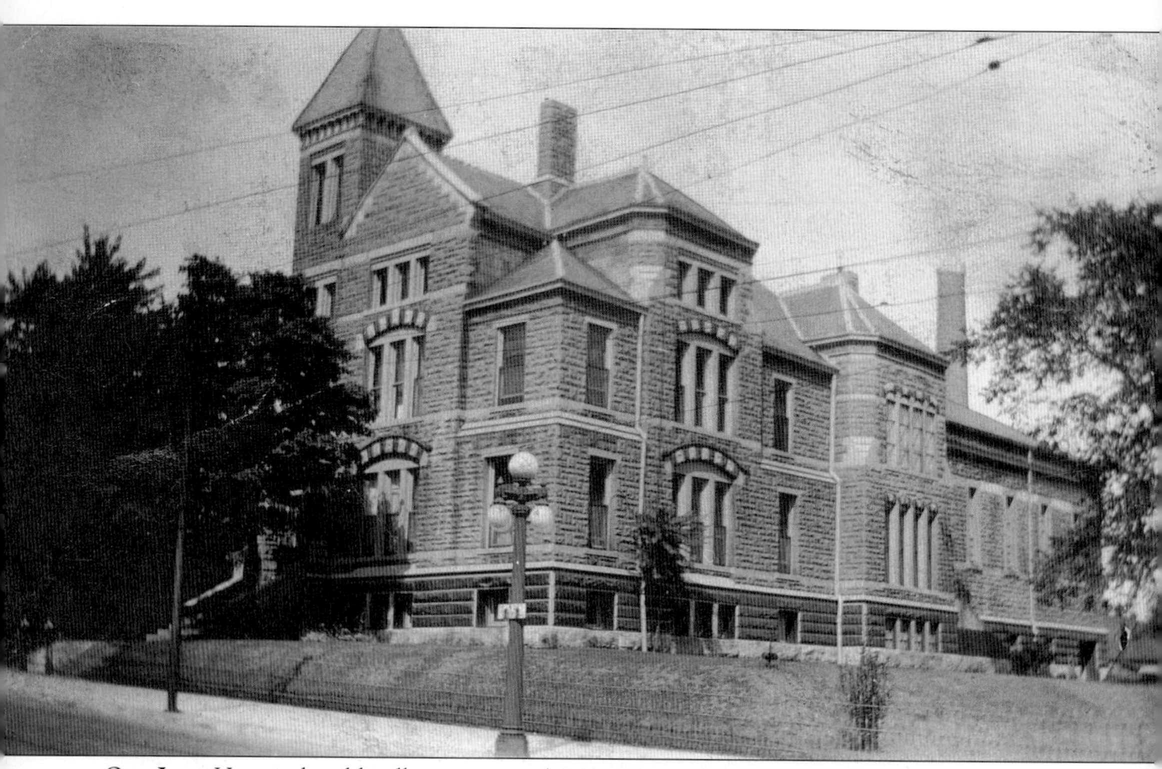

OLD JAIL. Here is the old jailhouse on south Main Street. It was torn down and is now a parking lot!

KRESGE'S *Specials* for TODAY

FRIDAY - APRIL 27th, 1956

* * * * *

....Fresh......Tasty....STRAWBERRY SHORTCAKE, w/Whipped Cream, 25¢

STRAWBERRY PIE, w/Whipped Cream, 25¢

#1 FRIDAY SPECIAL
French Fried Fish, Seasoned Green Beans
Chilled Macaroni Salad, Warm Roll and
Delicious Creamery Butter, 60¢

STRAWBERRY TART w/Whipped Cream, 25¢

VEGETABLE SOUP, 15¢

CHILI, w/Saltines, 30¢

#2 De LUXE LUNCHEON
6 oz. Salisbury Steak w/Bacon
Strip, Creamy Mashed Potatoes
Crisp Cole Slaw, Warm Roll and
Delicious Creamery Butter, with
Hot Coffee, 79¢

#3 CHEF SUGGESTS
Creamed Chicken Giblets on Home
Made Biscuit, Creamy Mashed
Potatoes, Crisp Cole Slaw, Warm
Roll and Delicious Creamery
Butter, ... 55¢

#4 TASTY LUNCHEON
De Luxe Barbecue on Bun w/Barbecue
Sauce, with Crisp Cole Slaw, 39¢

#5 TUNA SALAD BOWL
Tuna Salad, Sliced Hard Boiled
Egg, Crisp Head Lettuce w/Salad
Dressing and Ry-Krisp, 50¢

#6 VEGETABLE PLATE
Tomato Juice, Mashed Potatoes
3 Assorted Vegetables and with
Toast Points, 50¢

#7 DAILY LUNCHEON
Pot Roast on Bun with Delicious
Baked Beans and Sweet Relish,
..... 40¢

Delicious....
MALTED MILK, 25¢

SANDWICHES
EGG SALAD, 20¢
BARBECUE, w/Potato Chips, 30¢
BAKED HAM, 30¢
TUNA SALAD, 30¢

Grilled SANDWICHES
CHEESE, 20¢
HAMBURGER, 25¢
HAM, 30¢
CHEESEBURGER, 35¢

A SWEET CONCLUSION
HOT FUDGE SUNDAE, 25¢
STRAWBERRY SUNDAE, 25¢
STRAWBERRY SODA, 20¢
JELL-O FRUIT CUP, 15¢
Fresh.....
STRAWBERRY
BANANA SPLIT, 30¢

Fresh Baked PIES
APPLE, 15¢
PEACH, 15¢
RHUBARB, 15¢
LEMON, 15¢
STRAWBERRY, w/Whip Cream, 25¢

BEVERAGES
TOMATO or ORANGE JUICE, 10¢ & 20¢
MILK or CHOCOLATE MILK, 10¢
HOT CHOCOLATE, 10¢
HOT POT of TEA, ICED TEA, 10¢
LEMON, ORANGE, or LIMEADE, 10¢
ORANGE COOLER, 20¢
LEMON FREEZE, 20¢

.....Have BREAKFAST with Us!
Monday thru Saturday at 8:15 A.M.

To Avoid Mistakes Please Pay When Served

Mrs. Haselle
Food Dept. Manager

FORM 547

KRESGE'S MENU. Here is a menu from Kresge's Department Store in 1956. How would you like those deals today?

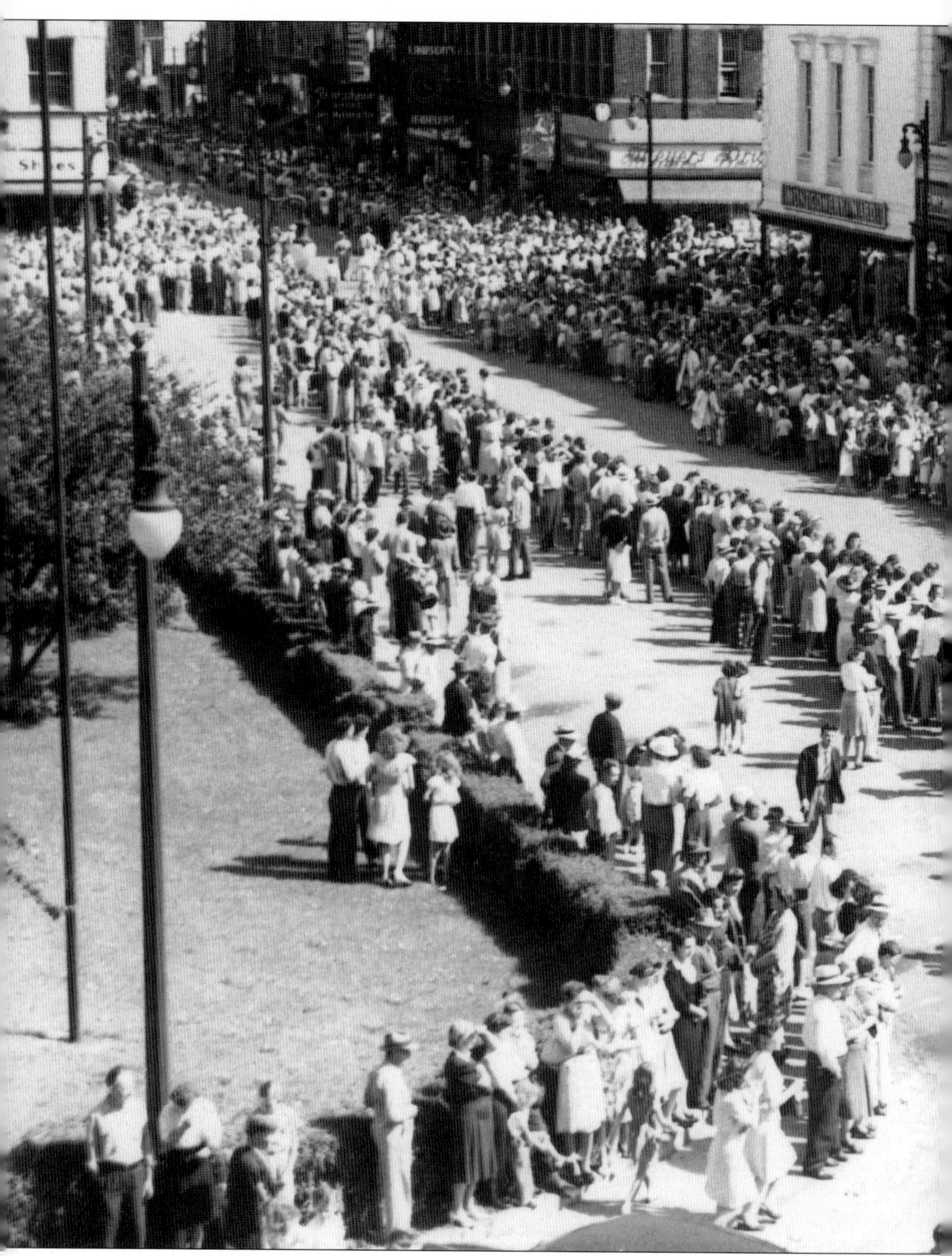

1940s East Side Courthouse. This picture was taken on the east side of the courthouse on north Main Street. The year was 1943, and Robert Davies took the picture. In our young hearts

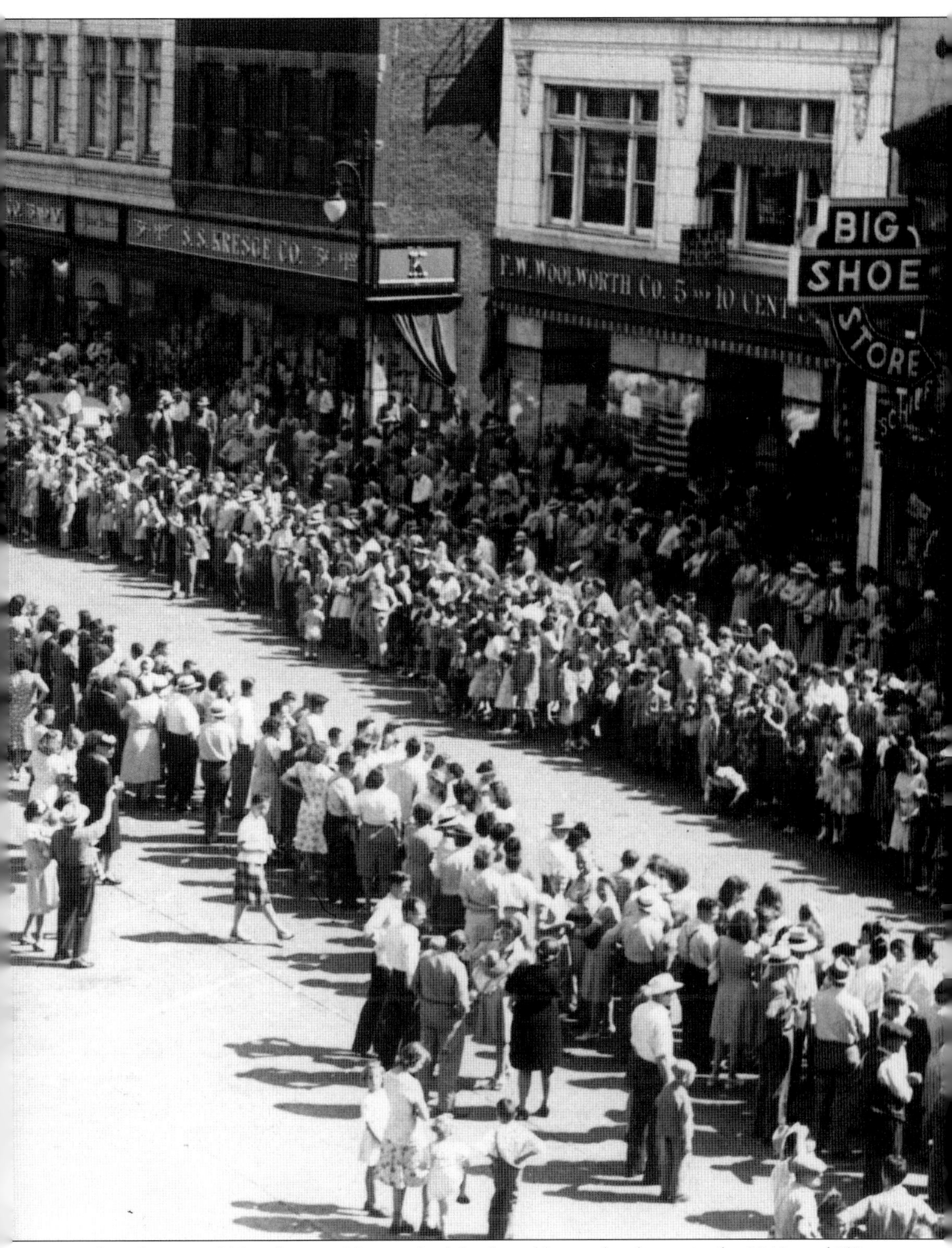

we thought it would last forever. Now we look back and know that living in the 1940s and '50s were the best years of our lives.

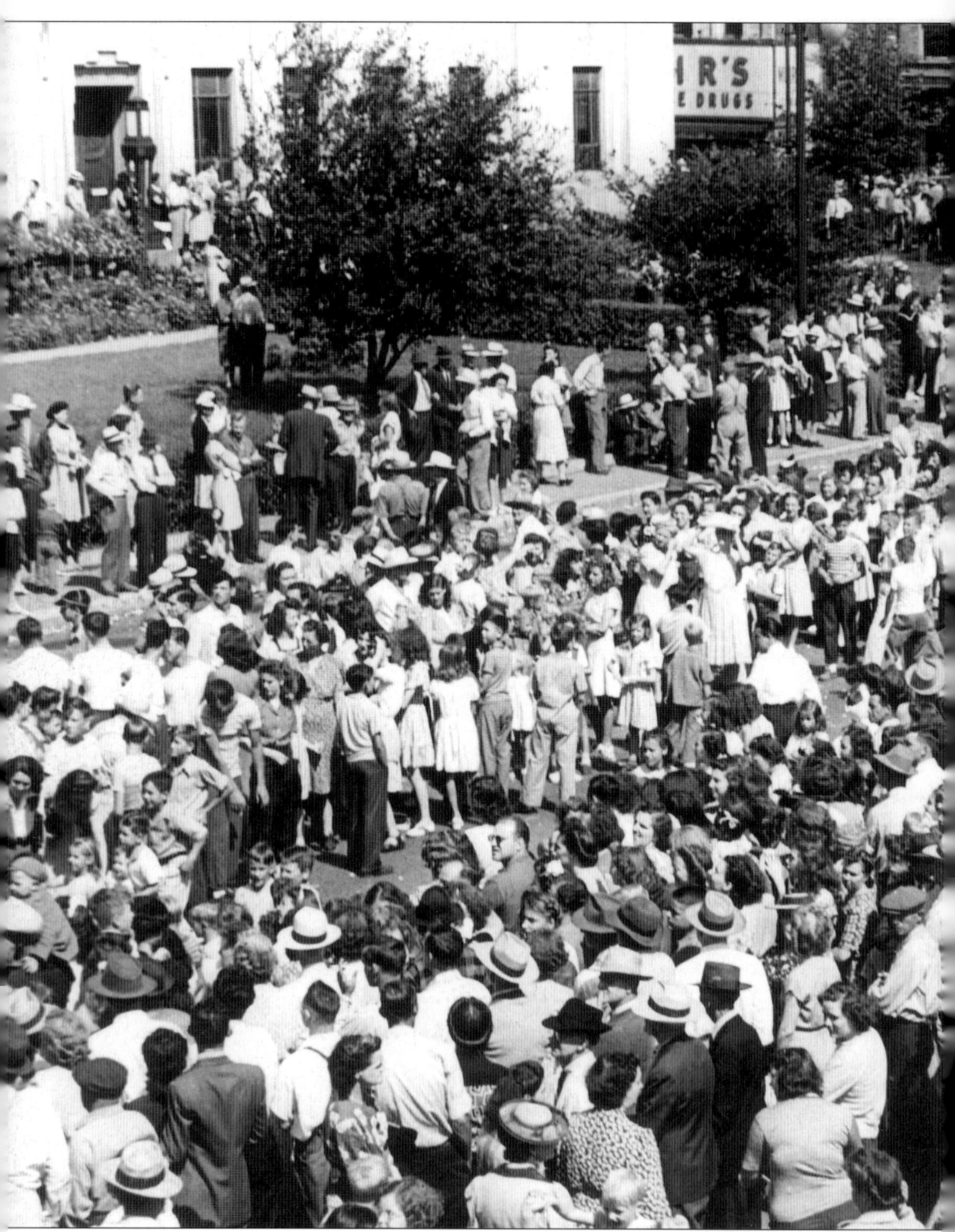

IN FRONT OF COURTHOUSE. Here is a picture taken in 1943 in front of the courthouse on north Main Street on the north side of the courthouse on Walnut Street. You can see

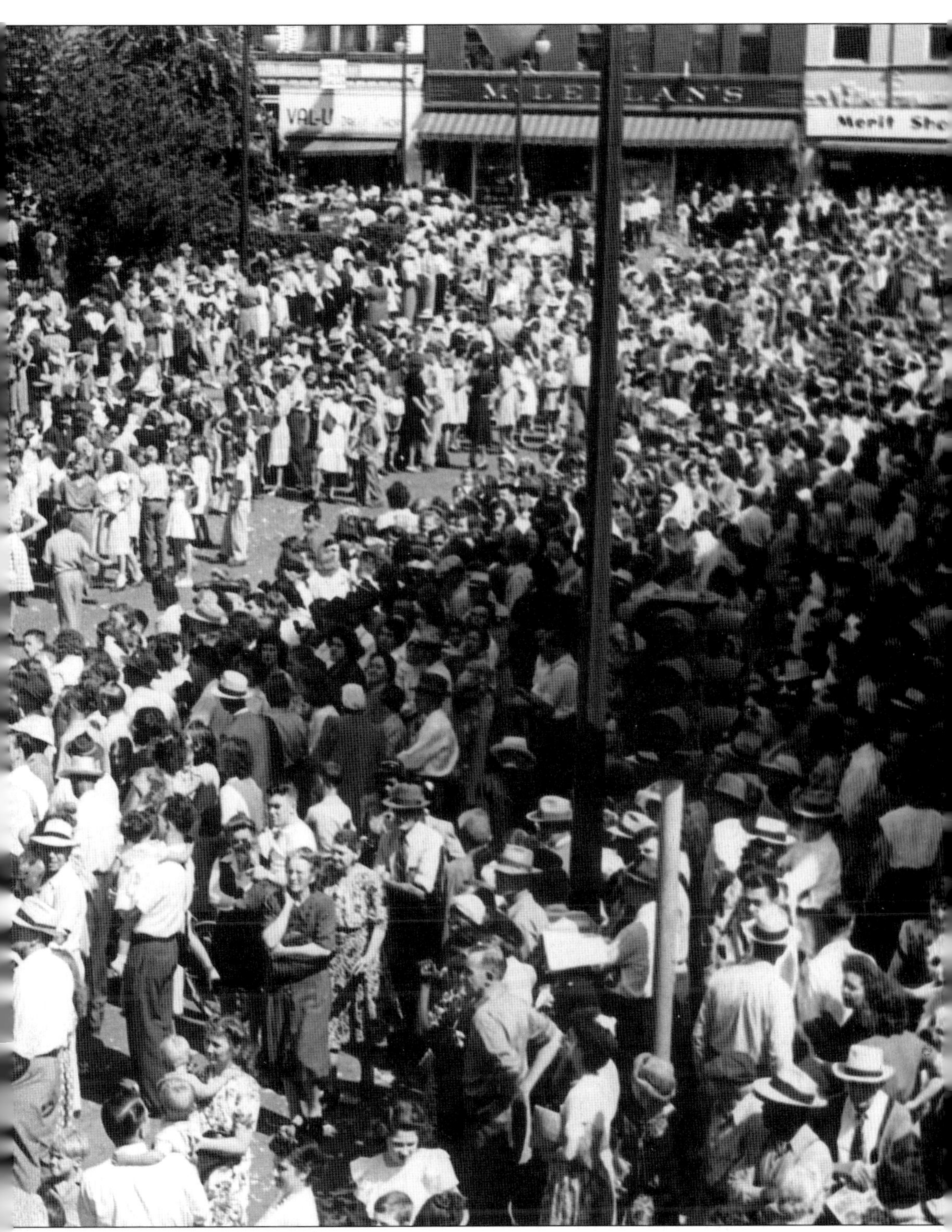

McLellan's, Merit Shoes, and Muirs Drugstore.

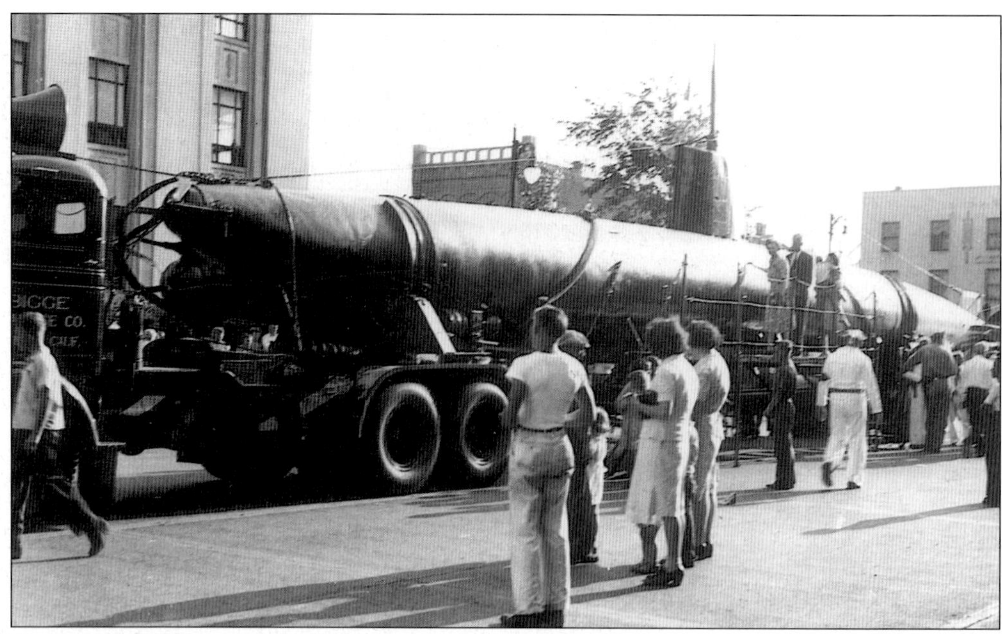

NAVY SUBMARINE. This picture was taken in 1945. The navy had brought a submarine to Kokomo, and the people were anxious to see it. Perhaps you are in this picture. The location was on W. Walnut just north of the courthouse, on the town square. (Photo courtesy of William Johnston.)

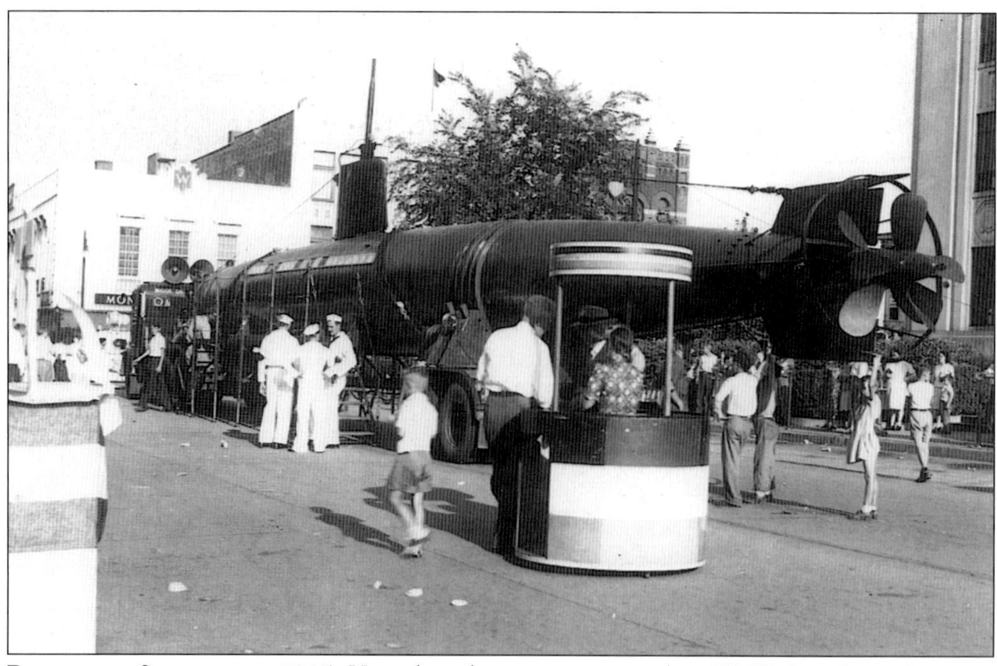

PICTURE OF SUBMARINE, 1945. Here the submarine is pictured on W. Walnut Street between Main and Buckeye Streets. (Photo courtesy of William Johnston.)

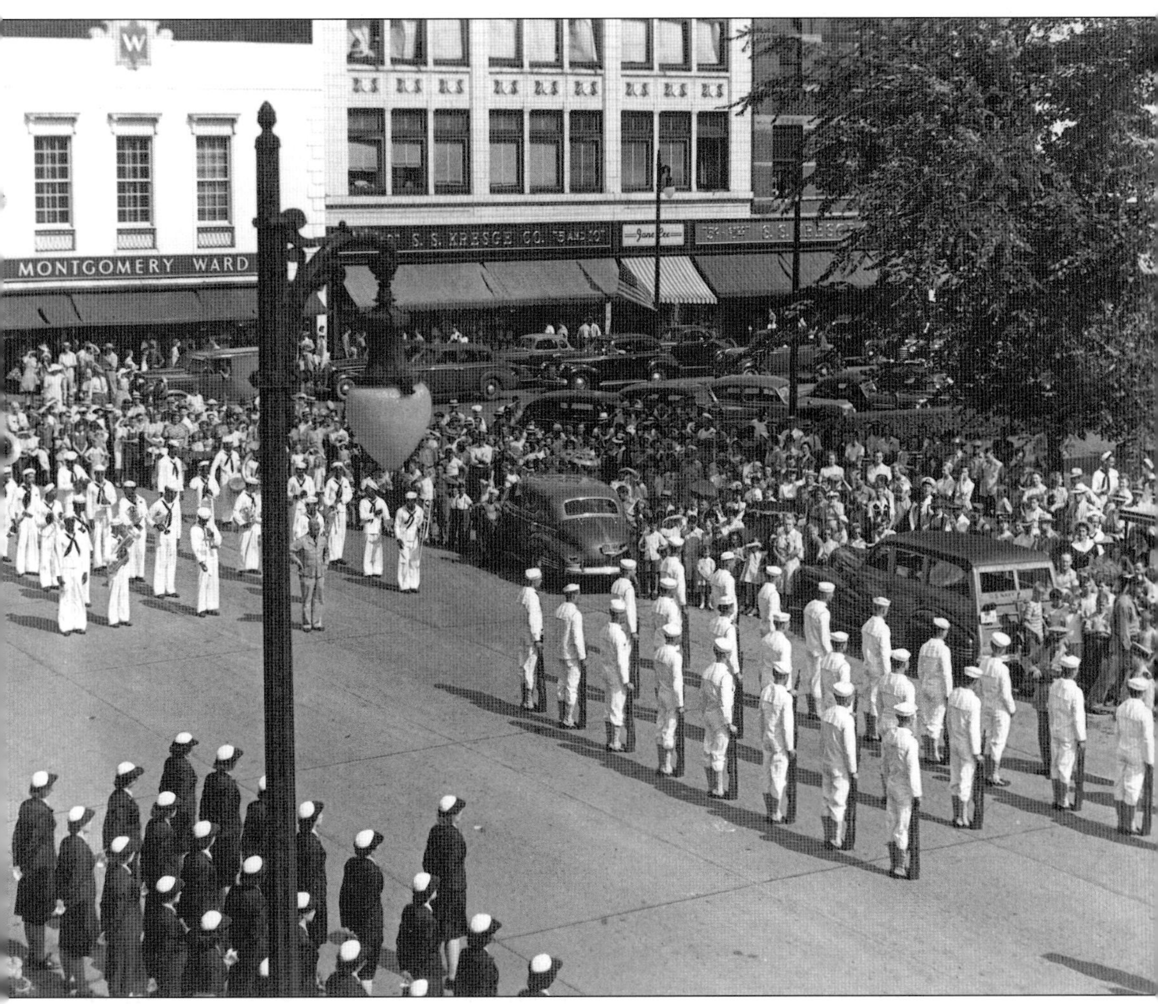

MAIN STREET. KOKOMO, INDIANA.

Two Ton Baker hits Kokomo

Kokomo In Pictures

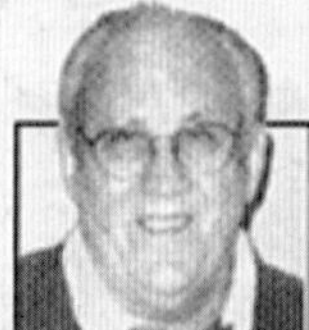

By Tom Hamilton

Perspective Generations Columnist

The year was 1947, and I was 14 years old. How many out there can remember Two Ton Baker? And, can you remember the song, "Kokomo, Indiana?"

Here is a window display in front of Kresge's in downtown Kokomo. In person! Two Ton Baker, Famous Mercury and WGN Singing Star will appear in Kokomo Thursday, July 17. To preview his new record release "Kokomo, Indiana." He will autograph your "Kokomo" record between 3 and 3:30 p.m. at Kresge's. Tune to WKMO for details. Eat your heart out, Indianapolis.

Kokomo was once again on the map! Not only were records being sold, but Kokomo was being mentioned in the movie called "Mother Wore Tights."

The Sipe Theater showed the movie in 1947. The stars were Betty Grable and Dan Dailey. Betty and Dan danced and sang to the tune of "Kokomo, Indiana." I was there, and even at 14 I was proud to live in Kokomo.

One of pinup girl, Betty Grable's, most popular films, as well as her personal favorite, this box office hit was packed with nostalgic moments and memorable song and dance numbers.

As I sat in my seat, I knew why everyone was there. Then, the magic moment came. Betty and Dan started singing "Kokomo, Indiana." You could not hear a pin drop.

One part of the song that will always stay with me is when they sing, "my heart will always be in Kokomo."

If you were born and raised in Kokomo, in your heart you will always be here! When I was overseas for 20 months, believe me my heart was in Kokomo.

Some of the hit songs in 1946 and 1947 were, "You Keep Coming Back Like a Song" and "The Old Lamp Lighter." And, isn't it wonderful to be a prisoner of Kokomo, Indiana?

The greatest people on earth live in Kokomo. If you smile and wave at someone, they always smile and wave back. Try it! It works!

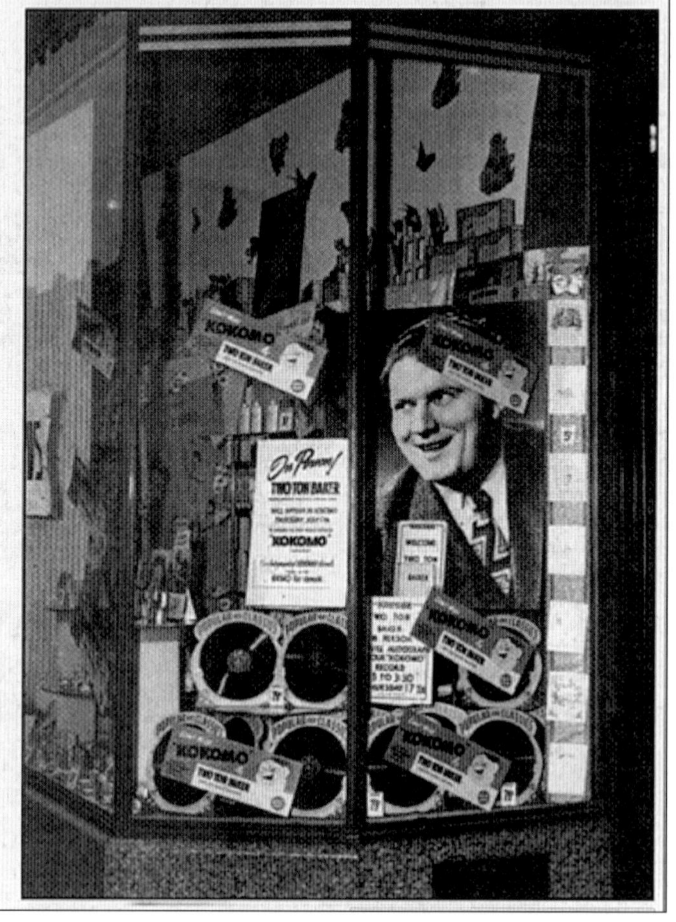

The following articles are from *The Kokomo Perspective*.

Songs helped us fall in love

KOKOMO IN PICTURES

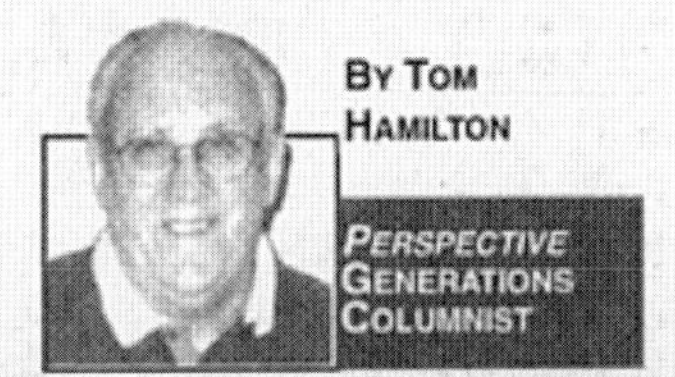

When we think of the 40s and 50s, we also think of the songs that helped us fall in love. And, this picture of Kokomo in the late 40s is like a pretty song. Doesn't it bring back memories?

Montgomery Wards is on the south east corner of Main and Walnut streets. If you look real hard, you can see the water fountain in front of the store. can you remember Leonard's Jewelers on the north east corner? The year was 1948 and a pretty day in August. Can you girls remember the La Mode? It was located at 208 N. Main Street. Can you remember the big clock in front of Lawson's? What were the names of the two stores between Leonards and Lawson's? And, did you notice all the women wore dresses?

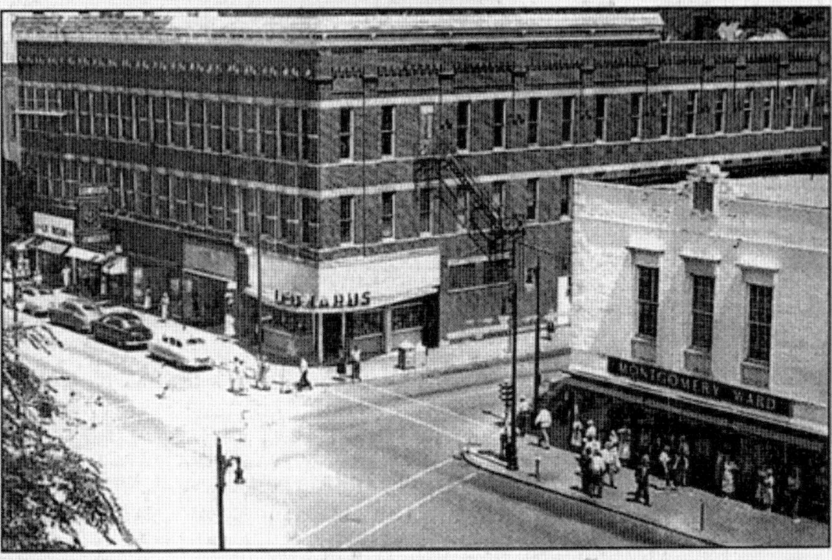

Can you remember your song? Was it, "Little Things Mean a Lot" by Kitty Kallen? And, who can forget Nat King Cole? He was my favorite! He gave us "Too Young" and "Mona Lisa" and the great "Unforgettable."

"A White Sport Coat and a Pink Carnation" by Marty Robbins was a smash hit. My favorite tear jerker was "Cry" by Johnnie Ray. Tony Bennett gave us "Because of You". Can you remember Guy Mitchell breaking our young hearts with "My Heart Cries for You"?

I was a young boy in a magic wonderland in Kokomo, Indiana in the 40s and 50s. I never dreamed that things would change. Perry Como, Frankie Laine, Doris Day and many others will never be replaced.

Remember the song "I'll be Seeing You"? The greatest songs were written in the 40s and 50s!

The night was like a lovely tune as we sat on the front porch swing. How much do you love me, she asked. I said, "See the stars in the sky? They tell you how much."

I got off the swing and grabbed her feet and started pulling her towards me. Then, she started laughing as I let her go. The moon and stars were just right as it lit up her face. I picked up her shoes and said, "The girl whose feet will fit there shoes is the one who will be my queen!"

She said, "Will you put my bobby socks on first?" I asked why and she answered, "I want to make sure they fit perfect!"

As I slipped on her shoes, I said, "Behold! My queen!" She asked if she could ride away on a white horse. The night indeed was like a lovely tune and one I will never forget.

Always remember...the moon belongs to everyone, The best things in life are free. (Remember, the *Kokomo Perspective* is free!) The stars belong to everyone, they gleam there for you and me. The flowers in Spring. The robins that sing, the sunbeam that shines. They're yours and mine. Don't forget to tell your wife you love her!

The owner of the little red truck

KOKOMO IN PICTURES

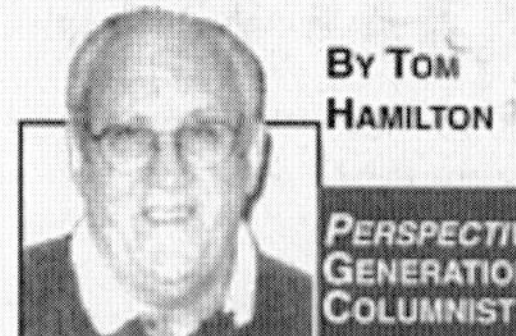

BY TOM HAMILTON

PERSPECTIVE GENERATIONS COLUMNIST

I recently received this letter from Lavonne Parsons about her father, Carl Wright.

"I am enclosing my one and only 'good' photograph of the Dodge pick-up. You asked your readers if anyone could identify the owner. He happened to be my father, Carl Wright. He purchased the truck new from Button Motors. In this larger version of the photo, the wording CARL WRIGHT, is clearly legible on the door.

"Our family moved to Kokomo in 1940, where my dad took a job installing furnaces for John Cleary. In those days, furnace work specifically was the conversion of the old coal-fired furnaces to natural gas.

"Mr. Cleary sent my dad to Columbus, Ohio, for schooling and helped him obtain a Lennox furnace franchise and to go into business for himself. A room was built onto the back of our home where he did all his sheet metal/duct work.

"When my brother returned from four years in the Marines, and subsequently the Korean War, he joined my dad in the furnace business. He well remembers building the sheet metal bins on the side of the truck for their tools. My dad eventually sold the Lennox franchise to Armstrong-Landon, while he and my brother continued to install Lennox furnaces for them.

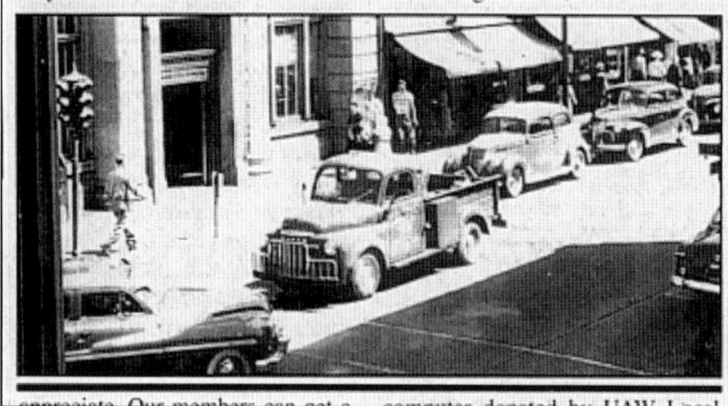

"On trips around town, my dad would point out various homes where he boasted he'd installed their heating. One in particular is now called the Bavarian Inn. My sister's son, Jerry Jackson, who is now a furnace man himself (for Griffey Contracting), upon working recently at the Inn, noted the perfect duct work still in place, only later to find out his grandfather, Carl Wright, had done the installing.

"I don't know how many years it was before Dad retired from the furnace business. The man was a perfectionist, both in the care of his new, little, red truck and his work. Many persons in the community had only high praise for his installations.

"He has four children still living, Lavonne Parsons of Kokomo, Margie Henry of Tipton, Bill Wright of Elkhart- where he continued in the installation of Lennox furnaces- and Carol Jackson of Galveston.

"Carl Wright lost his life due to cancer complications in 1975."

I want to thank Lavonne Parsons for this letter. Continue reading the *Kokomo Perspective*, everyone!

Stairway to the stars

Kokomo In Pictures

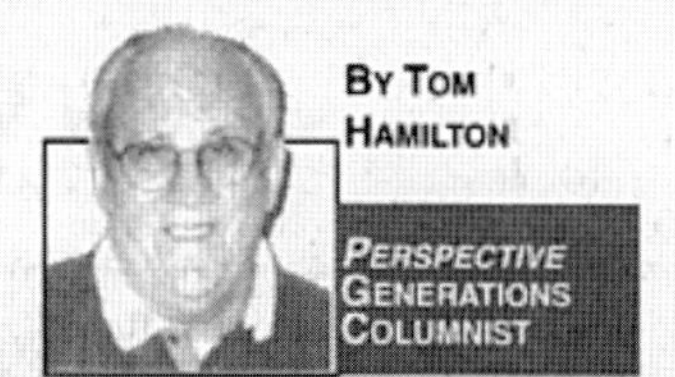

The year was 1906 and this picture shows Main Street south of Sycamore. Can you notice the first Armstrong Landon Building on the southwest corner? It was built in 1875 and was considered fire proof. Guess what? It was destroyed by fire in December of 1923.

The one we have now was built in 1924. On the southeast corner was the Farmers Trust and Savings Bank. Palmers Jewelers is now located there. Things sure change over the years, don't they?

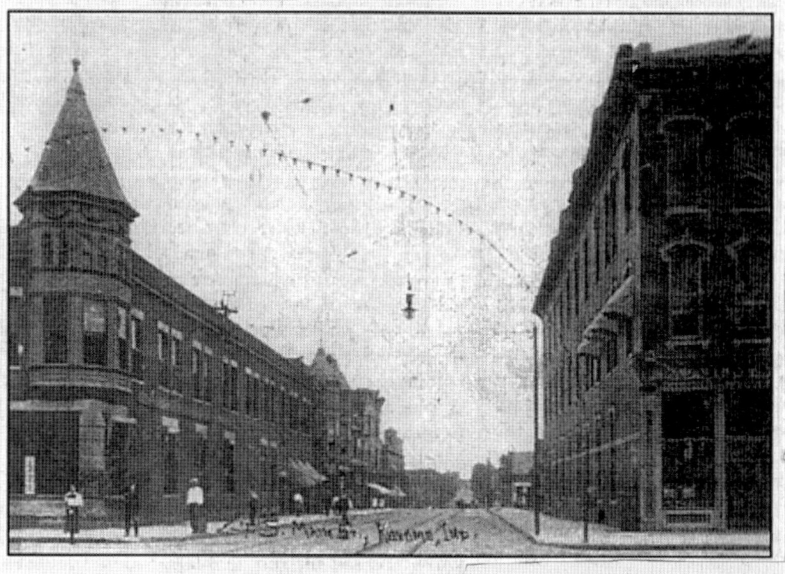

Did you ever go to your class reunion and see an old class chum of years ago? If it was not for the name tags, no one would know each other. Someone comes up to you and tells you who they are and you take one look and think, "My goodness they sure took a hit." What is funny, they probably think the same thing about you!

I like this picture because my grandfather's apartment was above where the old K&S Department Store was. Beckley's Office Equipment is there now.

There was a stairway up to his apartment. It was a stairway to the stars. There was a roof outside of grandfather's kitchen window. My girlfriend and I were heading up the stairway and she slipped and started to fall. I caught her just in time. She said, "I think I twisted my ankle."

She sat down as I took her shoes and socks off and started to move her foot around. I said, "Does that hurt?"

When I looked up at her, she said, "That's funny. It's alright now." I said, "You big faker."

She jumped up and started running up the stairway and into the apartment laughing on the way.

When I got there, my grandfather was grinning as he pointed toward the roof. She looked pretty standing there under the moon and stars.

I started to say something, but was lost somewhere out there in space. I had never seen so many stars. She said, "Look! A shooting star!" All I could see was her. She said, "Are you going to make a wish?" I said, "Only if you hold my hand and wish with me." While she was making a wish, I kissed her. I said, "My wish came true." She said, "So did mine."

My thanks to the manager of Beckley's for taking me upstairs to see the empty apartment and the torn down stairway. As I left, I thought I heard a young girl laughing as she ran down the hallway.

Do you know the FOP baseball team?

KOKOMO IN PICTURES

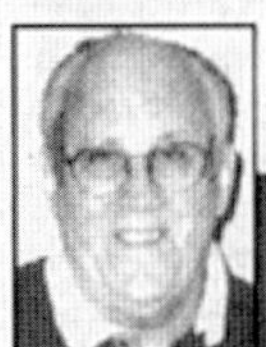

By Tom Hamilton

Kokomo Perspective Generations columnist

Back in 1948, the Fraternal Order of Police had a pretty good baseball team. How many of you can remember a local policeman by the name of Ray Lett? He is the only one pictured here without a uniform on.

Marian Heronemus Groves loaned me this picture of the ballplayers. My, what a group of guys these were!

Marian's brother, Dick Heronemus, is the fifth from the left in the front row. The third man from the left in front is someone who every "bowler" in Kokomo should recognize. His name is Wayne Kitts. In the back, second from left, is Joe Dillman. He was a foreman at Delco, and people speak well of him.

I called Carlton Hilton for more information about the amateur and semi-pro baseball teams in Kokomo. Carl is pictured here in the front row, with the number four on his sleeve.

He said, "We had an average of 75 percent wins over the years. Our most prominent year was 1950, when the Boosters -- whose record was 23-5 -- won the Indiana semi-pro tourney. That qualified them for the national tourney in Wichita, KS. But, we were unable to attend due to other commitments. The runner-up team went in our place."

Are you, or someone you know, pictured here? The picture was taken at Highland Park. Do you wonder about the lives of the people in the picture? I wonder if their future plans came true. I wonder if they ever hit the winning run, or caught the game-winning catch, or slid home for the hometown victory.

If I could go back in time, what year would I choose? How about you? Did you know that your mind is a time machine to the past? The wonders of it all! Have you ever gone to bed and dreamed of your childhood?

Sometimes, it is so real that I wish I could go back and dream the same dream. I even have dreamed of riding my bike all over Kokomo during the mid-1940s. I even woke up tired from riding!

As Rod Serling would say,"You have just entered the 'Twilight Zone.'" Wouldn't it be nice if we could just go back now and again and enjoy the delights of childhood? That is the wonderful thing about Christmastime -- we all can be kids again, at least for a little while.

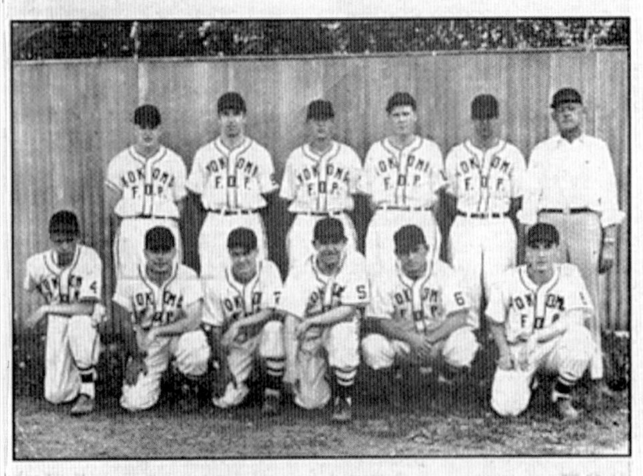

The Kokomo F.O.P. baseball team of 1948. Pictured are: (front row l to r) Roy Cargale, Carl Hilton, Wayne Kitts, Stan Kucholick, Dick Heronemus, Bert Lambert; (back row l to r) Finis Zugelder, Joe Dillman, Ralph Saul, Lou Wagner, Don Shick, Ray Lett. (Photo provided)

Play-by-play with Tiny Joe

KOKOMO IN PICTURES

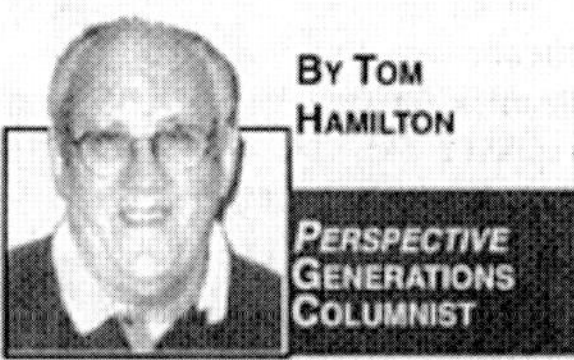

BY TOM HAMILTON

PERSPECTIVE GENERATIONS COLUMNIST

How many of you can remember the radio station called W.K.M.O.? It was located on the northeast corner of Main and Taylor. This picture, by John Ryan, was taken in 1942. Across the street from W.K.M.O., on the northwest side, was the Hotel Courtland.

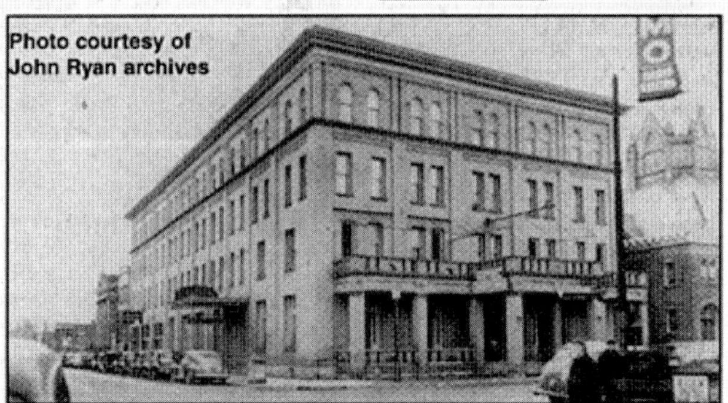

Photo courtesy of John Ryan archives

How can anyone remember W.K.M.O. and not think of "Tiny" Joe Jordan? He announced Kokomo High School ball games, and his voice became familiar to all Kokomo sports fans.

Tiny Joe had a way of keeping us on the edge of our seats! We were at home listening. The game was tied. Kokomo had the ball. Suddenly, with just five seconds to play, Bones Wagner took the last shot! All we could hear was screaming and the beat of drums. We waited for what seemed like an eternity. We yelled at the radio, "What happened? What happened?" The radio just sounded like a screaming machine. We never knew if it was our side or theirs doing the hollering. All at once, when you thought you couldn't stand it one more second, the noise would die down. It was then that Tiny Joe would simply say, "That's all, brother." That, my friend, was Tiny Joe's way of saying that the shot was good.

No sports announcer I have ever heard could make a listener feel the excitement of a ball game like Tiny Joe Jordan. Actually, he was not tiny at all. In fact, he tipped the scales at nearly 300 pounds!

Believe it or not, the Kokomo Wildcats played at Haworth gym. Does that name ring a bell? Remember Haworth High School? All of Kokomo High School's home basketball games from 1925 until 1944 were played at Haworth. It was named after C.W. Haworth, superintendent of schools and former principal of Kokomo High School. The first radio broadcasts of the games were from Haworth gym. It was destroyed by fire in 1944.

Correct me if I am wrong, and I could be, but I believe that Kokomo Wildcats played at the National Guard Armory at one time. One thing I am sure of, there will never be another Tiny Joe Jordan. In my opinion, he was the best! We could not listen to the game without biting our fingernails. If a turtle decided to cross the street, Tiny Joe could make it the most exciting thing ever broadcasted! It would be nice if I had a picture of Tiny Joe broadcasting a game. Does anyone out there have one?

Well, as Tiny Joe would say..."That's all, brother."